FOREIGNER

FOREIGNER

The story of Grace Morton
as told to

Stanley Roche

Oxford University Press

WELLINGTON

Oxford University Press
222-36 Willis Street, Wellington

Oxford   London   Glasgow
New York   Toronto   Melbourne   Wellington
Kuala Lumpur   Singapore   Jakarta   Hong Kong   Tokyo
Nairobi   Dar es Salaam   Cape Town
Delhi   Bombay   Calcutta   Madras   Karachi

ISBN 0 19 558044 3

Jacket designed by Lindsay Missen
Printed by Whitcoulls Ltd, Christchurch

Grace Botham at fifteen, a schoolgirl in
Chefoo, 1912

CONTENTS

FOREWORD

Papaioea Place, Palmerston North, looks rather like a picture from a child's colouring-in book. The houses have no fences; they sit in parallel rows on a continuous lawn, neatly mown by municipal gardeners and dotted with revolving clothes-lines and small tame trees. Though the houses are all the same shape and size, each is a different colour. A green one, a blue one, a cream one, a pink one, a buff one, and so on. Each house contains four units, and each unit contains a kitchen, a bathroom, a living-room, a bedroom, a sunporch, and one or two senior citizens – pensioners. Each unit has its own miniature garden plot, front and back, where flowers flourish, or vegetables, plaster gnomes, or ornamental shrubs.

There is something so bland and innocent about the place that you expect the pensioners, too, to have stepped intact from a picture book, complete with snowy hair, apple cheeks, and gold-rimmed spectacles. Of course, they are not at all like that. They are real people, each strongly marked by more than sixty years of tough human experience.

Nevertheless, when Grace Morton began talking to me, in one of the regulation sunporches, of executions and jewel smuggling, of Gestapo raids and mule bells, I was naively surprised. This in Papaioea Place?

The next time I visited her I took a tape recorder with me. It took us eight months of Saturday afternoons to complete the recording, and for two years much of my time has been filled with transcribing, condensing, and editing.

Whenever possible, I have checked Grace's facts and dates in our local library. Yes, Dr Wellington Koo did travel from China to Europe in 1936; yes, the Anschluss did occur on 12 March 1938; Alexander, the uncrowned king of Greece, did have an obsessive interest in motors, and did die as the result of a bite from a pet monkey; Henlein was the first Nazi governor of Sudetenland.

Again and again, Grace's memory was confirmed from outside sources.

Most of the words in this memoir are Grace's. Where I have intruded as a narrator, it is either to give background information or because, as she re-lived her life for me, there were moments when tone, gestures, and reticences said more than her words did. I think we have both enjoyed the exercise.

Stanley Roche

(1)

CHINA

I was born in the middle of a blizzard. My mother told me she couldn't bath me for two weeks because the water would have frozen in the tub right in front of the lighted stove. In eighty years I've never got over dreading the winter. If they'd told me hell was a cold place I would have been a good girl.

We lived way up in the far north-west of China in Lanchow, a city not very far from the borders of Tibet. My parents were missionaries . . .

This was in 1897. In distant England, Queen Victoria's Diamond Jubilee was being celebrated: sixty years of reign. Men wore boaters, women had wasp waists still, bicycles wobbled propelled by bloomered legs, and the map of the world was generously daubed in red. 'Soldiers of the Queen' was the pop-song of the music halls and it was lovely to be British.

China was not red in any sense – neither communist nor part of the Empire. She was more cultured than any other country and more barbarous than many. Her civilization was the oldest on earth; it had lasted 4,000 years. She was ruled by the Manchu dynasty, weary and corrupt.

Throughout the nineteenth century she'd been gang-raped by the western powers. 'We only want to trade with you,' they said with gunboats at the ready behind them to shell just a few towns, just enough to make their point. 'Trade is good for you.'

From the passages where they forced an entry, tea and silk and rhubarb flowed out in a satisfying stream.

'Trade is a two-way process,' they explained. 'You must take some of our goods now or the Balance of Trade will be disturbed.' Cotton goods from Manchester were landed at the open ports, but the Balance of Trade still swung unevenly. What else could they sell to stubborn China who didn't know what was good for her? It so happened that the British East India Company had a lot of spare opium grown on their estates in Bengal. Opium in vast quantities was landed at the ports.

11

The Chinese government had an absurd prejudice against having their country flooded with opium. They were disturbed by the monthly, weekly, increase in the number of addicts. 'No more opium,' they said.

The foreign merchants (and the Chinese ones) were indignant at this gross interference with the rights of free trade. The British merchants protested to their government and the gunboats came into position again and shelled a few more towns. Weary China again gave in.

More and more foreigners seeped into the Celestial Empire eager for the pickings. In the wake of the traders and the soldiers came the Christian missionaries to capture heathen souls. There was a military tune sounding somewhere in their ears and they could see the banner of Christ waving over their heads. They were brave, self-sacrificing, and narrow-minded; they had stiff upper lips and needed them. Onward Christian soldiers.

In England Nellie Barclay, reserved, intelligent, and high-minded, heard the call. She applied to the huge China Inland Mission in London, was accepted and trained and despatched with a clutch of seventy other British young to join the proselytizing army.

Thomas Botham was the fourth son of a farmer from the pious money-making midlands. The money-making strain led his three elder brothers to New York where the streets were paved with gold. The piety came out in Thomas (he had a sense of humour too, and the family penchant for adventure). They met, Nellie and Tom, in heathen China and married there.

The Manchu Empire was disintegrating into blood and dust. Rebels within and enemies without. It gave a last twitch of life. A secret society arose proclaiming death to the foreigner and support for the Manchus. Its members practised initiation rites and, with incantations and wild dances, worked themselves to a frenzy that made it a pleasure to kill. From certain physical exercises they practised to increase their spiritual mana they were nicknamed the Boxers.

All foreigners were their targets but they turned their attention first to the most innocent of them, the missionaries. Christian missionaries, they said, were poisoning the people. Christian missionaries practised cannibalism. Why did the foreign devils gather abandoned children into orphanages? Obviously they boiled them down to make evil potions from their livers and lights. The weight of their churches on the earth angered the gods. They were responsible for all famines and disasters.

'Sha! Sha! Sha!' shouted the Boxers, dancing up and down.

'Kill! Kill! Kill!'

Tom and Nellie Botham made their quiet missionary journeys on the Sian plains. Their first child was born – Mark, for the Gospel writer. They put his basket cradle and their little luggage in a mule cart. A placid cow kept pace with them. The next year Ruth was born and lived happily amid the alien corn for nine months, then abruptly died. Furlough in England and the third child, Olive (the branch of peace) appeared.

They were not ambitious people. They had learned to speak and think and even make jokes in Mandarin. They would have served happily as Christ's foot-soldiers for the rest of their lives. But the Inland Mission knew their worth. Tom was promoted to supervise all the Mission's work in the huge province of Kansu. They set up a home just outside the northern city of Lanchow. Nellie, with a baby on each knee taught illiterate women to read a Chinese translation of the Bible. Tom, travelling alone now, went to and fro, on and on, across his vast parish. Till he was bone weary, all over, all the time.

In 1897, the year of the blizzard, Grace (the favour of God) was born. But God's favour became rather hard to believe in when the next year Tom was brought home, collapsed and fever-ridden. They sent for the nearest European nurse, seven days' journey away, but he died anyway. It was typhoid, she said, when she arrived too late. A month later the last of the young Bothams was born – pretty Mabel with a secular name and the blondest of blond hair.

There's a lot to be said for a training in self-discipline and the stiff upper lip. Nellie cried herself to sleep every night for a year, but she kept the machinery of life operating.

By the beginning of 1900 the Boxers were slaughtering Chinese converts all over the neighbouring province of Shansi. In the towns a spate of posters recommended church burning as a civic duty, and by way of encouragement, added that anyone who sheltered Christian converts would have a match put to them too. Shortly thereafter, in a matter of days 230 foreigners were slaughtered – most of them missionaries; ten specifically for causing a drought in the province.

The Inland Mission sounded a temporary retreat. *Sauve qui peut.* Nellie, with four small children dependent, acquired a boat. It had a canopy of plaited reeds over the middle section and a long oar at the back for propulsion and steering. With two Chinese servants that she could trust she launched herself and her family on to the Yellow River. It wound its way to the coast right through the province of Shansi, the Boxer stronghold.

For six weeks, one thousand miles, Nellie and the children hid their foreign faces under the plaited reed canopy. At night they would float down below a village, tie up, and the Chinese servants would plod back to buy food and side-step curious questions. One by one the children took sick; Nellie prayed over them – there was nothing else she could do – and they recovered. Grace, a helpful two-year-old, tidied up by pushing the extra tins of food they'd brought into the river.

Shanghai, their destination, seemed like a myth to Nellie, a promised land. It was one of the Treaty Ports that had been forced open to trade. English voices, English faces, soldiers and safety. When she reached it she collapsed. Watching her dying, the missionaries sorrowfully parcelled the motherless lambs out among this and that family that would soon be going on furlough to England and could take them to their grandmother. Mark, a devastatingly good Christian at seven, prayed, 'Please God, take poor Mother to Heaven so that she can be happy with Father.' God didn't oblige. Nellie rose again.

Then it was Grace's turn. Bronchitis and abscesses in both ears. And this is the moment where memory begins.

I was lying in the cot and Mother and the doctor were leaning over the rails looking at me. Mother said, 'She's not asleep, she's pretending,' and I was furious because I wasn't pretending at all.

The past is dark. Memory sheds its bright light on random patches.

England. A little house in Bedford, a home of our own, a family home.
I started school alone. Olive had appendicitis. I had to go through the

14

park to get there. There were two old ladies at a table and little girls all the way down – ten or twelve of them. I was Gracie-at-the-head-of-the-table, not to be confused with Gracie-at-the-side-of-the-table.

At the Bedford house we had a little maid. She used to light fires and help in the house. The time I'm remembering must have been winter. I was feeling the cold as usual and I was allowed to go down to the kitchen where there was a big fire and get dressed there. It was early morning, still dark. There was a book there on the table called *Peep-of-Day*, a pious little book.

I couldn't pass anything without reading it. I was leaning over the candle reading this book and my hair caught alight. The little maid came in and slapped my head to put out the blaze. I was furious with her. I wouldn't speak to her for days because she'd hit me.

Grandmother's. Under her bed there was a box as big as a child's coffin. Laid out inside it was Harriet, the family doll. She was made of stuffed cloth with a china face and long dark hair. The hair had been Mother's once, cut off when she was ill as a child. Harriet had wonderful clothes, all the things that little girls used to wear thirty or forty years before. Long pantaloons, white ones with frills of lace at the bottom, and dresses with smocking and puffed sleeves, long cambric nightgowns. Olive and I used to dress her then take her for walks, each of us holding one of her hands – she was as big as a child. Once a lady behind us said 'I'm sure there's something wrong with that middle one's legs.' We were thrilled.

Mainly though in memory England is summer coloured, is located at Howbury Hall and inhabited by the Polhill children. Long, long, summer days, woods and hayfields, an enormous lawn, an enormous tree. England is safe and full of friends and laughter. At night the Botham children sleep in the Hall or the Polhill children come tumbling into the cottage. Somewhere in the shadows is a governess. Did she teach them all?

'Comment vous appelez-vous?' 'Je m'appelle Grace Botham.'

And from some mysterious place a kindly aunt pops up guiding her baby fingers on the piano.

French and music, the two great loves of my life. I've never been able to live without them.

And then abruptly everything has changed. Someone is missing. Is it Nellie's friend, Mrs Polhill? Does death live in England too?

They are on a ship again, back on their way to China. But only the three little girls this time and Nellie. Mark has been left behind in an English boarding-school to have his upper lip stiffened. He will spend his holidays with Great-aunt Alice and her brother,

15

Great-uncle Joseph, who live in a very quiet way on an inherited income in the gentle elegance of Queen Anne's Gate. It will be seven years before he sees his mother's face again.

The ship is a German one, the S.S. *Roon*. The little girls are racing up and down the corridors to find their own cabin which has mysteriously disappeared. Suddenly they see it and burst through the door to Mother. But it is not Mother. It is a huge female, all bosom and corsets who points at the door with a Valkyrie gesture and thunders at them, 'BE ASUNDER!'

'Later,' says Grace, 'we had races on board and I won a ring. I cried because I hated rings.'

The Boxer Rebellion, bloody and barbarous, was over. Matching barbarity for barbarity, blood for blood, an international military expedition had flattened the infected provinces.

The Celestial Empire lay dying and undefended, a prey to any nation with the strength to exploit it.

The foreigners flowed back into China.

❖   ❖   ❖   ❖

Chefoo was a northern coastal town. It had golden beaches where you could find cat's-eye shells and three schools where the assorted young of foreigners were educated. Most of their parents were missionaries. Most of them were destined to be missionaries. They were to go out and teach the Chinese to be good Christians – to forgive their enemies, do good to them that despitefully used them, and love their neighbours as themselves. Christianity was very good for conquered countries.

Grace was eight when she was sent with Olive to board at the Chefoo schools. They looked alike except that Grace's hair was curly and Olive's was straight. They loved each other and were mortal enemies and Olive was good and righteous and Grace was a rebel. When they had been at school a year Mabel joined them. She was fairer and prettier than the other two and she had the winning ways of a youngest child who has never been cast out of paradise.

There were three Chefoo schools, one for littlies up to ten or eleven, one for the big boys and one for the big girls. The children's nationality was 'foreigner'. That's how they thought of themselves

16

– not as English or American or Canadian, French or Australian, just as 'foreigners'. It didn't mean someone strange or alien to them. 'Foreigner' was the same as other people's nationality is to them; something homelike and comforting with a lot of superiority built in.

They were tarrying on the soil of China because that was where God had asked their dutiful parents to serve. Home was in a different place, usually England, and they were educated as citizens of that different place to which their living bodies would return some day as surely as their living souls would return some day to God.

So, though many of their compatriots had recently died victims of the course of Chinese history, the children learned *real* history, which was the history of far away England and Europe. And it wasn't Chinese they studied but *real* languages – French and German and Latin. They knew more about the emperors of ancient Rome and Caesar's Gallic wars than they did about the dynasties and wars of the ancient civilization that surrounded them. Botany was the most difficult subject because *real* plants, the ones in the books, flowered in English fields. It seemed there weren't many proper plants that you could learn from in China.

And in all this they were no different from thousands of other children dumped by the imperialist tide on to alien shores.

The teaching in Chefoo was thorough and if the children had any brains at all they had a reasonable chance of passing the Oxford Junior and the Oxford Senior Exams when they got to be big boys and girls. The questions, all officially sealed, were sent out from England; the answers, all officially sealed, were sent back to England; the results were cabled out from England. And that, mainly, was what you were educated for.

They were English schools as far as they could be. Cricket and soccer, hockey and tennis, and drill with dumb-bells and swinging clubs. Prep and detentions and conduct-marks, shrill little voices saying 'Ra*ther*!' and 'Don't be a rotter!' And sound-proofed music rooms.

Look: little Gracie Botham, eleven years old, is going up to the music room to do her practice.

She is wearing a pinafore over a blue serge frock, gathered from a yoke, with full sleeves, and a very white, newly-laundered tucker at

17

the neck. Her skirt hangs just a little below her knees, meeting black woollen stockings and, because it is late autumn, black lace-up shoes.

The path to the music rooms runs near the outer wall of the girls' school. Beyond the wall is the highway. From her side Gracie can hear the tinkle, tinkle, tinkle of approaching bells but the sound is so familiar she barely notices it. All day the mules go jangling past. Sometimes from this path she has heard the prolonged screaming of a pig being slaughtered on the highway and the horrible panic of the sound haunts her. Gracie loves all animals except cows and mice.

The highway, packed mud, is just beginning to freeze. The mules slither and slide. Soon it will freeze completely and for some reason it will freeze into exactly even corrugations like roofing iron.

Inside the grounds Gracie passes the amahs' rooms where the kindly waddling yellow women live. Thinking of them, she walks experimentally for a while on her heels. The amahs have no toes to walk on. Lily feet, bound when they were babies, no bigger now than a four-year-old child's. They wear little slippers, four or five inches long, as they toddle to their laundry work and mending. Imagine someone unbinding that four-inch horror of squashed flesh! Gracie stops walking on her heels.

The heavy work of the school is done not by the amahs but by Chinese 'boys' who are really men with pigtails and their heads shaved from the forehead right back to the crown so that they have huge egg-shaped faces. Funny faces, like Humpty Dumpty.

Though Gracie can speak pretty fair Mandarin – she prattled it to her amah as she prattled English to her mother – she knows that at school you don't talk to the servants. They say rude things that are not fit for the pink ears of little English misses.

Beyond the amahs' room Gracie suddenly changes direction and runs across to the lavatories, right in the far corner of the playground. When she comes out, the smell of lye disinfectant hovers around her like a moving cloud for all of ten minutes. Disinfectant is a life-saver in China. Diseases strike with murderous speed. The buckets of excrement below the wooden seats are a breeding ground. The Chinese are not interested in disinfectant. For them the excrement is a life-saver. They pay for the privilege of carting it away to increase the fertility of their fields. Girls' schools yield superior night soil because the product is mixed.

The school faces the golden bay and the sea. If it were summer she'd be swimming now. It is the pride of the Chefoo schools that every girl and every boy learns to swim. All summer there is a raft anchored in the bay. Gracie can swim, but the raft is still beyond her reach. Olive learned to dive off it last summer. Mabel can only dog-paddle in the shallows.

You always wear your pith helmet to the beach, even if it's six o'clock in the morning, or you'll get sunstroke. The last thing you take off before you get into your bathing suit is your cholera belt and it's the first thing you put back on, a nine-inch piece of flannel wrapped cosy round your tummy. Because if you perspire and dry off you can catch a chill and get cholera and die.

Another mule-cart tinkles by. Grace sees it in her mind, piled high with great sacks, as big as coal sacks, filled with peanuts. Each sack costs about ten cents. At school they mince the nuts to make peanut butter. Gracie loves it. Platefuls of bread and pean on the tables for tea. And cups of tea with condensed milk in it. In England milk comes from cows but (thank you, God) there are no cows here in northern China.

At the back of the school are the *kaoliang* fields, stubble now that the harvest is done. You make porridge from *kaoliang*. The teachers call it millet. The little foreigners call it birdseed and turn up their noses at it, preferring rice which is something of a luxury up here in the north. But the *kaoliang* fields were thrilling a month ago when the harvest was ripe. Like fields of wheat grown ten feet high with stalks as thick as bamboos. Autumn is the season for bandits. The crime rate rises as the *kaoliang* grows. It's as easy to find a mouse in a wheat-field as it is to find a bandit in a field of *kaoliang*.

Despite the bandits and the cholera belts, school (like China) is an ordinary place, secure and unremarkable, where the ordinary days mount to ordinary weeks and the ordinary years piling up beneath your feet gradually raise you from childhood.

But look back through the accumulated light of twenty-four thousand days and the ordinary hours of childhood glow luminous and mythical.

Remember the stories on Saturday morning, read by a tired

teacher while the little girls, each with her pile of mending in front of her, sew on tapes and buttons and with black wool weave the everlasting darns in the heels and knees of stockings. And, mouths moist and gaping, eyes hypnotized by the words, mend less and less, needles crawling to a halt.

Remember the Saturday afternoons tucked in bed in a silent dormitory to expiate your sins. Ten times late in the morning or talking in class and you've got yourself one black conduct mark. Every conduct mark costs one hour of Saturday's free time wasted in bored contemplation of the dormitory ceiling.

'Gracie Botham, three hours!' Gracie, though good at her lessons, is a naughty girl. 'Why can't you be like Olive?'

Sunday, the Lord's Day, and no mistake! A quarter of an hour kneeling by your bed when you wake up, then down to breakfast and for half an hour after it communal prayers in the big schoolroom. Then when you're neat and tidy in your best clothes form a crocodile in order of height and walk the two miles to the Union Church. In summer you wear your pith helmet and what with the heat and the grating rub and squeak of the brim of your helmet against your partner's, you're not exactly in a calm and holy frame of mind when you get there.

The Union Church is interdenominational. What kind of service are you going to encounter? It depends what brand of missionary is in the area. Only it won't be anything thrillingly evil like heathen or Catholic.

Gracie listens attentively to the sermon. Very attentively.

Two miles back in the re-formed crocodile. In summer there is lettuce salad for lunch, but this is China and everything has to be sterilized so the beautiful fine-chopped lettuce has had boiling water poured over it. It looks like dark green wrinkled grass, and slides down slimily.

Rest time. You can read if you want to or go to sleep. And it's time for the special treat – one sweet from the sweets in your very own tuckbox.

Monday. With the Lord's Day safely behind her, Grace re-enacts the sermon for her giggling friends. She squares her conscience by telling herself that she's not mocking the missionaries – merely copying them. It's not her fault if they're ridiculous.

If you've got a penchant for acting, private ridicule is the only venue open to you. Plays are read, set speeches learned by heart, but never acted. Acting, like dancing and card-playing are of the devil. 'It's not what they are, my dears, but what they lead to!'

But all the little female foreigners practise the royal curtsey in case they should encounter King Edward's queen.

Winter: and Grace's punctuality marks mount. The Chinese 'boys' rush steaming kerosene tins of hot water up the stairs to the corridors outside the dormitories. The little girls come running with their dippers and carry the water in, careful, careful, to their own basins to wash. If you're not quick when you hear the rattle of the tins the water will have a rim of ice round it when you get to it. Cleanliness is next to Godliness, but Grace, a slow starter in the mornings, often settles for a lower level of virtue and goes down unwashed.

But the quicker the water freezes and the worse your chilblains swell and itch, the closer you are to Christmas and two whole months at home.

In winter it was far too cold to be at school. So those whose parents lived too far away, in really remote areas, were moved into one building and the rest of us were shipped off home.

Oh, what a commotion there'd be! First of all the ones who were going to Shanghai by ship would start for the wharf – a long line of rickshaws pulled by grinning coolies with an excited boy or girl waving from each. Then the ones who were staying would be moved into one building with a lot of noise and running to and fro.

Then a jingling of bells and a clatter of hooves! The mule-litter for the Bothams had arrived.

There were two mules and a muleteer. The litter, called a *shantze*, was a tiny house of straw matting built between two long poles that extended fore and aft. The back of the house was made of blue cloth with a tiny window of mica; the bottom was just a sort of rope net.

First all our luggage was spread over the net then masses and masses of padded rugs and eiderdowns and cushions were piled over that. Then one by one Olive and Mabel and I would bend down and climb in. The servants would cover us up and tuck us in with eiderdowns all around us and stone hot-water bottles to keep our feet warm.

Then several coolies would come and help and they'd all lift up the rear shafts. 'Yah, yah, YOO-EH!' They'd give a sort of grunting yell as they heaved them. They'd push the back mule between the shafts. His nose would come right up to the window at the back of the wagon and we'd all have slid down and be almost falling out the front. Then with all the commotion, and the howling and yelling, and the shuffling of the mule they'd push the front one back into the shafts till his great hindquarters seemed almost in our faces. Then up would come the shafts with great yells and they'd fasten them on to his back. There we were at last on an even keel about five feet from the ground and wobbling like a ship in a rough sea as we staggered off.

Gradually the mules would settle down to a steady pace and we'd snuggle down under the rugs for it was bitterly cold. Twenty miles to go, but it took five hours. We travelled round the coast, right on the beach near the water's edge where the sand was nice and hard. We'd pass great drifts of frozen foam piled up as high as a house all the way along the beach like great mounds of dirty snow.

On and on the mules would trudge. We'd get so cold. We'd call to the coolie, trying to get him to lift us down so that we could have a run on the beach and warm ourselves. But usually he pretended not to hear us because it disturbed his rhythm. On and on he went steadily, asleep sometimes but still keeping on walking.

Finally after four hours we'd leave the beach and turn inland. Still three miles to go. Creak, creak, creak through the paddy-fields on a narrow path just big enough for the mules to walk along; because in China every bit of the ground is cultivated. We'd all be peering out by this time and at last we'd see them, the city walls of Ning Hai, twelve feet high and crenellated, but looking tiny at that distance, as though they were only a few inches tall. It was ages before they slowly got higher and higher. The walls were centuries old and the two gates we went through were at right angles to each other because devils couldn't turn corners. In between the gates there'd be a lot of noise – people bargaining and buying and selling. Through the second gate and straight down the main road, a mud and brick road crowded with all these buyers and sellers, oh, a fearful commotion – the noise and the press of people.

We went along the road about a hundred yards and we came to a high wall. And then a door in it, and bang! bang! bang! on that door. The gateman would come rushing out, they'd let the *shantze* down, Mother would come running, and all the servants, and oh! the noise, the shrieks, the jabbering in Chinese. The excitement! People unpacking the *shantze* and lugging our stuff into the right rooms and tidying up. All turmoil and joy. We were home!

In the silt of memory there is always one place, intact, that is more firmly home than any impostor of a johnny-come-lately. The smell of that bush by the gate, the texture of the veranda boards, that blue vase, speak to you in a mute and potent language. Under decades of living there is the Inland Mission Compound at Ning

Hai, with Olive and Mabel and Mother, waiting patiently for Grace. She goes in . . .

through the gatehouse where the gate-man lived and our sedan chair was kept. Past the first courtyard where the amahs lived. Then there was a three-roomed house for another family of foreigners, missionaries too of course. Through a gate and up some steps with a stone lion on either side and a swing in the middle. We'd named the lions Herminius and Spurius Lartius and the swing was brave Horatius in the middle. We had a very classical education.

Persimmons in the garden, and pomegranate trees. When the fruit was ripe Mother sent baskets of it to Chefoo. Once a year we were the most popular girls in school. In summer there were masses of cosmos and balsam all in bloom.

Our house had four rooms and a long veranda. Dining-room, playroom and two bedrooms. We took turns sleeping with Mother in her big bed. Oh it was lovely! How could anyone so small and thin feel so soft. And always warm. So clean, her flannel nightgown smelling of soap and her long hair in a plait.

There was no kitchen in the house. You went down a brick path and through a moongate to the cooking quarter. The servants lived there. We were allowed to talk to the servants in our courtyard but we weren't allowed in the kitchen with them because they loved to teach us swear-words. Mother never knew it but I did learn some – very lovely and effective! I can still say them in my mind. Years and years later one of the old Chefoo boys in the First World War told me what they meant and I promised not to use them again, and I never have, just for love of Jack.

The kitchen-boy used to carry our meals, all covered over, across to our courtyard. I remember one lunch-time, we were really hungry. Just as he stepped out with the tray a thunderstorm crashed down. We had to stand there and watch our lunch separated from us by a wall of water.

Beyond the kitchen was another courtyard. There was a pergola with pumpkins climbing over it and a chapel where we had services. A Chinese Christian minister lived there with his wife and family. They had two little children who used to come and play with us. We always talked to them in Chinese. I can remember one of them, a little girl younger than we were, looking up at me and indignantly saying, 'Don't call me An-wei! Call me Miss Chou!'

I was always happy when I had a piano or organ to play, so when we were home for the holidays it was my job to play for the chapel services. It was one of those little pedal organs; you pushed with your knee to make it loud or soft. One note didn't go at all and there was another that would go on and on every now and then like a stuck car horn. One day after service a dear old woman came up to Mother and said, 'You know when that Number Two Missie plays the organ I feel as if I'm in Heaven!'

So I've done my Christian work. I've sent one woman to heaven.

One of the first things we did when we got home was rush down and visit the amahs. We'd always had amahs; we learned Chinese from them as we learned English from our mother. It was only coolie language though – the simplest kind of Mandarin.

When we were little the amah used to sing to us. I've always remembered a lovely song about a little mouse that ran up a lamp and found some oil to drink. He wouldn't come down again, so the mother mouse had to go up and carry him down. There are two words for carry – *pao* and *pei*. *Pao* means to carry in your arms as you would a baby. *Pei* means to carry something slung over your back. *Pei* is the word that's used in the song. That always tickled us, the picture of Mother Mouse with little oily Baby Mouse slung by his tail over her shoulder.

There isn't really a tune to the song; the amah would sit and croon it, swaying all the time. Many years later I wrote a song about it for my own son; I used the tuneless bit as the chorus. He loved it and now my grandchildren love it too.

> At night when he was tucked in bed,
> My little boy would say,
> 'Tell me about when you were young,
> And lived so far away.'
> And what I told brought back to me
> That far-off land across the sea –
> Way back in China – in old Cathay.

> *Hsiao lao-shu*
> *Shang teng-t'ai*
> *T'ou yu ha (n)*
> *Hsia pu lai*
> *Chiao t'a ma-ma*
> *Pei hsia lai.*

> And that's the song my Amah sang
> To lull me off to sleep.
> 'Once have got one piecie mouse,
> He climb up lamp to peep.
> Findee plenty oil to dlink.
> Talkee, 'No come down I tink,'
> Call he mama cally he down,'
> Sh—sh—go sleep.

24

Little mousie
Climbee lampee
Findee dlinkee
No come downee
Call he mama
Cally he downee.

I heard the mule-bells tinkling by,
I heard the temple gong.
And sometimes there were fireworks
That crackled all night long.
But close beside me Amah stayed,
Lest I should wake and feel afraid,
While swaying from side to side she sang
Her tuneless little song.

Hsiao lao-shu . . .

My son's own children now come near
To hear the lullaby . . .
The story of the little mouse
Who climbed a lamp so high.
And when he'd filled himself with oil
He wouldn't come down again.
So call his Mum to carry him down,
And sing the old refrain . . .

Hsiao lao-shu . . .

At Ning Hai there was one amah that we were especially fond of. She had a big *k'ang* in her room, a brick bed as long as a divan with an opening in the front and a fire burning in it continually. It's a lovely way to keep warm. She used to sit on it all day doing the mending. In the middle of her room was an exciting stone manhole that opened into a cellar where the whole floor was covered with fir-cones. We used to love jumping down and playing there.

One day I said to her, 'Why don't you sleep down here? It's lovely!' Oh, she was so angry! She went to Mother and said, 'That Number Two Missie says I've got to sleep down the hole and I won't!' I'm afraid Mother had a lot of trouble from that *er kuniang* (Number Two Missie). Olive was *da kuniang* – the Big Miss. And Mabel was *siao kuniang* – Little Miss – but I was nothing but a number. The middle one always has the worst of everything. 'Olive must have it first because she's the oldest!' 'Mabel must have it first because she's the youngest!' The poor old middle one never gets a look in. I used to complain about it all the time. That's why I was so naughty I think.

Soon after we got home it was Christmas and that was the great time of the year. One of the coolies would walk back to Chefoo. He'd be away three days. The first day he'd walk the twenty miles to Chefoo. Next day he'd collect all the orders Mother had given him and the mail – parcels from England from grandmother and my aunts and uncles, all posted three months in advance. On the third day he'd start early in the morning and tramp all the way back with a long shaft over his shoulder and a huge basket hanging from each end of it, both of them bulging with goodies, all sorts of tinned stuff and luxuries that you couldn't buy locally. Oh, those wonderful parcels from Grandma, full of dresses and fine-knitted woollens and dolls and all kinds of toys!

And after Christmas – still all those weeks of holidays. If the weather was fine and not impossibly cold we'd wrap up in all the winter clothes we had, all the woollies from Grandma, and go for a walk or a ride. The Chinese didn't wear wool; they had padded clothes and they got fatter as winter advanced. Three-coat weather, four-coat weather. The very coldest was seven-coat weather. The little boys ran round like little fat scarecrows with their arms sticking out stiff from their sides. They didn't get washed the whole winter. We did; the coolies would carry hot water across from the kitchen and pour it into a tin bath.

Our favourite walk was round the city walls. They were ten or twelve feet wide, wide enough for a carriage to go along; made of mud and bricks but broken here and there. You went up from a ramp on the city side and to walk right round took us exactly an hour. When we went for a ride it was on Patience. We weren't allowed pets – cats or dogs or anything – because they carried diseases. Once there'd been a missionary who'd died at school through being bitten by a rabid dog. But we did have Patience the donkey. And we loved her more than anything else in the world, I think – even each other. When we went back to England we couldn't understand why Patience couldn't come with us. Our hearts were broken.

Ning Hai was in a peaceful part of the country and sometimes the *mafoo* (the man who looked after the donkey) was allowed to take us out alone. We'd all three sit on Patience's back in a row and walk between the fields. We used to come to places where no white person had been seen before and the Chinese would stop working and stare at us with their mouths open. Once we came to a pagoda on a little hill and Patience decided to walk up to it. It was quite a steep slope and one by one all three of us slid off over her tail into a giggling heap.

One day a really strange thing happened. We were out with Patience and the *mafoo* and we came to a little hill that we'd never seen before. It looked like a miniature volcano, not more than twelve feet high with a crater in the top. I had to get off of course and scramble up it. It was all dark, but the hole didn't stop and there were steps leading down from it. I poked my head in. It was quite dark. Then as my eyes adjusted I saw below me a whole mass of faces staring up. The big egg faces of Chinese men. They were at benches making something – sewing I think. I suppose I must have blocked out the sunlight because they were all staring up, gaping. I wonder what they thought when they saw this weird foreign creature peering down. I scrambled out and ran away as fast as I could with my heart beating. Much later I found out that factories were sometimes built like that, like igloos of mud. It kept the cold out in winter and the heat in summer.

When it was too cold to go out, or wet, we did what all children do in the school holidays. We'd play in the playroom where there was a *k'ang* or we'd sit around the huge stove in the dining-room and Mother would read aloud to us while we did our crochet or knitting. She was a wonderful reader, she could make anything exciting. I remember when she read us *The Rise and Fall of the Dutch Republic*. Nowadays I don't suppose people have read it – it would be boring to them. But we thoroughly enjoyed it and got excited over it. Erasmus seemed like a family friend to us.

We read a lot. Edith Nesbit was a favourite – *The Red House* and *The Five Children*. We loved *Lays of Ancient Rome* – that was what we named our lions from – and *Greek Myths and Legends*. *The Black Tulip* – how excited we got over that! And I remember so well the first time I read *Les Malheurs de Sophie*.

Our grandmother used to send us marvellous games from England. Though we weren't allowed to play cards, in the ordinary sense, we had a sort of Happy Families substitute. There was one set where all the cards were pictures from the Tate Gallery and the idea was that you collected all of one artist's paintings. When I went to the Tate Gallery years later I recognized all the paintings from our cards. We used to make up limericks too – we got very good at that – and play chess. Mother was a fine chess player. She was good at such a lot of things.

As we got older we used to be given assignments to do in the long holiday. Olive and I were stuck one day over a problem in algebra, and we were fighting about it. Olive was good at maths, much better than I was, but she wasn't a good teacher. 'How does it come to that?' I'd say and all she'd answer was, 'Well, it *has* to be that.'

This time while we were fighting Mother came in. 'What's the matter?' she said. 'Can I help?'

We were very scornful. 'You wouldn't know,' we said. 'We're doing *algebra!*'

She looked at us and said, 'My dear girls, I did all those exams long before you were born.' So we showed her the problem and she solved it without any trouble at all and explained it in a way that I could understand. She was a very accomplished teacher, and well-educated. She gave up a lot to become a missionary.

I don't know why Olive and I fought so much. Different natures I suppose. We'd be at it like a pair of tigers, snarling and fighting. Then Mother would come in and immediately Olive would be sweet and nice and

27

I'd get all the blame. I'd go for Olive afterwards. '*Why* do you go on like that? *Why* do you pretend you weren't fighting too?'

'I can't help it,' she'd say. 'When Mother comes in I just don't feel angry any more.'

I'd keep on feeling the same whoever was there. So that really it was as much her fault as mine. Or even if it were all mine, she changed so much when anyone else was there that I just took it as hypocrisy – getting out of trouble and letting me get in. Perhaps there was jealousy between us. Neither of us fought with Mabel. She was very different from us, very pretty and loving and lovable. Hair the colour of honey. We both used to look after her and protect her.

It was as hot in summer as it was cold in winter. The temperature used to go up to somewhere between 100 and 105 degrees Fahrenheit. But Chefoo was by the sea and you could bathe and swim and row there, so during the August holidays instead of us going home Mother used to come to Chefoo and stay at the school Sanatorium. Even when it wasn't holidays she would turn up sometimes in the summer and stay there. At those times we were allowed to go across and sleep with her, one at a time.

We used to take turns and it was marvellous when your turn came. From the girls' school you went down a path into a shady gully, very deep and cool. At the bottom there was a little stream with a bridge across it. Then you'd go panting up the other side and there was the San, a lovely big house in a beautiful garden, and there was Mother in it.

One day, when I was thirteen, Mother was in Chefoo and it was my turn to go and stay the night. But just before I left Mabel came to me and said she had a tummy-ache and could she go instead of me. I was disappointed, all day I'd been looking forward to it, but I could never refuse Mabel anything so I swapped turns with her.

The next morning the headmistress sent for Olive and me. She looked very strange when we went in and she said, 'I have something very sad to tell you. Last night the Lord took your little sister.'

The next day they buried Mabel. We went to the funeral. It was cholera. Not the kind that makes you vomit but a violent intestinal infection that in those days, before there were injections, killed you in five hours – you were just dried out from it. Everyone was very frightened because they thought there would be an epidemic at the school. But there wasn't. Mabel was the only foreigner to get ill.

It felt very strange to me after Mabel was dead – apart from the grief. I don't think I ever got over it. It was a shock of course, but more than that, it left us incomplete. I couldn't remember the time before Mabel was born. There had always been three of us girls and me in the middle. The 'three Bs' they used to call us at school. I never felt quite so special again and life never seemed as safe as it had been.

I don't know how Mother felt about Mabel's death. She was a very brave woman and she didn't show her feelings. Once when we were at school she arrived in Chefoo and it was three days before they told us she was there in hospital. She had been at Ning Hai, the only foreigner on the compound at the time. The weather was icy and she slipped and broke her leg. She lay there with the servants standing round looking utterly helpless. She told them to take a door off its hinges but they wouldn't believe that she really wanted them to do something so peculiar and it was ages before she could convince them. Finally they did manage to get the door off and under her directions with a lot of handling and pushing they managed to get her on to it. She got the amahs to fetch blankets and cover her up and she had to lie all night like that. When the night finally ended and daylight came she sent a coolie to get a *shantze* and they manhandled her into it. She had to endure the five hours jogging till they reached Chefoo and the relief of English doctors and nurses. She'd endured so much pain that she wasn't fit to see us for three days, but when they finally sent for us, she told us the story as though it was the greatest joke in the world and she had us crying with laughter as she described her conversations with the servants trying to get them to take the door down. It was years before I realized what an excruciating experience she'd been through.

That was the kind of woman she was – she thought more of our feelings than her own.

I think it must have been after Mabel's death, what with all the sorrow, and people saying, 'She is with her father and Our Father,' that I felt very religious and decided to be confirmed. I know Mother was very pleased about it. She'd never said anything but I think perhaps she'd had some doubts already about my spiritual state.

I learned all the Church of England catechism – 'What is your name? Answer N or M. Who gave you that name? My Godfather and my Godmother at my baptism . . .' and so on. But that year no C. of E. clergyman turned up in the area so I had to be dipped with the Baptists.

They did it in the sea. The wardrobe mistress had us all dressed in our white summer clothes – white shoes, white stockings, white dresses. But she insisted on our wearing dark knickers so that we wouldn't spoil our white ones. We were dipped in and we came out dripping, all white but with this great big dark patch showing through. It took away the glory and solemnity of the performance.

But in spite of the black knickers I really did believe. I had faith and I knew faith could move mountains and if you prayed for anything with true faith in your heart God would answer your prayer. In winter, when we went to church in the crocodile we wore our best Sunday clothes and our own hats; the pith helmets were only for summer. The wardrobe mistress was a great friend of Mother's and I suppose she wanted to help us in any way she could. I needed a new hat so – Heaven help us – she made me one. A dreadful affair it was, made of velvet in two shades of grey with a little brim and two feather-shaped pieces of velvet sticking up like deformed ears. It might have been suitable for a fifty-year-old missionary. But I was thirteen and self-conscious and even in those days I had a little bit of taste. And I would have to wear it in the crocodile as we passed the boys on their way to church. It was more misery and humiliation than I could bear.

My dormitory window looked east towards the sea and that Saturday night I sat up in my bed all night and prayed for the end of the world. Perhaps it wasn't all night. Perhaps it was only to ten or eleven o'clock but it certainly seemed like all night. I had faith. I sincerely believed that the Lord would come in all his glory so that I wouldn't have to wear that hat to church. But He didn't. I did have to wear the hat, right past all the boys. I lost my faith in the efficacy of prayer that Sunday and I've never regained it.

After Mabel's death Olive and I drew closer together. I found I didn't much like being alone. I used to try and avoid spending hours by myself in bed on Saturday afternoons because of conduct marks.

I said to Olive, 'If you don't get enough bad marks to send you to bed for at least one hour next Saturday I'll . . .' Well, I don't know what I threatened her with. Anyway she didn't like the thought of my being all alone either. She really was very kind to me in spite of our fights. So one week we both really tried. Olive was late all week and inattentive whenever she thought it would be noticed. And do you know what happened? They said, 'Olive dear, you're not feeling well, are you?'

I performed miracles of punctuality and I scarcely talked at all in class. I got through with only nine bad marks for punctuality and attention – not enough to earn me a single conduct mark. We had to record our own marks and hand in the total at the end of the week. I think everyone was honest about their marks – I know I was. Scrupulously honest.

I handed in my nine marks and the mistress said, 'Grace Botham, you've kept back one mark!' So I was given a conduct mark and had to go to bed on Saturday afternoon as usual. Do you wonder that I'm sceptical of professing religion?

When that happened I went to the person who'd done it to me and I said, 'I hate you!' She said, 'What did you say?' I wouldn't answer. She called me up to her bedroom – Miss Wilson, it was. She taught history and I've never liked history since. I wouldn't tell her what I'd said. I said, 'You heard me didn't you?' She said, 'You are to confess what you said.' I still wouldn't speak. She said, 'That tongue which has said wicked things shall not speak again until it has confessed its fault.'

My mother happened to be in Chefoo at that time and we went to visit her in the afternoon. Every girl in the school could communicate in deaf and dumb language – we were so often kept in silence at the table. Olive and I went over to see Mother and I didn't speak a word. I'd been told not to speak. I didn't speak. I talked in deaf and dumb language all afternoon and Olive translated it. It was quite fun.

Not just fun, though. Even though I was out of sight and hearing of the school and Olive certainly wouldn't have given me away I felt obliged to carry out the punishment. Otherwise I would have felt dishonest. We had very strong moral values. I can't tell lies even by implication. Only once in my life have I ever knowingly told a lie and then it was a desperate situation of life or death. That was why I was so hurt when I was accused of lying.

I kept up the silence for three days and then I got bored with it. So I went up to Miss Wilson's room and banged on the door. She told me to come in. 'Miss Wilson,' I said, 'I said I hated you.' And I went out. She rushed out and caught me and took me into her room. She knelt me down beside her bed and prayed over me. She went on so long that I just crept out and left her praying. I'd like to have seen her face when she opened her eyes but she never said anything about it.

Most of the girls took all this moral and religious attitude for granted and they carried on with it. Nine out of ten of the people I knew at Chefoo became missionaries or are still very religious but I was beginning to question it. It used to worry me that the missionaries quarrelled among themselves. The Methodists would say that the Baptists were wrong and the Baptists would say that the Presbyterians were wrong and they would all say that the Catholics were wrong. I used to wonder what the Chinese would think. Wouldn't they say, 'If they are all quarrelling surely they may all be wrong!'

Mind you, I'm not a heathen. I believe there is something – something we'll never know. But I can't believe in an anthropomorphic God.

That year something did happen that impressed me with the wonder of the universe more than all the Bible and the religious talk could do. It was 1910 – the year of Halley's comet. One evening when it was dark and we were all in our dressing gowns ready for bed we were told we could go down to the hockey field, because the comet was passing overhead. So we all trooped out, past the tennis courts and the garden – all the familiar places looking mysterious in the dark. Then down a very steep bank on to the hockey field. It was a wonderful place to see the comet from. The high enclosing bank narrowed our view so that this huge thing seemed to extend right across – oh, a third of the sky. The brilliant head and the long, long tail. It seemed to move so slowly that it lighted up the whole world. And when the head and the bright part of the tail had passed out of sight there were still flakes of light trailing behind. I don't know if that's accurate but that's how it is in my memory.

The hockey field always had a flavour of strange wonders for me, because in that steep bank was a locked door. We never saw it open. Behind it was the ice cave. In winter the coolies would go down to the beach and cut away great chunks of ice and carry them, dripping all the way, up to the school to store them in the cave. So there was the frozen foam deep under the hillside waiting for summer. Then they'd bring it out in blocks for the ice-box – literally an ice-box in those days.

31

About this time, or a little earlier, there was an outburst of bubonic plague right across the province. Apparently it starts with a big black lump under your arm and then you die very quickly. They sealed off the whole compound – schools, Sanatorium, hospital and staff houses . . . there was a wall right round it anyway. All the gates were sealed except one and a quarantine station was set up there. The only people who were allowed in and out were certain coolies who had to go and bring water in from the artesian wells. The water was meant to be absolutely pure, untouched by human hand, but I once saw one of our coolies stop on the way back and give a rickshaw coolie a drink. The rickshaw coolie just dipped his own mug into this so pure water.

Mother was at Ning Hai at the time of the plague and they sent for her so that she could be in quarantine with us in case anything happened. On the last day before she came in she was kept in someone's house, or a Chinese Inn, all by herself for twenty-four hours – that was the incubation period. She said that was the one time she felt in danger. All night she could feel the lumps starting under arms. But it was only imagination. Nothing happened.

I remember during that time being on the boys' football field. We'd gone down to watch a match and I got bored and wandered away near the wall. I managed to peer over it or through it and there on the road, quite close to where I was, was a dead man – just lying there. That was at the height of the plague. No one at school caught it.

*   *   *   *

Grotesque, myopic, the Manchus still basked in the eye of Heaven, though their throne was tottery and rotten. One decent shove and it would fall.

The foreigners shored it up contemptuously. Better to deal with the deluded Manchus than some unpredictable upstart government. The Manchus for all their illusions of grandeur understood a simple bargain – money for privilege. The foreigners advanced enormous loans to the Emperor; in return their trading rights were guaranteed and expanded.

Below the opulent Manchus were the Mandarins, a class of government officials who had won their privileged position by success in the gruelling three-day examinations on the Chinese classics. With the help of a large dollop of corruption and extortion on the side they lived very well. The merchants, both foreign and Chinese, amassed fabulous fortunes.

At the bottom of the structure the peasants tried to force

exhausted limbs and shrinking lands to yield enough to cope with the monstrous taxes loaded on them. Often they failed and joined the semi-starving – the landless poor, the urban workers, the beggars.

The rich oppressed the poor. So it had always been; it was a fact of life. Only when the oppression became more than flesh could bear would there be a revolution. A dynasty would topple, a new one be hoisted in its place, promising redress, blessings, the good life. And for a while, a decade, a century, life would be easier. Then the old system would re-assert itself. The rich would oppress the poor. It was a fact of life.

But now that China was more or less in touch with the rest of the world, a new group arose who, having lived abroad and seen how other countries organized themselves, could contemplate alternatives. The voice heard most clearly and most often was Sun Yat-sen's.

'We are the poorest and weakest state in the world, occupying the lowest position in international affairs; the rest of the world is the carving knife and the serving dish while we are the fish and the meat.'

His remedies sounded so simple. Depose the Manchus. Cast the foreigners out of China. Let all Chinese feel themselves one of a single vast family working and caring for each other. Let them rule themselves as a democracy. Let the wealth belong to those who produce it: let poverty be banished.

But how could anyone change the structure of the world like that? Change the things that had always been and would always be?

It seemed that quite a lot of people were willing to try. Nine revolts in ten years; the tenth on the tenth day of the tenth month, in the year 1911 was successful. More or less. China became a republic and Dr Sun Yat-sen was asked to be its president. But there was a complication. An ambitious and devious official of the Manchu government, Yüan Shih-k'ai, with his private army had seized control of three provinces, including the city of Peking, the home of the Emperor. The Republicans depended on popular support. They had no army strong enough to dislodge Yüan. It seemed desirable to negotiate. The bargain that was struck was disastrous but inevitable. If Yüan would force the Emperor to abdicate, Sun Yat-sen would yield to him the presidency of the new republic. Yüan accepted enthusiastically.

The revolution went on for several years with the fortunes changing this way and that. We didn't know much about it at school. We knew the names of the leaders, Yüan Shih-k'ai and Sun Yat-sen, but we were children and to us the detention you'd just been given and the result of next week's hockey match were more important than anything outside the walls. We did know that there was fighting going on in Chefoo and that people were being taken away and executed by one side or the other.

I saw it happening once. I'll never forget it as long as I live. There was a field not far away with a tall hedge of bamboo in front of it. That was supposed to be the place where they executed people – cut their heads off. We used to pass it on the way to church. One Sunday when we were walking home from the Union Church a group of soldiers came towards us. When they got close we saw they had two men with them, two prisoners with their arms tightly bound with ropes. The soldiers were shoving and prodding them along. And one of them – one of the soldiers – had an axe up on his shoulder. An enormous great big thing with a huge blade. You could see right away what it was. It was horrible.

But the really weird thing about it was those prisoners. They were being shoved and forced along and, do you know, they were laughing. Looking at each other and grinning and laughing. The soldiers pushed them in behind the bamboo hedge and the man with the huge axe followed. It was such a familiar place to us that it was hard to believe what our eyes were seeing. I kept thinking of those grinning heads rolling bloody on the grass.

Mind you, we saw some extraordinary sights in China. There was always a lot of cruelty. The punishment for a thief was to have his legs cut off just below the knees and many and many a time we'd pass legless beggars who'd been thieves. They had pads under their knees that they knelt on. They couldn't walk of course, but they had things like flat-irons with wooden handles in their hands and they used those for their forefeet and went along quite merrily on all fours. When someone came they'd leave go of one of the irons and hold out a hand grinning and calling out. If we weren't in the crocodile we'd throw money to them and they'd laugh away when they caught it. The point about the punishment was that they couldn't reach to steal any more.

The thing that made us most aware of the revolution was the servants' pigtails. Pigtails were a Manchu convention and wearing them was a sign of subservience to the Emperor. The first time the republicans rose in the town a lot of the men were so excited and thrilled that they cut off their pigtails.

But then the royalists managed to retake the town. And they cut off the heads that had no pigtails. After that most people played safe – our servants among them. When the republicans were on top the men of the town would wrap their pigtails round their heads and hide them under the little skull caps they always wore. When the royalists came they'd let them down again.

Ordinary people manage like that in troubled times all over the world. Later in China when the north and the south were fighting, the shopkeepers kept two flags in the back of their shops. 'Who won last night? Oh, the north,' and the northern flag would be put out till the tide turned. And in Nazi times I've seen people, crossing the frontier from Germany, take off the little swastika badges they wore and pin them under their lapels.

The republicans ordered the women to unbind their feet. But that was impossible. The little girls suffered agony from the binding of feet, but once they were adult and their feet had stopped trying to grow they didn't suffer any more pain – only they could never do more than toddle along. When they tried to unbind their feet after the revolution it was as agonizing as the binding had been. So in the end all they did was unbind the feet of the children who were just a few years old – they were in pain anyway, the poor little things. And of course the babies were no longer bound. When I came back to China it was an amazing thing to see little girls running – actually running – as freely as the boys.

I'd lived almost all my life in China and to me a Chinese man didn't look like a *man* at all. Not in the way foreigners were men. He was just a Chinaman, which was something different. Then gradually as they cut off their pigtails and began to grow their hair where it had been shaved before, they began to look like ordinary humans. Like *men*. I began to see that some of them were very good-looking.

I don't think they thought of us as humans either. At home in the holidays we'd often go out for picnics in places where white people had never been seen before. We'd think we were right away, no village anywhere near, and we'd sit down and start our picnic, and before long – I don't know where they sprang from – there'd be a complete ring of people all around us, staring. We had a technique for dealing with it. If they moved close in, crowding round us, one of us would whisper, 'Look at their feet!' We'd all swing solemnly round and stare at their feet and after a moment or two you'd see those feet begin to shuffle and back away.

They never offered any violence, but they used to call us foreign devils. There was a chant they had – 'Devil, devil with eight legs!' they'd shout at us. A spider has eight legs and it's a sort of nothing because it isn't an animal and it isn't an insect. I think we seemed unnatural in the same way. But they were always good-humoured about it. They'd laugh and call out, 'You old devil!' We could speak Chinese so we'd turn round and say something back to them and – oh, then they realized that we were human!

It was different of course with the ones we knew – the ones that worked for us. People have said to me in New Zealand, 'Fancy you having servants, treating people like slaves, and making them work.' But the Chinese were anxious to work for foreigners because they paid well and the conditions were good. And a bond grew up between us. My amah cried like anything when I couldn't take her to England with me. And we were fond of them. We were all part of one household.

Round about this time I was due to sit my Oxford Junior Exam. I'd been working for it in an haphazard sort of way, but I was depending a lot on getting work done in the week immediately before it – Revision Week. At the beginning of that week I went up to do my practice in the music room and I fell asleep. The next girl found me like that with my head on the keyboard. I went back to the classroom and I fell asleep there. They couldn't wake me up. So they put me to bed. I kept on sleeping so they sent for mother; they thought I'd got sleeping sickness. I don't remember her being there at all. I slept the whole week and at the end of it I woke up again perfectly all right. Except that I hadn't done any revision. I sat the Exam. knowing I'd fail and not caring in the least. Finally two months later the results came. They read them out in the big school room and when Olive heard my name in the pass list she burst into tears of relief. I just felt mildly surprised.

By this time Olive had taken her Oxford Senior Exam. and Mark had finished school in Bedford and was working in a bank and taking a language course at London University. Mother was due for a furlough in England. It was time we all went home and started being a family again.

They travelled by way of the newly-opened Trans-Siberian Railway. This was in July 1913.

Russia was like a great pupa straining to free itself of its restrictive cocoon. For decades successive Czars and their ministers had been explaining to the pupa that it wasn't in a cocoon, that it hadn't outgrown the cocoon it wasn't in, that it wasn't hungry, that if it wriggled and heaved it would be punished, that a cocoon was where God wanted a pupa to be, especially if it was a Holy Russian pupa, and that to think of breaking out was suicidal and blasphemous.

The pupa still wriggled and heaved. Right now it was reaching such a climax of movement that it seemed that this time, this time, the bonds must break.

There were more than two thousand strikes in Russia in 1912. Over half of them were for 'political' reasons.

Siberia wasn't a place to the non-Russian world; it was a word that meant punishment, expiation, the slow death.

Most recently it meant a massacre. The gold-miners of Lena worked for a starvation wage for about fourteen hours a day. When they struck for the means and the right to live the Czarist Government sent troops in and 170 workers were shot.

You thought of Siberia in those terms: agony, exile, blood on the snow and a demented howling of wolves.

Yet when we got there it was full of flowers. And oh, so hot! Even on the ship that took us across if you lay down on the deck you left a damp silhouette of yourself in perspiration. And at the branch-line station they had rush mats on the couches so that you wouldn't stick to the surface.

The sky was so blue in Siberia – like an up-turned blue saucer. We put out our hands, Olive and I and the young bride who was travelling with us, and our hands came back to us clutching masses of flowers. Blue and white they were with long, long stems. We decorated the compartment with them, flowers everywhere, but of course they drooped and died almost straight away.

The young bride was soft and glowing with love and frustration. There'd been a mix-up over the bookings. Mother and Olive and I had a four-berth compartment and a man had been put in with us in the fourth berth. The Russians are like the Japanese; they're not worried by things like that. In the end the young bridegroom on his honeymoon had to share with the man and the poor little bride had to move in with us.

(Sixty-five years later Olive in an English home for retired missionaries heard an old, old voice crying in the darkness, 'Mother, mother, I don't want to die tonight!' In dressing-gown and slippers she padded down the passage to find the source of the voice and offer any comfort she could. And found what time had done to the bride with her hands full of flowers.)

On the stations in Siberia you could buy milk – actually fresh milk! – and lots of fruit. But if you stepped out on to the stations it was like stepping into an oven. They were still working on the line and for the first time in my life I saw foreigners (white people) doing manual work. I was shocked. They had black mosquito netting hanging down from their hats to keep the flies and insects off.

I remember how we skirted round Lake Baikal, down one side, across the bottom and up the other side and on that one stretch we went through *eighty tunnels*! I remember the names Omsk and Tomsk, and how we arrived at Chelyabinsk on Wednesday morning and left it again the night before. That was where we crossed from Asia to Europe.

We changed trains there too and in the new train a Russian man was given a seat in our compartment for the day. He was Mr Sigismund Novitski. He began a conversation with Mother in French. They talked all day. He had a son, he told her, seven years old, and this little boy was ill through worrying over politics. Olive and I gaped. Politics! Why should anyone worry over politics? Especially a child! And to get ill with it! We couldn't understand it.

Mr Novitski begged Mother to write to him from England and tell him if there was any possibility of his being able to immigrate there. When we got to England Mother tried hard but she couldn't work anything out for him.

She wrote to him but had no answer. It seemed as though what he was afraid of had caught up with him and crushed him.

At Moscow we changed trains again and everything was cleaner from then on and the train was faster and more comfortable. Three days later we reached England. We'd been travelling for a fortnight and though it had all been fun we were very dirty and very tired.

*   *   *   *

1913. Georgian England. Shirt waists and leghorn hats. Gracious manners and, despite the suffragettes, a stable social structure, and peace that felt as though it would last forever.

When we arrived two very satisfying things happened in quick succession. We met Mark again after seven years and we all had deep hot baths. I had to have two rinsings. It was lovely to see all that Siberian filth go down the drain. Someone had lent us a house for three weeks and Mother, Mark, Olive, and I installed ourselves as a family. Oh the amazement, the joy, of having a brother! Some of the girls at school had had brothers in China but we were among the ones that never spoke to a boy, never saw a boy really – just fell in love at a distance with the captain of the cricket team. But to have your own brother! And living in the house with you! He was over five years older than I was. When I'd last seen him he was a schoolboy and now he was a grown man. I was about sixteen and I fell in love with him, just adored him. And he was so nice, so good to us. And so happy himself to have a family after being so long alone living in other people's houses.

A maid used to come in for a few hours to clean up the mess we'd made and cook one meal for us. Apart from that we were on our own. To any New Zealander this sounds ridiculous, but to people like us who'd always had Chinese servants and to Mark who'd lived in a boarding-school or in a house where there were English servants, part of the delight of those weeks was being left to do for ourselves. Mark used to put on an apron and flop around in slippers concocting the most amazing meals – he'd never been allowed in Aunt Alice's kitchen. Olive and I had great fun doing what we called cleaning and dusting. The maid was very nice about it and she kept things in order but I bet she had great tales to tell them when she went home.

We were so light-hearted. Mark was taking a course in Arabic at London University – he was preparing to work as a missionary among the Moslems in China – and he used to practise phonics in the bathroom, the weirdest noises echoing through the house. He was very witty and could make up poetry and sketches that we all acted in the evenings. The Polhills whom we'd known when we were small had a big town house in London. They used to invite us over for parties where everyone was in evening dress. I was nearly always called on to play the accompaniment to whatever was happening and Mark who had a nice tenor voice used to sing parodies of popular songs that he'd made up himself. He had a tremendous sense of humour and we used to laugh till the tears ran down.

Meanwhile, Mother had been getting us settled in England. She found a pleasant little private school in London, called Wynaud House, and I was installed there as a weekly boarder. There were only two of us boarding there and we slept on the top floor of this high, narrow house. My days were filled with music. Mother had found me a very good teacher and I used to practise for four hours a day. I used to work on scales and arpeggios for an hour before breakfast every morning. When the breakfast bell went I'd jump up and start running down the stairs. I always fell over as I ran. My fingers had been going two-two-three, two-two-three, and I couldn't stop my feet doing the same thing. I tripped on the third step every single morning.

The work at Wynaud House wasn't hard. I heard of a girl from Chefoo, Mildred, who had come to England about the same time that I did. The girls at the boarding-school she was sent to were told by the headmistress, 'You must be very kind to the little girl from China because she'll be out of her element and there'll be lots of things she won't understand.' Mildred was tall and blonde and beautiful. By the end of the first term she was captain of the hockey team and had been put in a class a year above the other girls of her age. I didn't become captain of the hockey team but I did win the French prize without too much effort. They gave me *Les Misérables* in three volumes and that made a difference to my life later on.

All the same there were things that were strange to me in England. When I first arrived I thought, 'What a lot of foreigners there are walking around these streets!' It took me a long time to get used to the idea that the 'foreigners' were the natives here. I couldn't understand the language that a lot of them spoke. Once Mark and I passed some men working on a building.

'What language is that they're talking?' I asked him.

'English, of course,' he said. I didn't believe him. It was Cockney they were speaking. I'd never met any English people who weren't educated. These seemed like a different race to me, strange and incomprehensible.

I suppose I would have felt a lot stranger than I did if it hadn't been for the China Inland Mission House. It was in the north east of London. Rows and rows of Coronation Street style houses and in the middle of them a long, long drive leading through enormous grounds to a four storeyed house with rooms for forty or fifty people.

All the business for the Inland Mission was done at that house. By that time there were thousands of missionaries in China. It was headquarters for any of them who were home on leave and for all the boys and girls whose parents were in China.

After the house we had borrowed reverted to its owners we all stayed on and off at the C.I.M. House and I spent every weekend there. The matron was Miss Hibble, a very prim and proper spinster, but kind-hearted. She and I didn't always see eye to eye. We weren't supposed to go to the theatre of course but Maskelyne the famous magician's show was approved of. One day I had been out with two friends. When I got back Miss Hibble called me into her room.

'You've been to the theatre,' she said.

'No I haven't,' I said. 'I've been to Maskelyne's.'

'I know,' she said, her lips very tight, 'that you have been to the theatre.' So the next day, for the very first time in my life, I did go to the theatre. When I came back I went to Miss Hibble and said, 'Miss Hibble, I can't bear to think of you telling a lie so I have now been to the theatre.' I can't say I found it very corrupting. The play I'd seen was Maeterlinck's *Blue Bird of Happiness*. Gladys Young was the star.

By the time I'd finished school, Mark had completed his university course and he and Mother were ready to go back to China. Olive wanted to be a missionary too but she'd decided to train first as a nurse at St Thomas's Hospital.

The only thing I was sure about was what I didn't want to be and that was a missionary. But I had to decide on something and there were really only two choices for upper-middle-class girls in those days – nursing and teaching. 'I may as well be a nurse too,' I thought.

Aunt Sarah, my father's sister, was the matron of a hospital. She arranged that I was to be shown over the whole institution. I went along but whenever there was something unpleasant to be seen I fainted and had to be carried out. Nursing was not for me: I had to be a teacher. I was too young to be admitted to training so it was arranged that Mother's brother Jim would be my guardian and for the next year I'd live with him and his wife.

Mother left Olive and me with a lot of instructions as to how we should behave ourselves. The bogey of the time was the White Slave Traffic. Mother had heard a story about a very nicely dressed man, very proper, with a rose in his buttonhole, who got on a bus and sat next to an innocent girl. He drugged her, or she fainted or something, and he carried her off the bus and she was never seen again.

'Mother,' I said, 'I solemnly promise I'll never speak to a man with a rose in his buttonhole.'

All the same we did feel bereft when she and Mark sailed away and once again our family was scattered over half the world.

Grace finished school in July 1914. About the same time the Archduke Ferdinand was murdered in Sarajevo and the national greeds of the previous century climaxed in the First World War. Thousands of amiable, kindly, young men rushed helter-skelter to the recruitment offices to offer themselves as killers of other amiable

40

the recruitment offices to offer themselves as killers of other amiable kindly young men. The gracious manners of the time did not preclude this.

Grace was touched by the war only through her love of other people more closely involved. It was her fate to live half her life on the edge of other people's wars. When it broke out she was with her aunt and uncle in their quiet home near Manchester.

Uncle Jim was the nearest thing to a father I've ever had. He had no children himself and he was so good and kind to me. There was a whispered story that Aunt Mollie, his wife, had been in an orphanage. Why it was whispered I don't know. Perhaps it's always disgraceful to be unfortunate. She was a very beautiful woman and they were deeply in love with each other all their lives. She was good to me in her way and I never had to do anything for my keep but I always felt that she resented my coming to this private Eden of theirs. I spent most of my time practising the piano.

I was a rather delicate girl in a prehistoric Victorian way. I'd been anaemic and I was very, very thin and I used to have quite a lot of pain every month when I menstruated. The doctor ordered me the 1914 version of an iron tonic. I had to put some big rusty nails at the bottom of a glass, fill it up with water overnight and drink it off in the morning. I don't know that it did me any good.

Every now and then I'd leave this quiet domestic atmosphere and go down to the Mission House in London for a holiday. There it was a different atmosphere entirely, full of excitement and high spirits. Olive and I would meet there and all the other boys and girls whose parents were missionaries in China. It was almost like a big house party, especially at Christmas. There was very little flirting went on. We were like members of one family and we had fun together the way brothers and sisters or cousins will. Even that first year most of the boys were in uniform, young officers all of them. Even if they enlisted as privates, with their education and background they were told to take commissions.

Oh, the antics we got up to! We behaved like children and really we weren't much more. Telephones were still a novelty. I remember Ray coming in one day and saying, 'Let's ring somebody up!' So he opened the London Telephone Directory, shut his eyes and put his finger on a name. Ziffo, Paddington 2458. Ray dialled it.

'Is that Mr Ziffo?'

'Yes.'

'Paddington 2458?'

'Yees, Meester Zeeffo 'ere.'

Ray said, 'What time's the wedding?'

'Vat vedding? Zees ees Zeeffo! Paddington 2458!'

'Yes, that's right! What time is the wedding?'

There were eight or ten of us and every day for about five days we went to different boxes all over London and we rang to ask what time the wedding was. The next Christmas Ray happened to be home on leave again and we were on holiday, so he rang up and said, 'Mr Ziffo? What time is the christening?' Nobody could ever catch us because we rang from different phone boxes all over London. For four years we kept it up each holiday. The last time I was in London I looked it up in the telephone directory and there was still Ziffo, Paddington 2458. But that time I didn't ring. Mysterious telephone calls were no longer a joke.

I remember going out with Ray once when he had just been made a captain. Very modestly he took off his splendid new uniform and wore mufti. On the way home we called into a little chemist shop to get some rolls of film. A tiny little runt of a man served us. He looked Ray up and down, making comments about people who didn't enlist and talking about white feathers. I was just going to rage at him but Ray got hold of me and pinched me to keep me quiet. When we came out of the shop I said, 'Why didn't you say something? Terrible little creature!'

He said, 'You wait.' And the next day he put on his full captain's uniform with his little cane and puttees and we went in again. He didn't say anything – just asked for some more rolls of the same film. I've never seen anything like that man's face. Absolute purple. That was a gorgeous moment.

I said that all the boys there at the Mission House were like brothers or cousins and yet there was one that wasn't – Cowan. I think he was a New Zealander but we didn't ask what anyone's home background was. We were from Chefoo and we spoke English and that was our nationality. China was our home and we were all 'foreigners'.

Cowan was tall and craggy. He looked a lot like Edmund Hillary must have as a young man – perhaps that's why I think he was a New Zealander. And he and I . . . there was something that flashed between us. But we were so young. I was seventeen. Today I suppose it wouldn't seem so young. But in those days it was. We never even kissed each other. But there was this thing – this consciousness – between us. He came and said a special goodbye to me when he went off to the war, at the end of his final leave. The others went out of the room. They all knew that Cowan felt that for me and I did for him. He went out to France, to the front, and all the boys who saw him there said that he was talking about me all the time.

He wrote for a while. Then silence. Not a word. We got news of the others. You could always get news of officers through Cook's Bank. That was a sort of exchange mail place for officers and people wanting news of them. But no one got any news of Cowan.

I was still at Aunt Molly's and Uncle Jim's then. 'Oh, he'll be all right' – you know how people go on – 'It'll be all right!'

Then one morning I woke up with a terrible pain in my jaw. I'd had a dream. I dreamed that Cowan was wounded in the jaw. I went down to breakfast and told Aunt Mollie about it. 'I know Cowan's been hurt,' I said. 'I know he's been wounded in the jaw. I dreamed it and I can feel it still in my own jaw.' She said it was all imagination.

About two weeks later the news came through. He had been very badly wounded and was in a hospital in Holland where there was a jaw specialist unit. I never saw him again. His jaw had been badly shattered, but what was worse – he'd lost his memory and he never regained it. From what I heard years afterwards, he married the nurse who looked after him. For nine or ten years after that I was inoculated against love. I always thought, 'Suppose Cowan gets his memory back!' I wouldn't have cared if he'd got a wife or not. I would have gone and been with him.

When the next college year started I was old enough to enrol at Cambridge. I would have loved to have gone to the women's university college there, Newnham. But it was terribly expensive, well beyond our pockets. Even to go to Homerton, the Teachers Training College, you had to pay substantial fees but somehow we managed it. I felt humiliated though walking around as a sort of poor relation of the university students. Especially through *those* streets, for I fell in love with Cambridge.

Homerton was supposed to be a good Teachers Training College and I dare say it was. Mother had decided on it because she had a friend, an elderly lady, (or so I thought at the time; I suppose she was fifty) who was the matron there. She had been in China and she took a motherly interest in me, inviting me to Sunday tea in her own flat sometimes. Crumpets and things!

There were 200 girls and we each had our own bed-sitting-room. The work wasn't hard and the lectures were interesting. We all had to do our homework in one room, like prep at school. Since I usually finished quickly I used to read French novels afterwards to keep my hand in. I unearthed my Victor Hugo prize and read *Les Misérables* that way. I think the other girls were rather impressed by this odd accomplishment.

I got along quite well with them – they were quite a pleasant lot of girls – but I made my friends amongst the people I met at Mr and Mrs Oswald Smith's place. They were a very Christian couple who were extremely interested in missions and missionaries and I just qualified as the daughter of missionaries. They had a big flat over a shop on one of the main streets of Cambridge and every Sunday they held open house there for all sorts of young people – at the university, from the army, or just living in the town. Delightful times we had there, and delightful friends I made – medical students from Emanuel and boys from Christ's and King's.

We did all the traditional things: punting on the Cam, gliding past the grassy backs, canoeing up to Grantchester. I can still recall how I felt running in my white dress along the towpath during the May-week bumping races, or wandering through the quads of Trinity or King's, or having tea in front of the fire with my friends at Emanuel. And above all, the loveliest memory is of going to King's College Chapel for Evensong on a Saturday.

I used to sit there in a stall opposite the choir with my arms resting on the same wood that had touched the arms of so many people in the past – great and famous people – hundreds of years ago. I'd look up, up, at the high vaults and hear the sound of that lovely choir echoing from them. Away above the organ loft I could see not a gruesome crucifix but two angels with their trumpets raised. I used to think that they were trumpeting away to something still higher, something unimaginably greater than anything I could conceive of.

Cambridge is the only place in the world where the actual sticks and stones mean anything to me. I feel as if it's part of me and I'm part of it. It must be the feeling that people who have family homes feel for the place where they were born. I wasn't born there; and yet in a way I was. Because it was there that I felt the missionary-spun cocoon I'd been in begin to split. I began to emerge as me.

I learned to dance at Cambridge and I went to the theatre quite often. Some of the girls from Homerton used to go to nearly every theatrical performance that was on, queueing for cheap seats in the gods. But that wasn't my style. When I went to the theatre I sat in the best seats, and I wore my best and most appropriate clothes and I had an escort who knew how to behave. Otherwise I'd rather stay at home.

It wasn't just me who was changing. The world was altering round us, becoming mechanized. Cars began to appear in the streets. I remember one day – a shocking day in my life it was – there was an university boy at the Smiths' who had a little open car, a sportscar. It was very, very smart indeed to have one in those days.

I said, 'How do you drive this thing?'

'Get in,' he said, 'and I'll show you.'

He stood outside the car and told me what to do and I did it. Off I shot at full speed not knowing why! Luckily it was Sunday – no traffic. I didn't know how to stop, or steer, or what made the thing go faster or slower. I just sat there grabbing the wheel. I shot on to the pavement between a tree and a shop – there wasn't room to get between them but I did – then back on to the road again.

I thought, 'No, this is the end. This thing will go up to Petty Cury and I'll smash into it and die!' Just as this flashed through my mind I saw the word OFF on the dashboard. I switched it off. It made an awful row but it stopped with a jerk.

I got out and staggered back. A crowd had gathered and a policeman. On the ground was a little girl. I'd knocked her over when I shot on to the pavement. I was certain I'd killed her.

I panicked. I ran through the Smiths' house to the kitchen and hid there. Bessie was there – she was a sort of char who helped on Sunday afternoons.

I said, 'I've killed her!' and Bessie said, 'I'd better make you a cup of tea, Miss.'

Then Mrs Oswald Smith came running through. 'It's all right!' she said, 'She's quite all right!'

I wouldn't believe her, but it was true. The child was quite unharmed. There was a court case about it. The boy whose car it was was summonsed and he refused to name me at all. He said a young lady passenger accidentally started it. He paid the fine and wouldn't let me share in it.

I was still wobbly. The next time I went into town I bought the biggest doll I could find with my precious money from Uncle Jim, and a box of chocolates, and a friend and I took them down to the place where the child lived. It was a tiny house, one of a row in a slummy street.

The child's mother came to the door and I said, 'How is she?'

'She's all right,' the woman said, 'there's nothing wrong.'

I said, 'Thank God!' or something, and the woman said, 'I think you're worse than she is, Miss!' I kept on having nightmares about it for a long time.

In those days policemen were very fatherly figures. One term holiday when I'd gone to stay at the Mission House and Olive was at St Thomas's we used to meet at a spot halfway between every afternoon and have tea together. We used to take turns at paying but then Olive let me pay three times in a row so the next day I just didn't take any money. We had our afternoon tea then I said, 'Well, I'm jolly well not going to pay for this lot! I haven't brought any money, so there!'

She looked at me, appalled, then she whispered, 'But I haven't got any money! Why do you think I left you to pay?'

We scraped through our pockets and purses and between us we had just enough to the last halfpenny to pay the bill. We slunk out of the shop without leaving a tip, which is most embarrassing in England. 'What'll we do?' we said to each other because we had no money now and we both needed bus-fare to get home. We were in the middle of West End. There was a policeman there directing the traffic.

'You stop in the doorway of this shop,' I said. 'I'll see if he'll lend me some.'

I went up to him. He stopped all the traffic and asked me what the matter was.

'I've done a silly thing,' I said. 'I've come out without enough money to get me home.'

He opened his pocket slowly. 'How much will you need?'

I told him, sixpence. He pulled out half-a-crown and gave it to me saying, 'Now Miss don't you do that again. That's a silly thing to do. Always come out with enough money to get home,' and he held the traffic still while I crossed back.

The next day I was ill and couldn't go out. About three days later when I was well again, I went to pay the policeman back. As soon as he saw me he stopped the traffic and said, 'Miss, did you come on Saturday?' I told him no, I wasn't able to. 'Well, that's good,' he said, 'because I was off this beat then and I wouldn't have wanted you to have a trip for nothing.' I gave him the half-crown and got another fatherly lecture in exchange.

Meanwhile the war that everyone had said would be over in a few months dragged on into its third year. It didn't affect me personally at all. I didn't even notice the rationing – I'm not particularly interested in food. The nearest I got to real involvement was when a zeppelin came over Cambridge while I was at Homerton but as I was in the lavatory at the time I didn't even see that. But there was the constant worry about the boys at the front and about this time I had another dream. I dreamed I was in the trenches and I was just behind an officer. I couldn't see if it was Ray or Len. Suddenly he went over the top and I went over too. I must have been floating because there was no effort involved. I was just behind him, behind his left shoulder, when suddenly he fell and I woke up.

I went down to breakfast and said to the girls at the table, 'I know I'm going to have some bad news,' and sure enough it came. I got the letter three or four days later. It was from one of the other boys telling me that Len had been killed. It mentioned the time and the day that Len had died and it fitted in exactly with my dream. Why I should have known I don't know. There was nothing between us except friendship and a brotherly affection. It's inexplicable. Just a freak wavelength of thought? I don't know.

While I was at Cambridge I made one rather odd friendship – odd but pleasant. This was with Mr Wilkinson. He was an ageing man; I thought he was about a hundred in the shade but I suppose he must have been in his fifties. Whether he was a widower or a bachelor I don't know. There was a girl whom I knew who was very, very delicate, a fragile girl, and Mr Wilkinson had taken her as a sort of protégée. He used to invite her over to his house and let her sit in his garden whenever she wanted to. A big house and a big garden. There was nothing furtive about him. He was just a kind elderly man. One day when she went to see him she took me along. He talked to me and found me an oddity, I suppose, and after that he used to invite me over to see him. I don't know what he did for a living – he was always rather a mystery to me – but I know that he was a member of the University Senate. He used to do a lot of travelling all over England and whenever he came to a place that was famous for some speciality he would post me a sample of it. For instance, if he was in Bath a little parcel of Bath Buns would arrive. Never anything expensive, just a pleasant surprise.

While I was in Cambridge, the Prince of Wales, who later became the Duke of Windsor, was awarded an honorary degree at the Senate House. Mr Wilkinson had a ticket for the investiture of course and he gave it to me. So I sat and watched this gorgeous golden-haired, blue-eyed prince get his degree. Nowadays I think a Mr Wilkinson would be looked at askance and thought of as an old perv. That's a pity. He was a gentle, formal old man with a kindly heart.

I did have one unpleasant experience at Cambridge. Most of the girls were about eighteen or twenty when they were at Homerton and most of them were quite nice people. But two or three doors down from my room there was a poor old thing of nearly thirty doing her training. She was very much out of her element and I felt sorry for her and I showed her round a bit. She began coming into my room to ask me things and to talk. It got to be a bit of a nuisance. Then notes started appearing under my door; 'To the Angel of the house,' and things like that. By this time I couldn't stand her; she was a soppy-looking thing.

One day she came in and suddenly flung her arms round me and started kissing me. It dawned on me then what was the matter with her. I said, 'Get out of here!' and pushed her out the door. She didn't stay on for the next year. Just as well, she would never have made a good teacher.

When I finished at Homerton I felt that I didn't want to go and teach. Before I knew if I'd passed my exams or got my certificate I went up to London and started working as a volunteer in the War Office. It was a huge place; letters came in all day long. They seemed to go round and round. Most of them had stamped on them, 'Passed to you for further notice', and were signed Lieutenant So-and-So. Or Captain, or Colonel and so on, up and down the hierarchy. I only got as far as having to pass them on to a captain. Some of the letters were tragic and some were bizarre. I remember one from a man claiming a very large pension because he'd been wounded in the leg and had lost the pleasure of dancing properly.

Even though it was volunteer work I got paid for it. I remember thinking, 'This is very much easier than teaching and I get paid as much. So why teach?' However the news came that I had passed my exams and I thought, 'Oh well, I suppose I'd better do the job I've been trained for.' So I applied for a position I saw advertised and I was accepted.

The position was in a private school in the country not very far from London. I've forgotten the name of the place and very glad I am to forget it. The headmistress was a snobby person, very pleased because she had the daughters of quite a number of titled people at her school. They were nice children and I enjoyed teaching there until one day she sent for me to come to her office. A letter had arrived for me with the name Homerton College on the envelope. She asked me to open it in front of her. It was simply a formal letter stating that I was now a certificated teacher. She asked me to show it to her and I did, quite innocently.

'Homerton College!' she said. 'I thought you were from Newnham! THIS is not the sort of teaching you were trained for and THIS is not the sort of school you should be in!'

I said, 'Right! I'll leave today!'

'Oh no, you won't!' she said. 'You'll stay for two weeks and serve proper notice!'

'Nothing doing! I'm not going to stay where I'm not wanted!'

I packed my things and the senior assistant, a nice woman who really was from Newnham, drove me to the station. So I landed back on the doorstep of my grandmother in London. It was the first but not the last time that I've done that to a school. I'd rather starve than be treated that way.

I got in touch with Miss Allen, the principal of Homerton. She told me to come down immediately and when I arrived she told me she had a position for me in the College Demonstration School – what you would call a Normal School. It was lovely. I could still visit the friends I'd made at Cambridge and spend Sunday afternoons at the Oswald Smiths'.

I rented two rooms, upstairs bedroom and downstairs parlour, from a delightful little person for a pound a week including food. She cooked the meals and served them to me in my parlour, made my bed and did the cleaning. She was a lovely little person. She used to stand and talk to me often while I was eating. One day when I was going out to a party she said, 'You're very pale – I'll tell you what to do. I've got some geraniums out there. It's the best thing you can have instead of rouge, it looks so natural.' And she fetched geranium petals and rubbed them on my cheeks.

One day I said to her, 'I can't understand it, my room looks so untidy.'

'Well, why don't you tidy it up?' she said.

I looked at her for a minute while the idea penetrated. Then I said, 'Thank you. I never thought of that.' Because it hadn't entered my head that that was what you did. In China the amahs put everything away as soon as you used it and even in England I'd always been where there were servants to tidy up. She did all the cleaning and it hadn't dawned on me that I was the one to keep it tidy.

I tidied up and I said, 'Oh, what a difference! Thank you ever so much for suggesting it!' I think she thought I was mad, and looking back now, I think I was mad, but you only understand things from your own experience and I'd never seen a 'foreigner' tidy a room.

I taught for two years in the Demonstration School. During that time the armistice was signed and the war ended. It became possible to visit Europe again. One day Miss Allen sent for me.

She told me that she knew I was well versed in French; she remembered that when I was at college I used to read French novels in preparation time. 'I suggest,' she said, 'that you take a third-year specialist course in France and that will give you a qualification equivalent to a degree. You can get a bursary to cover your living expenses if the Board of Education in London are satisfied that you're a suitable person likely to benefit from advanced study. Do you think that's a good idea?'

I thought it was a great idea. I went up to London to the Board of Education and a Mr Twentyman had a conversation with me in French and I was granted my bursary.

Mr Wilkinson came down to see me off. In his top hat and gloves he stood waving to me as the boat pulled out into the Channel.

❉   ❉   ❉   ❉

France 1920. A world had died on this soil. More than half the fighting men of the country either lay beneath it now or went on it maimed. But if you didn't know what had happened, could you possibly have guessed?

I travelled south to Agen, a town not far from the Spanish border. It was Victor Hugo's birthplace. I was assigned to an *École Normale*, a Teachers Training College.

There were sixty-four girls boarding there and they all slept in one enormous dormitory. Bed-table-bed-table-bed-table, all the way down. But I, thank goodness, didn't live there. I was put on the staff. I had a private room with a little entrance hall from the passage. The bursary allowed me all expenses in return for five hours a week conversation with the girls. I used to go for walks with various groups of them and they'd talk away in English to me. It was a very easy way of earning bed and board.

In the first group I went out with, one girl took it upon herself to lead the conversation because she spoke such good English. She made herself the guide to all the sights of the town. She pointed to a big building on the right and said, 'Zees ees zee casernes of zee soldiers!' and then to one on the left, 'Zat ees zee barrack of zee foolish.' *Caserne* is a word for barrack. Her 'barrack of the foolish' was the asylum of the insane. On the way back we came through the town. There was a notice that I liked over the door of a teashop. 'Ici on sert le "five-o'clock" à quatre heures.' 'Five-o'clock' is their word for English afternoon tea. Later we used to go in there often. They served the most superb *éclairs* and *babas-au-rhum*.

Everyone had difficulty with my name. The nearest they could get to it was 'Botam' which they spelled *beau temps* – fine weather. When I told them that my christian name was Grace, they laughed because they thought I'd used the word for grease – the fat that you cook with – and I was extraordinarily thin. So I pronounced it grass and that made them laugh even more because of course *grasse* is the adjective for fat – a fat person. Finally they worked out the meaning of Grace and called me Mademoiselle Gracieuse Beautemps – Miss Gracious Fineweather.

The concierge simply settled for 'Mademoiselle Miss'. He was M. Pochou, a funny old man who lived in a little house at the gates and was responsible for locking them at night – a girls' school, you know. The French are very careful.

M. Pochou thought I was a shocking character. I arrived there in September. It was very hot and there were mosquitoes everywhere. I asked for a mosquito net.

'Go to M. Pochou,' I was told. 'He'll fix you up with one.'

So I went to him and said, 'M. Pochou, I cannot sleep without a *mosquitaire* on the bed.' He was horrified. It seems that I'd asked for a musketeer to sleep with. On top of that, I wanted a bath every day. Unheard of! I had to go downstairs in my dressing gown, through the long dining-room, through the kitchen quarters, round the back and there amongst a whole lot of pipes were the baths.

Finally M. Pochou decided it would be less trouble if he put a *sitz* bath in my entrance room. He carried the water up for it every morning. Looking back, I can't blame him for looking at me askance.

One of the conditions of my bursary was that I had to present a thesis at the end to the British Board of Education to show that I had used my time to good effect. I chose for my subject 'The Teaching of the Mother Tongue', so I studied their teaching of French to French children and I was able to go into any lecture I liked and listen to it, and into any class in any school in the whole district, so that at the same time I was able to improve my own knowledge of French. As well as that I took an extramural course at the Sorbonne. It was a cultural course in French and there was a lot of material in it on Norman and Gothic art.

At Christmas I went to stay with a family in Bordeaux. By that time I'd improved enough to be able to make the one and only French joke of my life. At New Year the daughter of the house who was a musician and her friend, a poetess, took me – another oddity, being English – to a party. It was in a studio and there were a lot of artists there, mainly men. That was the first time in my life that I ever saw bearded men. At first I didn't say very much. One of the young men came up to me and said, 'I'm afraid that you feel a bit out of it because you won't understand all the slang (*argot*) that we're using.'

'Oh, I understand very well,' I said, 'Why, just at the moment I'm studying *art gothique!*' (Gothic art). He flung up his hands and cried, 'Listen, listen! Be quiet everyone and listen to what the English girl has said!' From that moment I was in among them all and when midnight sounded I've never had so many bearded kisses in my life.

When I had been there a few months, I had a letter from another English girl at Carcassonne, an old Roman city not far from Agen. She was on a bursary from Durham University. She asked if she could come and see me and she shared my room for three or four days. She was a dear little soul and in terrible trouble. She had become engaged to a boy at Durham. When he finished his course he was offered a job which was specifically for a single man. He took the job, she was awarded her bursary; but before they parted they married secretly. She'd only been in France a few weeks when she found she was pregnant. She was horrified and didn't know what to do. People felt a lot more strongly then than they do now about illegitimate pregnancies and fallen women and though she was married – I saw her marriage lines – she had no visible husband and no ring. For weeks after she stayed with me people kept eyeing me up and down, especially M. Pochou.

Finally she went back to England and even then her wretched husband didn't acknowledge her. She just went and stayed on a farm and was there living on her own till after the baby was born. At Christmas time I sent her a box of *prunes d'Agen*. Agen is famous for them; the stone is taken out of the prune and an almond paste put inside. She wrote back saying it was the only present she'd received. Her father and mother had cast her off too.

The person I remember most vividly from my days in France was an old, old woman whom I met only once. She lived in a place a few miles away called Marmande. Someone who knew her took me to visit her as a kindness. And she talked and she talked and she talked. She told us all about the days when she was young. How she'd never been allowed to be alone with her future husband until her wedding night. When they were courting, her mother would let her walk up and down the road with him so long as they remained in sight. 'But, oh,' she said, 'he was the most wonderful man!' They had been married so long and so happily! And he was so big and strong! When he was ill, dying, they had bled him. It was not leeches they used then but *ventouses*, a kind of suction cup about the size of a little meat paste jar, that sucks out the blood. And to cover his great wide back they had needed forty-two. 'Quarante-deux ventouses!' she said, still amazed and still so proud. 'Quarante-deux ventouses sur le dos!'

I had a lovely year there in France *but* . . . There was one big but. We had a Spanish cook and everything she cooked was done in oil and I could not digest it. All my bursary money went in buying myself food that I could eat. It got to the stage where I was so ill I couldn't continue. I had finished my thesis but a month before I was due to take my Sorbonne exams I had to go back to England. It was very disappointing and I never did finish my Sorbonne course.

*   *   *   *

It was seven years since Nellie and Mark had gone back to China. All the Bothams were adventurers. The Christians in the family put their trust in the Lord and the Lord led them into strange places.

He led Mark to the Moslem communities of China. A generation before, Tom Botham had bemoaned the fact that there was no missionary to talk to these people in their own tongue. Mark had acquired the rudiments of Arabic at university. Using that as an opener, he lived in Moslem villages till he could talk and think and make jokes in Arabic. He visited their wise men and listened quietly till he understood their philosophy and their passions.

51

He travelled the old Marco Polo road from east China, exploring on horseback as far as Lake Kokonor in Tibet. When he sent an account of this journey to the *Royal Geographic Magazine* in London it was accepted immediately and he was made an honorary member of the Royal Geographic Society.

In Tibet he was twice granted an audience with the Panchen Lama, a godlike being as rich in spiritual mana as the Dalai Lama. In the ritual exchange of gifts that decorated the visits Mark received two delicate little silk scarves. He posted them off to his young sisters.

Olive put hers away very, very carefully. I of course had to wear mine. It was a pale blue, a very fine loose weave and strongly starched. It was so pretty as a scarf, it tied and stood out. But when it got dirty, I washed it and it turned into a slimy little handful of stuff in my hand. Olive used to scold me – why didn't I keep a treasure like that instead of wearing it? Well, she lost hers in China. They had everything they possessed stolen and I'd have lost mine in Czechoslovakia in any case, but at least I had the fun of wearing a real scarf given by the Panchen Lama for a few weeks.

Nellie, now nearly sixty, whether from saintliness or exhaustion was beginning to look oddly insubstantial.

'You need cups of tea and kisses,' said Mark. 'You'd better go to England and fetch Olive.'

He persuaded her. They began to make their way south, Nellie travelling in a litter and Mark, for company's sake, riding alongside for the first few days. They stopped at a mission station for the last night that they would be together before Mark turned back again; during that night the biggest earthquake that either of them had ever known rocked the little village. It was terrifying but the damage seemed slight. Clay walls had cracked, one or two of them had tumbled but nobody was killed or even injured.

The next morning they said goodbye to each other – goodbyes always wrench the heart, no matter how perfect your faith, when distance is measured in thousands of miles. Mark turned north to make his way back, Nellie continued south. Almost immediately both realized that the earthquake was not a matter of a few cracked walls. Years later Grace found it listed in a roll-call of major natural disasters of the world. Olive wrote an account of it from what her mother had told her of the experience:

Day after day Mrs Botham passed through ruined villages, often having to make long detours to avoid cracks in the ground, or great falls of earth and stones from the hills. Night after night she spent in her litter, well away from walls which might fall in the many smaller shocks which followed that first terrible one.

The people who had escaped with their lives, huddled together in fear saying, 'Heaven has decreed that all men shall be slain.' Even hawks crouched in the holes in the cliffs, afraid to swoop on their prey. The awful news of the catastrophe came to the traveller as a dreadful exhibition of power. 'Such mighty power,' seemed to be repeated in the creaking of the litter poles, till suddenly came 'The Mighty Power of God' – and 'and He is on our side' she realised in joyful relief.

The earthquake was not the only disaster of the journey. The other quieter personal one was more devastating to the Bothams in the end. Mark took ill with what proved to be an attack of rheumatic fever. He recovered, but, as usual in those pre-penicillin days, his heart was affected.

In her old retreat, the Mission House in London, Grace was recovering from her overdose of Spanish oil. As she got better she began to worry about earning her living again. The rest of the Bothams knew what they were born for; she felt rudderless and drifting. She had never wanted to teach in the state school system. England was not her country and working-class people of any country seemed alien and unattractive to her. She was certainly not prepared to expose herself again to the humiliation of trying to hold a position in a private school.

I knew Olive would be going to China as soon as she'd finished the last little bit of her course. It looked as if I was going to be all alone in England, and I didn't like the idea at all. Mother, Mark, and Olive were all dedicated Christians. My ideas were beginning to be quite different – but to be separated from them by so much land and sea! It felt terribly lonely.

Then suddenly out of the blue like a sort of grotesque good fairy came fat old Miss T—. She was very pious and very dull and I suspected right from the beginning that she didn't live up to her beliefs as the missionaries, for all their funny ways, do.

But she was saying, 'Come and teach in China!' It wasn't a missionary school; it was Miss T—'s very own. A little school for English children at a health resort way up in the mountains in the middle of China. Of course I'd be hundreds and hundreds of miles away from Olive and Mother and from Mark but at least we'd all be in the same country.

'I'll come,' I said. I was to teach French and English and be the House Mistress in a dormitory cottage where seven or eight small boys slept. It sounded demanding but not impossible. I wasn't completely well yet but Miss T— was on furlough and wouldn't be ready to leave for some weeks.

'I shall require a medical certificate,' she said, looking me over suspiciously.

I took myself off to the doctor. 'She is not strong,' he wrote on the certificate, 'but is able to do the work she has undertaken.' He gave me a great big pickling jar full of pills, several years' supply, and a few weeks later Miss T— and I were on our way.

It was the worst journey I ever had! The ship was going by way of Suez. Miss T— had booked a four-berth second-class cabin. I hate sharing a room and I hate travelling second-class. She was big and fat and so were the other two women we shared with. The cabin was bulging with all this flesh and I didn't like any of it much.

To make matters worse Miss T— thought it was her duty to chaperone me and guard me from the evil attentions of any males of the species. It was awful. I was a very different person by this time from the girl who'd come to England straight from a mission school. I enjoyed the theatre, I'd learned to dance and I loved it, I could play cards, I liked nice clothes. All so innocent when you're not in a missionary circle but so wicked when you are. Miss T— brought home to me how narrow that pious outlook was. My own people were never like that, especially Mother and Mark, but lots of the missionaries, and lots of the pious do-gooders like Miss T—, disapproved of nearly everything except their own lives.

I got away from her as much as I could in the daytime. I remember the absolute beauty of the Mediterranean and that Mt Etna was in eruption as we passed by. And I remember Miss T— popping up at my elbow as I gazed at it.

The journey took six long weeks. When we reached Shanghai we transferred to a steamboat and continued up the Yangtse River to Kiukiang. Those few days were the worst of all because I was alone with Miss T—. There was just no escape.

The China Grace returned to was a sadder more pitiful place than the one she had left. The revolution had failed. Yüan Shih-k'ai, the president of the new-born republic, had proved to be short on principles and long on personal ambition. At first he had the support of his own loyal army and of the revolutionaries. But he reformed nothing, ignored and demeaned the infant parliament. And there were plenty of ambitious men with loyal armies behind them to

the bearers would lose his footing and begin to slide off the side. He'd just hold on desperately till the others could heave him up again. I've been up in heavy snow when you couldn't see the path or the edge of the precipice. I've been when it was so windy that you were certain you were going to be blown over.

But that first time it was beautiful – fine, and the air so fresh. The bearers trudged up the three thousand feet with just one stop at the half-way place for a smoke and a cup of tea. They were cheerful and happy and they talked among themselves all the way.

At three thousand feet you got to the Gap, a little Chinese village; then on and between two huge cliffs you came to the head of the valley. A beautiful valley, very green with trees and a river running down the middle. Mauve azaleas growing wild all over the hills.

Just where the river rushed past there was a big building with a hockey field in front. Behind it up the hill were three or four houses that were the dormitories for the bigger children. It looked a pleasant place but I soon found out the catches.

Miss T— had just one other trained teacher on the staff. The rest were just young people helping out. Pretty soon I found myself teaching nearly everything. I even took hockey. I didn't have a minute to myself all week. Mind you, I enjoyed it but it was very, very tiring.

When I arrived there it was early winter and I hadn't been there very long when we had the famous ice storm. It was raining and as the rain fell to earth it froze. At the same time there was a steady wind blowing. We came out in the morning into a crystal world. Every single twig, every single branch had about four inches of ice pushed out to one side of it, like a crystal shadow. There were little crystal trees and every one with its own shape blocked in beside it in ice.

There were rough stone steps between the little house where we slept and the school. To get up them that day took you a quarter of an hour on hands and knees. To get down them, two seconds flat, sitting.

The long holiday was in summer. I used to go camping with friends I'd made there – but not the rucksack and sleeping-bag camping New Zealanders go in for. We did it in style. About twelve of us, men and women, would have ourselves carried up to the summit of the mountain, another three thousand feet, then we'd make our way down the other side. As you got lower, all the accumulated water from the mountain was flowing in a very swift and narrow river that widened every now and then into a still basin like a tiny lake, then plunged down again through a corridor of rock to the next basin. There were four pools and you could swim in all of them and drown in all of them just as easily. If there was any cloud on the mountain you were taking your life in your hands to swim. Any rain above and the water would come dashing down the mountain and the pools would rise six feet before you had time to get out. And you'd be swept away. But if it was all clear above it was the loveliest place in the world to swim.

Just near the lowest pool there was a Chinese temple and we rented that for the holidays. We took our servants down with us and there were the chair coolies too to help with the work. All day we lounged on padded mattresses on the great big veranda stirring only to plunge into the pools. Our servants would bring our meals out and serve us there and at night they took the mattresses through to the temple rooms and made them up into beds. We did nothing except swim, sit around, eat, and sleep.

It was a lovely life but during the term I had to work very hard and as usual I became ill. At the end of my second year I had to have an operation. I was carried from the hospital to the home of some friends of mine further up the mountain. This was summer time, September.

There was an old Chinese prophecy that the world would end on the 23rd of September – our calendar. And there was a missionary at Kuling, a Mr Coates, a man with six children. We used to call them his six little jackets. The Lord suddenly revealed to Mr Coates that the world was indeed going to end on the 23rd of September – that year. On the 23rd I was in bed in the house of these friends of mine, the Sharples. And it began to pour with rain. And it poured and poured and poured. Alice Sharples had some friends in the other room and I could hear them laughing and talking. Then there was a fearful noise outside. I gave a shriek. Alice came running in and we both watched a tree, then another, sail past my window down the hill. Upright still, just sliding past. There'd been a landslide from way above. We thought the house was going, but no, just these two trees only a few feet from my window.

I said, 'I am going to get dressed and come out. If we're going to die, I'd rather die dressed.' So she helped me and we all sat round in the other room and waited for the world to end. You know when every one's in the same state of danger you don't feel it so much, or show it. The really frightening things are those that happen when you're completely alone. We sat around singing and playing games of all kinds. But with one ear cocked too for the roar of a second landslide. In the evening it stopped raining, and gradually over the next three days it cleared up and it wasn't the end of the world after all.

The funny part was that Mr Coates had taken his six little jackets and his wife and a goat and he had sailed down the river. Whether he thought he would escape the end of the world that way, I don't know. A sort of Noah trick, I suppose.

Meanwhile we'd had unexpected news from west China. Mark, this old bachelor brother of mine, was getting married. He was over thirty now and he was marrying another Olive, an independent missionary from the same station as him. That meant she had lots of money – private means – and didn't have to rely on the mission for support. She met Mark up in Lanchow where she founded a girls' school and ran it. Later she founded a soldiers' home in Cairo and ran it. Later again she founded a soldiers' home in Jerusalem and ran it. She was always founding things and running them. Well, she had the money to do it and she did it very well.

She and Mark were very much in love but almost immediately after the wedding he went down with another bout of rheumatic fever. I've never forgiven the mission for sending him back to the same place where he had his first attack. He was the only person capable of speaking Arabic to the Moslems but it was like signing his death warrant to let him go back there.

He was terribly ill and he and his Olive came down to Kuling where I was. It was supposed to be a health resort but there was Mark ill at one end of the valley and me ill at the other. He got worse and worse. Three times I was sent for – they thought he was dying. I had to get a four-bearer chair and go up the valley to him. I remember once he was alone with me (his wife had gone out of the room) and he said, 'Don't be frightened! I'm not frightened. Of dying. But it's a lonely business.' The third time I was sent for was the last time I saw him.

Then, of all people, it was Miss T— who arrived one morning to give me the news that he'd died in the night. It was dreadful. She tried to be kind. And then to have to cable the news to Olive and Mother!

He was buried in Kuling. My father was buried in west China. My little sister was buried on the coast in east China. Mark was buried in central China. I've been bitter about it because China and the mission killed every member of my family except me and Olive. And they changed Olive so that we were always apart.

Whether it was Mark's death or not I don't know, but I got worse and worse. Soon it was clear that I wasn't going to shake off my illness and return to teaching. I felt dreadfully ill, as though I were dying too, and all I wanted to do was get to Mother and Olive. They had arrived in China but they were at Kaifeng and that was thirty-six hours away by train.

It wasn't only the thought of the journey that daunted me. The country was in a terrible state. There was anarchy with various warlords and their armies fighting everywhere. But I felt so desperate I didn't mind what happened so long as I could get to Kaifeng.

I found there was a middle-aged man from Kuling making the journey too and oh, he was so kind to me! He managed to get me the whole side of a compartment to myself so that I could lie on the seat and rest or doze. I had my dog Bruno with me too. I was never without a dog if I could help it ever since the time we were children in the mission and weren't allowed to have pets and longed for them so much. Dogs have been like friends and family to me.

It was a dreadful journey, hazy and confused like a nightmare. I remember looking out of the window and seeing a soldier taking aim, just for fun it seemed, at an old farmer in his field. Pot shots for practice! Later we were held up for five hours at one station because a troop train had drawn up a short way from the siding so that the soldiers could have their meal. A five-hour meal! And the great Blue Express had to wait for them to finish!

Finally we reached Kaifeng and I was taken to the mission station and put straight to bed. But you know what the missionaries are like, they wouldn't have a dog on the place. They took my Bruno and they murdered him. I've never forgiven them for that. They were terrified of people getting rabies.

There I went to bed and there I had to stay. Flat on my back for five months. I had every meal from a tray on my chest, not even allowed to sit up for it. It was a complete physical breakdown. I hadn't been strong and Miss T— had given me so much to do I'd collapsed. That and Mark's death.

The awful part about it was that there wasn't anyone I could talk to – they were all either Chinese or missionaries. The books were all about missionaries – pious devotional stories. They'd come to me and say, 'Here's an interesting book for you,' and I'd start it and find it was the story of Mary Slessor or someone, a missionary anyway. It might have been interesting but I just couldn't bear any more missionaries. I was reduced in the end to having my Beethoven sonatas propped up in front of me so that I could play them through in my mind.

They had big services every Sunday that all the Chinese women converts attended. They'd all heard that the younger sister of the nurse was there and they wanted to see me. Olive and Mother were very embarrassed about it because I didn't look the same as the missionaries. I had short hair and short sleeves on my nightdress. They all had little buns of hair and long sleeves and well-covered ankles. (Mother used to ask me, 'How do you know that that woman's a missionary, dear?' I'd say, 'Because her skirts are long.' But if the fashion had been for long skirts the missionaries would have been wearing short ones.)

This Sunday I was fast asleep and I suddenly woke up. I was looking up from the bottom of a well that went up two or three feet solid with faces. All these women had crowded in and made a solid phalanx round the bed, all their faces staring down at me. They were gasping and looking at me and talking about me. I could speak Chinese still and I heard one of them say, 'She is prettier than her sister, isn't she?' But that wasn't true. Olive and I were alike but she was better looking. I had curly hair though.

Those five months made me aware of how much I'd changed. I was just where I'd wanted to be, with the only surviving members of my family. Although we were so often away from each other we'd always been a close family. But now I couldn't see eye to eye with them at all. I thought their ideas were narrow and they thought mine were sinful. I was the outsider. Mother was upset about it but I could no more go against my own conscience than they could against theirs.

It was a relief when the doctor said I was well enough to be taken down to Chefoo. Mother and Olive had some leave due to them so we all went together. It was a horrible journey – by train first and then by bus the rest of the way. From the railway station to the bus depot you had to travel by taxi. The road had been used by Chinese carts and the wheel ruts in it were at least a foot deep. The taxi wheels were not wide enough apart to straddle the ruts and were too wide to go between them. So one wheel was always down in a rut and the other up on the crown of the road.

When we got to the bus depot the bus hadn't arrived. We all wanted to use the lavatory so we found the comfort station. It was a brick wall raised up parallel to the road. You just squatted behind it.

The bus journey was a nightmare. I felt so ill and the bus was ramshackle and bumpy. The passengers were mainly Chinese but there were two other foreigners in it. Continental business men they were, German, I think, or Dutch. I had fashionable clothes on but I looked dreadful and I knew it. The two men began talking about me in loud voices. They spoke in English – showing off. One said to the other, 'You zee zat one. Zhee zinks zhee ees very beautiful but zhee ees not. Zhee oter one ees more beautiful!' And if ever I didn't think I was beautiful it was then!

At last we reached Chefoo. I was put to bed and I began to get better.

٭   ٭   ٭   ٭

Nellie and Olive left Chefoo when their leave was over. They wished Grace well, they would pray for her. She wished them well, she would not pray for them. Letters would be exchanged, family news, birthday greetings, presents, money; affection remained. But it was no use pretending that it wasn't, in a fundamental sense, goodbye. Both sides knew it.

There were as many dead Bothams now as there were living ones. Grace herself had almost made it four to two. She'd always had an appetite for life and now as strength came back a positive joy in living flooded her. She wanted to be light-hearted, have fun, be amused.

As I began to get well again I picked up a lot of pupils, people who wanted to learn music or French or English, I could see it was possible to make a living from private teaching if only I had a house to live and work in.

In those days when I wanted something it usually turned up. This time it was Nancy Chan who was the good fairy. Nancy was an American woman so beautiful that you just couldn't take your eyes off her. Not pretty or good-looking – beautiful. She'd been raised on a farm in America, very little schooling, just an ordinary girl except for her astounding looks. At sixteen she got married and had a little son, Edward. Her young husband was horrible to her and after a year she left him and was divorced. To earn a living for herself and the baby she worked in a boarding-house. A Chinese student on a government scholarship came to board there. He fell in love

60

with her and he promised if she would marry him he'd be a father to her baby and she'd never have to work again. And he kept his word.

When I met them Mr Chan was district head of the government inspectors of salt. Like most government officials in those days he'd made a lot of money. Nancy was a lovely person though rather unhappy, I think, even then. We became friends, but she was never really accepted in Chefoo because she had married a Chinese. Later I was involved in the sequel to her story when I knew her son in Shanghai.

Nancy persuaded her husband to offer me a house. I could rent it quite cheaply – fifty Chinese dollars a month (that was about ten American dollars).

It had four bedrooms, a dining-room, a drawing-room and, down a passage, the kitchen and servants' quarters. There was no running water and only the old type of san lavatory. The coolie had to see that that was cleaned with lots of disinfectant two or three times a day and he had to carry hot water for a bath for every foreigner in the house each day.

To get servants I had to find a good cook. The cook was always the boss of the servants. You engaged him, told him how many servants you needed and he produced a handful of assorted relatives to fill your requirements. If the other servants did anything wrong you never spoke to them about it. That would have been an insult and they would all have left. You simply told the cook.

I had a cook, an amah to do the washing and be my personal maid, a table-boy to serve the meals and do some of the light work, and a coolie for the heavy work. They were an interesting lot.

The coolie was a character. He was an earnest soul but so dumb. One of those people who's always having ludicrous accidents. The amah was making my bed one day and she screamed. I rushed to the bedroom to see what the matter was. She was standing there panting and pointing at the corner of the ceiling. I looked up and there was a human leg hanging down. The coolie had gone up to the attic to get something and had stepped on the plaster instead of keeping to the beams.

Another time I noticed that the corner behind the piano was dirty and I asked him to clean it. He pulled the piano out, cleaned behind it, and pulled the piano back trapping his own head between it and the wall, his body and legs sticking out in the room. That's quite difficult to do.

The table boy was tall for a Chinese, about six feet. He'd been in the army for ten years he told me. He liked the army because even if they didn't pay you you were sure of your food. You can always get food from someone if you have a gun to wave at them.

'Why did you leave?' I said.

'Oh, it got dangerous. They started fighting.'

But the cook was a genius. He'd worked for both American and French people so he had marvellous recipes. I'd say to him, 'I'm having eight people to dinner tonight and we'll have such-and-such and so-and-so to eat.'

'Yes, yes. All right. Very good!' he'd say. But we never had a single thing that I'd mentioned. Instead he'd produce an eight-course dinner that was a work of art.

Sometimes he would make it to a single colour-scheme. The vegetables, the fruit, the sweet, the flowers on the table would all be subtle variations on the same combination of colours, and the fingerbowls would match too.

An American woman who was having dinner at my house said one night, 'Oh, these are such pretty fingerbowls! Would you mind telling me where you got them? I'd like some myself. I promise I'll never use them in China.'

'I'd like to know myself,' I said. 'I've never seen them before.'

The servants all knew each other and it was they who did the borrowing. Nobody minded. Often I've looked up to see a strange boy waiting on my table and maybe if you were out to dinner in a friend's house you'd find your own boy serving you.

Once when I was giving a dinner party my next-door-neighbour Sonny, the American Vice-Consul, was there. So were Dr Spence and his wife, very good friends of mine. Sonny wriggled in his collar and said to Dr Spence, "Your shirt's a bit tight in the neck, isn't it?'

'Oh, so that's where it's gone!' said Dr Spence. Sonny had been out to dinner every night that week and his shirts hadn't come back from the laundry. So when he said to his boy, 'Bring me a dress shirt,' the boy had popped across to Dr Spence's boy.

It was an odd life. I lived in an eight-roomed house with four servants and Sonny lived in a seven-roomed house with four servants. If neither of us was going out to dinner, Sonny would pop over the wall and his boy would come and stand behind him and serve his meal and mine would come and stand behind me and serve mine, then when we'd finished Sonny and his boy would pop back again.

Even when I was alone I was always served a three- or four-course meal. Otherwise, the cook would have been insulted. There was only one foreigner I knew in Chefoo who couldn't keep servants. That was the missionary dentist's wife. She would insist on going into the kitchen and cooking. The servants lost face because they worked for a woman who lowered herself to do menial work.

When I first had my house I shared it with two American girls from the Y.W.C.A. That helped with the expenses and later when they had gone I often had navy wives staying with me. The Chefoo I was seeing now was very different from the one I'd known in my days at the missionary school.

The port was a summer station for the American navy. The sign that summer was coming was the arrival of a ship load of White Russian prostitutes. They'd set up in town. There'd be notices down the Chinese streets that we never dare to walk along – PRETTY GIRLS AND CLEAN BEDS. Then the Americans would arrive, thousands of them. Coming home from a party I've sometimes seen a stream of rickshaws, several hundred of them, and in every one a drunken sailor, all being taken back to the liberty boats that would return them to their ships in the harbour.

It was with the Americans that I had my first experience of anti-Semitism. Mr and Mrs Strausser were both millionaires. He was an exporter of silk and lace and she had had an inherited income. We had some ridiculously formal customs at Chefoo, like having 'At Homes' and leaving visiting cards. Mrs Strausser used to save all the cards that were left at her place and when she accumulated half a dozen of your cards she'd return them saying, 'You might want to use these.' 'No wonder she's a millionaire!' people said cattily. She played the violin and I often accompanied her on the piano so we came to know each other quite well.

They lived in an enormous mansion of a house on top of a hill that was all garden. There were strange wonders in that garden.

One day they rang me in the morning. 'The cactus flower has opened! Come quick!' I raced up there. A big trumpet, pure white at the top and gradually deepening in colour till at the very bottom it was deep dark green. It lasted one day and it bloomed once in a hundred years. I'm glad I saw it. The house was a museum of antiques from all over the world. 'Your house is more comfortable,' she used to say, but she cherished her lovely things all the same.

One day Sonny said to me, 'You know the only thing that people don't like about you is the people you mix with. You make friends with Jews.' I was amazed. I'd never come across that attitude before. Next to the Germans, the Americans were the most anti-Semitic people I ever met. Lots of them would accept the Straussers' invitations to their formal dinner parties but they'd never ask them back or make friends with them.

Meanwhile the war lords who used to terrorize the country had disappeared and the fighting had settled down into a war between the Kuomintang, the People's Party, who were revolutionary and the party who'd taken over in the north.

For the people who suffered it was the same thing. They didn't care about the rights and wrongs of it. It just meant soldiers wandering round and fighting in the streets and sometimes a nine o'clock curfew. And for shopkeepers having to keep two flags so that you could show your loyalty to whoever had the power to shoot you.

I had been to a dance once with some Americans. Two or three of them were seeing me home – it was well after nine o'clock, of course. We were walking along the road to my house when suddenly a Chinese sentry with a rifle and bayonet fixed leapt out of the dark in front of us.

He yelled at us in Chinese, 'What are you doing? What are you doing?' – very fiercely.

'Good evening,' said one of the Americans, cool and cheerful.

The sentry yelled, 'What did you say? What did you say?'

For the life of me I couldn't think what 'Good evening' was in Chinese.

'It's all right,' I said. 'He wasn't saying anything bad.'

As soon as he realized that I could speak Chinese he came up behind me and put his bayonet against my back. I could feel the point pressing on my coat. And he walked behind me shouting, 'What did he say? Tell me what he said!'

Then suddenly I remembered. 'He said, "Have you had your rice yet?" ' Because that's a sort of formal remark that's used in China as a greeting – much in the way that we say, 'How are you?'

The sentry grunted and lowered his bayonet. One of the navy men pulled out his wallet and gave him a visiting card. He looked at it upside-down and put it in his pocket. That was all right: he'd got a printed permit for us to pass.

In the winter-time the navy and their wives went away so that I was usually alone – except for the dog and the cat and the servants. One night I woke up hearing a fearful commotion. I got up and raced downstairs. The door between my part of the house and the kitchen had a glass pane in it. I looked through and saw a lot of soldiers there. They had my cook down on his knees. They were holding him and they had revolvers in their hands.

I opened the door and said, 'What are you doing here?'

They turned round. 'It's all right, all right. It's all right Madam! Your cook is a very good man. All we are doing is looking for something. It's all right!' The amah, she was the cook's wife, was kowtowing – down on her knees banging her head on the ground and begging them to let him go. They shouted, 'We'll bring him back. We'll bring him back. It's all right!' and they disappeared with the cook and left the amah howling.

I immediately rang Dr Spence and he and another Englishman came along with their revolvers ready to protect me, but there wasn't a sign of anybody there. They waited around for a while, then they decided nothing was happening so they said, 'You'll be all right. Ring us up if anything happens,' and they went home.

I didn't know what to do. I'd had a dinner party that night and I was tired and confused and excited. The amah had gone off to her quarters wailing away. I went back to bed.

About an hour later, bang, bang, bang, on the back door. I went down and opened it. There were the soldiers but not the cook. I let them in. 'We want you to watch,' they said.

Outside, between the house and the servants' quarters was a meat-safe made of wire. They went out there and one of the soldiers put his hand up and brought down from the top of it a big bundle tied up in a white square of linen. They all leaned over and the one who was the leader made me come and look too. They opened the bundle and inside it were a handful of long-nosed bullets, three revolvers and – just for a second I saw it – a roll of money, a long roll about the diameter of a silver dollar. And then suddenly almost as soon as I glimpsed it, the money wasn't there any longer. Just the revolvers and the bullets.

The spokesman told me that the bundle had been put there by robbers who were cousins of my cook and that he was in collusion with them. The cook didn't come back. Bit by bit I pieced together the whole story.

Three men from the cook's village had deserted from the army. (In China everyone from the same village is considered a relation – they usually have the same surname.) The three men had taken to the hills, turned robber, and attacked an old man and his wife. Later they were caught by the police but they wouldn't tell where the money and their revolvers were. They were tortured and finally one of them confessed, saying that they'd left the loot with a friend who worked for a foreigner. After more torture they identified the foreigner and that was when the police came and took the cook.

The cook's story was that when he was busy cooking for my dinner party the three men came to him and asked him if they could leave a parcel with him. He knew nothing about the robberies and the men were from his village so he agreed. 'Stick it on top of that safe and you can collect it later.'

The police pretended to believe that the cook had taken the money. Criminal law in China was terribly brutal and accused people had no protection. They put my poor cook in gaol and kept him there, chained to the floor, for five months. During that time they brought the others out and one by one executed them in front of him. But still they could get nothing more from him than he'd told them in the beginning.

I used to send the table-boy with money to buy food for him because all they had to eat in prison was what their friends brought them. We did all we could to help him but that wasn't much.

We thought that possibly the governor's wife might be able to help. My Y.W.C.A. friends had met her up at the Yamen – that's the governor's residence. We couldn't approach the governor direct. A woman can only approach a woman; but we thought that the wife might be able to influence her husband. We made an appointment and at the proper time we were allowed past the guard and shown in. She was lying on a *k'ang*, a big well-padded one covered with beautiful woven carpets. She was leaning against cushions and beside her was a spirit lamp and her opium pipe. It was about eighteen inches long with the most minute bowl. A servant stood there cooking something over the spirit lamp, turning it and turning it and finally out from the flame came this tiny little black thing like a seed. It was put into the bowl of the pipe and the Taitai (the governor's wife) took it and smoked it. Just two or three puffs, all the while listening to our story. She smoked three or four pipes while we were there, nodding occasionally and looking very calm and pleasant.

Finally she said she would speak to the governor about the case. As soon as she had said that, she ordered tea for us – that's a sign that it's time for you to go. The tea came in tiny bowls, green China tea, and we drank it, bowed, and left. Nothing happened.

Quite soon afterwards there was a change of government. The old governor disappeared and the new one announced a general amnesty for all prisoners except communists and parricides. So the cook was released. I tried to take him on again but it was hopeless. He'd started smoking opium himself and was an addict, dirty and shaking. I suppose, poor fellow, it was the only thing that helped him endure those dreadful months. But he was quite incapable of working.

With the cook, of course, I lost all the other servants too. They were his team. So I began looking round in a hurry for replacements. The first cook I tried couldn't cook. The second had trachoma, an eye disease very prevalent there and very catching. The third couldn't cook. The fourth spoke a different dialect from me and had no English either. I forget what was wrong with the fifth, sixth and seventh, but they all had fatal flaws.

Then came the eighth, a little round ball of a man, and he was a dear – little Humpty. That wasn't his name but you couldn't look at him without thinking that it should have been. He arrived with his wife who was to be the amah. I didn't like her much but it was a package deal. He employed a boy and a coolie. The boy was a bit useless so in the end Humpty said we'd be better off without him. He did both jobs himself from then on and did them very well.

He and his wife had a baby, a little tiny fellow not eighteen months old. He could just run about. One day I was having an afternoon tea-party, an 'At Home' with all the ladies being polite when suddenly there was a roar of childish laughter and in came this tiny thing. I'd given some dolls' clothes – goodness knows where I'd got them from – to the amah and she'd put one on him. A little doll's dress that didn't come past his waist. Below it he was all bare. And he rushed in shouting with laughter. He was so sweet. And so shocking to some of the ladies.

The dog I had at this time was Michael who was a bit of everything. Pug face, short legs, curly tail, and outsize intelligence. He and Humpty developed a deep and abiding affection for each other. Every morning they'd come up together with my breakfast tray. There was always a spray on it from my own garden and a message that Humpty would deliver. 'My son sends this flower to you.' Then I of course had to send a present back to him.

That year there was great excitement in the Chefoo schools. At the end of the long winter holidays the schools used to charter a coastal ship so that all the children from the south could gather in Shanghai and return together. It took three days up the coast. This year the ship didn't arrive on the third day. Nor on the fourth or the fifth. Telegrams were being carried up from the town to the school and back again. Yes, it had left Shanghai as scheduled. Phone calls to consuls, cables to parents, police, navy. Then, worse and worse, a rumour steadily gaining confirmation that the ship had been seized by pirates.

Everyone was worried sick. There were 200 school children on board that ship. Finally when everyone was beginning to give up hope a message came from a fishing vessel that if a launch was sent to such-and-such a bay the children would be returned unharmed.

It was all a mistake of course on the pirates' part. They'd had information that a ship with bullion was leaving Shanghai on a particular day. Maybe it was. But they seized the wrong one and all they got was this swarm of young foreigners. They locked them in the saloons and the cabins and ransacked the ship. But the only treasure they found was a term's supply of oranges, dried fruit, biscuits, condensed milk, etc. The Chinese are a philosophical lot so the pirates had a feast themselves then started passing the goodies through the windows to the children. A good time was had by all and the children couldn't stop writing essays about it for the rest of the term.

Spring came and brought back the White Russians and the notices in the alleyways. The Y.M.C.A. arrived and opened up their huge establishment in town with cinemas and boxing rings and cafeterias where you could buy anything under the sun, just as Americans do everywhere they go. Last of all the ships arrived and the liberty boats came swarming into shore.

That year the Gospel Hall people were worried about the immorality all around and they decided they'd take a rest from the Chinese and give converting the American sailors a spin. They set up a hall where there was free coffee, biscuits, and hymn singing. A lot of the sailors were from the Bible belt in America and quite a few went along and had a good time thumping out the old rousing favourites. I knew a missionary girl who was concerned in it and she was chatting one night to one of the sailors there when he suddenly said, 'I gotta go!'

'Oh, won't you stay?' she said. 'We're going to have a service in a few minutes.'

'No,' he said, 'I gotta go.'

'Why,' she said (she'd been getting on rather well with him) 'why do you have to go?'

'Honey,' he said, 'if ya must know, I gotta get me some sex.' She was so horrified she never went back again. She didn't know there were people in the world like that.

Once again navy wives came to board with me and with Humpty at the helm we had marvellous picnics on the beach. Down to the beach we'd go, a crowd of us, and swim out to the raft – the same old Chefoo raft I swam to as a child. We'd dive there and sunbathe, then, always at the same time, we'd see little fat Humpty come down the beach with the coolie behind him carrying two baskets over his shoulders. He'd lay a cloth on the beach and we'd sit in our togs and be served this beautiful meal. Then while we kept on lounging and swimming he packed it all up and went home to get dinner ready.

One day I was sitting on the beach with a crowd of navy people – a beautiful sunny day it was – when one of the girls looked up and pointed. 'Whatever's that over there? That cloud?'

It was a big cloud, solid black, and about thirty or forty feet wide. And it was flying towards us. It came nearer and nearer and passed over us not more than five feet above our heads! And the noise! A solid mass of locusts, just like a carpet, casting a deep shadow. We tossed sand up and some of the locusts fell down beside us. The cloud rose above the high cliffs backing the beach and disappeared. We heard later that the swarm had flown on over two provinces and had come down in the third, hundreds of miles away. The crops had been completely denuded, not a leaf left anywhere.

There was another memorable picnic when we went along the coast to Wei-hai-wei, the British naval summer port about twenty miles along the gulf. One of the navy boys organized it. We were going to drive there; three cars with five people in each. Because we were in the Chinese war zone we had to get passes, masses of them telling who was going, rank or occupation, reason for going, length of stay and so on. But the boys finally got them all, everything under control.

We drove along the beaches where we used to travel in the *shantze* but now there was a road. We stopped for a swim then drove on with the boys still in their togs till we came close to Wei-hai-wei. Right in the middle of the road was a sentry box and a Chinese soldier stepped out from it with his rifle with the bayonet fixed. We stopped, out got our Leader in his 1920s bathing suit and handed all this mass of papers to the sentry, with great pride and joy. But the man looked at them and shook his head making grunts of refusal.

Our Leader shouted, 'Look! Look!' jabbing at the paper with his finger and the sentry jabbered back at him and neither could understand a word the other said so they came and fished me out of the car to translate.

'You can't pass,' said the sentry.

'But we've got all the papers,' I told him.

He stared into the distance and said, 'New government!' Nobody ever knew what was going on. It was just the background of life all around us. Sometimes it was more relaxed and at other times it was very tense, but foreigners were never in much danger; it was a Chinese war.

Well, he wouldn't let us pass. So my friends said, 'Oh well, never mind, we'll go back and have another swim.'

So I said to the sentry, 'It doesn't matter, we'll go back!'

'No,' he said, 'road closed.'

'Well, let us go on to Wei-hai-wei.'

'You have no passes!' He was like the military all the world over.

'Don't be so silly,' I said. 'If we can't go on, we must go back.'

'Road closed.'

'Oh, the silly idiot!'

The American and I just got back into the car. He swung it round and started driving back. The sentry with his fixed bayonet jumped on to the running board. We dashed along and one of the boys leaned out and pushed him. He fell off, rolling over. By the time he'd picked himself up all three cars had passed but we saw his mate go back to the sentry box and we knew he'd be phoning someone or other.

So we drove back to Chefoo. When we got to the outskirts there was a whole posse of Chinese military police waiting for us. They took charge and herded us in the cars through the town into the pig sales yard. Then the police got out and locked the gate behind them. It was a big yard with a high wire fence all round it. The military police stood outside on guard with their bayonets fixed.

It happened to be just the time that people were coming out of church. They streamed along from the Union Church right past the pig sales yard. It didn't matter for the others but for me it was embarrassing. The missionary churchgoers saw me there clothed rather peculiarly (we girls had hastily pulled our frocks over our bathing suits). And with all those *awful* Navy people! One of the saintly Bothams! I always knew that middle one would come to no good.

They turned their Christian noses up and walked by on the other side.

But then Dr and Mrs Spence came along. They'd been to church too but they were not the missionary type. All through my life I've found more kindness and understanding from Christians who quietly live their belief without trying to convert other people. They went to church. If I didn't they weren't bothered. They took me as I was.

Dr Spence came straight up to the sales yard and said, 'What on earth has happened to you?' I told him and he said, 'Just hang on. I'll phone the magistrate and see what it's all about.' And within half an hour they unlocked the gates, ushered us out, and we all drove home.

Shortly after that I went to the Union Church for the last time. The Spences were sitting in front of me. They were such kindly people and they'd been such good friends to me. The night before Mrs Spence and I had seen a film together at the American Y.M.C.A. theatre. We still had ministers from different denominations taking the service each Sunday. The one who got up to preach this time talked about worldly pleasures, the terrible people who go dancing, the sinful people who go to the cinema and how God had turned his face away from them. And there was lovely Mrs Spence in front of me, more Christian than anyone else I knew. I thought, 'That's the end for me. If you're not welcome here because you go to the cinema – well, I prefer the cinema!'

Almost all my life in China there'd been a war going on, but it wasn't anything that concerned me. But after the non-picnic at Wei-hai-wei it seemed much closer.

An absurd little incident happened about this time. It must have been just after the navy left at the end of summer. I was alone in the house and I telephoned someone to ask them to tea. The telephones were manual so of course the exchange operators knew everything that was going on in Chefoo. This day, though, I couldn't raise the exchange at all. I rang and rang. No go.

I sent for the rickshaw coolie and he took me down to the exchange to see what had happened. When I got there the door was shut. I pushed it open and went in. Not a single person there. All the counters and chairs as usual but completely deserted.

I banged on the desk and called out in Chinese, 'I want some service!' Immediately lots of heads came up from under the desks. They looked at me, then they laughed and laughed. I was furious. I thought they were laughing at me.

'What's the matter?' I said. 'What's all this about?'

Finally one of them told me. 'We thought you were the army!' There'd been another change in control of the area, another victory or defeat. They'd heard about it on the telephone and were expecting these new troops to burst in any moment. So when they heard someone come pushing at the door they all hid. I never did find out why they weren't answering the phone.

There was never any actual fighting where we lived but we sometimes heard gunfire. My Y.W.C.A. friends lived closer to the Chinese part of the city. Once crowds of men streamed past their windows with guns and long knives in their hands. And they heard the chant, 'Sha! Sha! Sha!' which means 'Kill! Kill! Kill!'

About this time too I noticed a change in the Chinese. I wasn't much in contact with them so it must have been a widespread change for it to have impinged on my world. I had had a request to take an evening class, a small group of seventeen-year-old boys. It was the first time I'd ever taught Chinese people and this group anyway were very pleasant, intelligent boys and most conscientious. Only one of them was ever absent and then for only one session. The next time I took them I said to him, 'Where were you on Tuesday night?'

The others did a modest little giggle, and he said, 'Oh, I was unable to come. I got married.'

The change that I'm talking about struck me when I was marking one of their essays. In it the boy had written something about 'my country'. Those were the words he'd used – 'my country!' I had never heard that said before in China. My village – yes. Or my family, my shop, my son, my house. But never my country. That was not where loyalties lay. But now since the revolution and the wars, and particularly I think since Japan had grabbed some Chinese territory there was this new spirit, this sense of nationality.

I had been in Chefoo nearly three years when a little old lady called on me one day. She was a religious lady with plenty of money and she'd come out to do good for the Chinese. She wanted to found a school for Chinese girls, not a missionary one, just one where they'd be well taught. Somehow she had heard of me and she asked if I would establish it for her. She had already had the offer of a building and she wanted to pay me a very good salary so I accepted. I was feeling well now and ready to take on something new.

70

I had arranged to let my house for a year when suddenly she had to abandon the idea – something about the buildings I think. She was a very honest and particular person. She came and told me what had happened, very apologetic.

'Oh, it doesn't matter,' I said. 'I can get my private pupils together again.' But she insisted on paying me a whole term's salary as compensation. I really admired her for that.

When my Y.W.C.A. friends heard about this they told me that an American Presbyterian College near Canton was desperately looking for a teacher for one year while one of their staff was on leave. Would I take it on? It was a sort of Teachers Training College for Chinese girls run by the mission.

Well, I'd arranged to let the house and this seemed a way out of the muddle. I wrote to the college and had an eager acceptance from them. Just before I left another letter came saying, 'We trust your first aim is to bring people to the Lord.'

I wrote back saying, 'It certainly isn't. I was coming to do a good job of teaching and to get paid for it. So I'll take back my application since there seems to have been a misunderstanding.'

I had a telegram back immediately saying, 'Please come.'

So, with my dog Michael, I went. We said a very sad farewell to Humpty who was staying on to run the house for the new tenants. There were tears in Humpty's eyes as he and Michael parted.

✻   ✻   ✻   ✻

Down the coast to Hong Kong. For one hundred yards while Grace crosses British territory between the coastal ship and the river boat, Michael is an illegal immigrant.

Grace is twenty-nine now, but looks younger. She is five foot six and has the approved slim boyish figure of the 1920s. Under a soft panama hat her hair is short, light brown, and curly. Eyes of a brilliant English blue, clear skin, firm features. She wears a dusting of powder but needs no other make-up.

Her dress, blue voile with openwork embroidery, is Parisian Vogue by way of a Chinese tailor. The waist is low below the belt, the skirt short above the knee. White court shoes and the very latest flesh-coloured silk stockings. They flatter her legs which, long and slim, are worth the attention. Under the dress she is wearing a single garment called a 'teddy' – embroidered silk, cut with a sleeveless bodice and culotte legs.

Over her arm she carries a coarse linen coat, white like her shoes and hat. She is elegant, looks alert, cool, and at this moment, amused.

One sleeve of her coat is unaccountably active, jerking and swaying with a life of its own. Michael, a stowaway under the coat has got his excited head wedged in this odd linen tunnel.

They travel by night to Canton and wake in the morning, blue September weather, to the Pearl river, rich with life. Sampans by the hundred where the water people live out their lives never touching dry land. Little children with corks bigger than their heads tied on them, crawl and toddle on the decks. If they tumble overboard they'll bob up again. Michael barks an introduction and a fine rich dog chorus answers him from the boats.

At Shameen, the little island where British residents live and where no wheeled vehicles of any kind, not even rickshaws, are permitted, they transfer to a launch. Twenty minutes upstream is the island of P'ak Hok Tung – the White Crane's Nest.

Banana palms and orange groves, rain in the night and days of sunshine. The tables stand clumsily with each leg in a bath of kerosene to keep white ants at bay. Grace's white court shoes turn green overnight with tropical mould.

This is the far south where coolies have the delicate hands of artists and all the women look like flowers. Remote from the clashing ambitions of the northern warlords a vision of a new China is sprouting in this tropical warmth. Sun Yat-sen's People's Party, the Kuomintang, has sustained a ten year old rebellious secession from Peking, with a government based at Canton. But Sun Yat-sen is dead now and the idealism of the Kuomintang is becoming a little tarnished as a young militarist called Chiang Kai-shek forces his way to power.

But politics, ambition, and war seem remote from the White Crane's Nest where 200 graceful southern girls are being taught how to teach English and music and maths to Chinese children in the mission schools. The 200 in their blue trousers and jackets are so orderly and decorative that they seem to Grace like a formal garden of flowers all sown from the same seed. But as her eyes grow accustomed to this light she sees that each face has its different and individual beauty.

Grace teaches them English and forms them into a choir where they sing in parts and harmony. She is shown a large blank classroom and asked to help the flower girls transform and civilize it. Together they shop for Chinese carpets and lamps and low blackwood tables, and marry them to western casual couches and armchairs. (This is an American College and money grows on trees.)

In an old house down by the jetty live two young Germans, commuters from Canton where they export fine Chinese silks, and carved ivory and jade.

'Rather snazzy, especially the tall guy,' says Lillian, one of the American teachers, capturing Grace to make a fourth for table-tennis.

'But I barely know how to play!'

'They'll teach you.' Then with a sigh, 'I wouldn't mind that Otto teaching me a thing or two. But he doesn't seem to want to.'

The little ball ping-pongs across the table weaving a relationship. Grace is outclassed.

'You'd better team up with Otto. He's the champion,' says Lillian, handing out a thousand-volt smile.

Otto, six foot two, has the speed and co-ordination of a trained athlete. And the gentleness of an expert. He nurses his partner along. 'Good, very good. We will win the next game, yes?'

By the end of the week they are playing fast with much laughter. The ball leaps and dances between them. An excitement seizes them disproportionate to the game. Partnered, Grace and Otto are invincible as though they were playing to a secret strategy learned long ago.

Then unexpectedly their rhythm hiccups. For a split second both pause and an easy shot is missed. Both bend to retrieve the ball. Blundering hands bump each other. 'Sorry!' Their glances catch and lock. Abruptly, with a kind of jerk, Grace breaks the contact. For the rest of the game they play clumsily and Lillian and Ernest have an easy win.

The flower girls are copying into their neat exercise books a neat solution to the problem of X the unknown. They sit in a long curve on chairs that have side-arms for writing, each in the same pose, body slightly turned, dark head gracefully bent. Their beauty and docility releases a ludicrous spring of tears behind Grace's eyes. Like a frieze of sorrowing women, she thinks.

Is it something in the air of P'ak Hok T'ung that makes tears start so easily and beauty stir this pleasurable sadness?

The Chinese graves are pyramid-shaped mounds, shoulder high. There's a little opening at one side so that the spirit may pass out as it wills without inconvenience. The dead are kindly treated here. The shadow of all that they may need in the world of shadows has been burned at the graveside. Paper money, paper food, a paper sedan chair. The rising smoke will go with the rising spirit on its journey.

Grace and Otto walk at night among the graves. At the edge of the cemetery the land slopes away. Spicy scent rises from the groves of mandarin orange trees below them.

'My brother,' says Otto, 'was wounded in the war. He was hurt very badly. My father was sent for to the hospital and he was told, "Your son is dying. There is no hope." My father was a doctor himself. He had a large practice then in Hamburg. He was a very good man, very loving to his family. When they told him my brother was dying he said, "If there is no hope I will take him home."

He arranged for an ambulance and somehow he got my brother home alive. He gave up his practice and nursed him with his own hands. Day and night he was always with him. And very slowly my brother recovered. He is married now with children of his own. If my father had been any other sort of man he would be dead.'

Grace thinks, 'Otto must be like his father. I can imagine him doing the same.'

Later they walk in the orange groves. He shows Grace what she never before noticed – that the trees bear ripe golden fruit and small green fruit and white blossom at the same time.

'All is there together, fruit and flower and leaf.' The tropical night is warm. He is a sense of peace beside her. Flower and fruit and leaf.

The river swarms with life, and not just sampans. One afternoon there are four naval vessels lying in the Pearl River. One carries the flag of the Peking regime. What is it doing here? An armed local vessel watches it sullenly nearby. A British gunboat is anchored close, and beyond it another ship, more guns, and the flag of the Rising Sun, a kind of horror to the Chinese now they know or think they know that Japan plans to gobble them up, bones and flesh.

The White Crane's Nest, the shabby domestic sampans, look pathetic and vulnerable beside the brute metal of naval guns.

And it's guns and aircraft that wake the river and island people in the morning. The four teachers who share a house rush to the window and find, incredibly, that an anti-aircraft post has sprouted on their lawn. They rush out, four female foreigners in their nightgowns, and shoo the soldiers like wandering cattle. 'Get off our lawn!' The soldiers with Chinese good nature say, 'Oh, all right,' and let themselves be shooed. They set up on a neighbouring lawn.

There are no cellars at the school but the 200 and their teachers manage to squeeze themselves down half-underground amongst the foundations of the building. They crouch there all morning. They hear more aircraft and the recognizable stutter of the anti-aircraft guns. And every now and then deeper booms that may be naval guns or bombs. Much is happening outside. They have become a theatre of war. (Whose war?) It is very serious but huddling there they feel ridiculous and they giggle their way through this baptism of fire.

By afternoon the firing has petered out. They crawl up into the light of day stretching away their cramps. What's happened? Who won? Who was fighting who anyway? The world is perfectly ordinary, just as it was. Perhaps they imagined it.

Otto knows he didn't imagine it. He has been phoning P'ak Hok T'ung all day but the exchange has been jammed with inquiries. When he does get through there is no answer from the school. No launches are prepared to trust themselves up the river.

'I was convinced you were dead,' he tells Grace. She is touched to see that his eyes look faintly bruised. His voice is uncertain.

That night they dance to Otto's wind-up gramophone, holding each other with considerable urgency.

Spring comes. It is Michael's season, probably his finest hour. Not only does he sow a crop on at least sixteen houseboats but he makes a spectacularly successful stage début. The college concert: Grace's choir do her credit but a more personal item is expected from the staff. Grace walks on to the stage rocking in her arms a shawled baby. Appreciative giggles from the graceful girls. At the end of the stage Lillian shows a biscuit to the audience and hides it ostentatiously under the sofa cushion. The baby metamorphoses into Michael (loud applause). Michael obeys simple commands, 'Sit, go, lie down!' (polite applause). Grace suggests 'Biscuit?' Michael displays enthusiasm. 'Go find biscuit, Michael!' Michael circles, sniffing, leaps on sofa, nuzzles behind cushion, emerges triumphant, and eats biscuit (very loud and prolonged applause).

Otto brings Grace an ivory fan delicately carved and a mandarin robe of embroidered silk. Later as they walk in the Chinese graveyard his voice comes abruptly out of the darkness.

'There was a girl in Hamburg. We were betrothed. That is very important in Germany – a very important ceremony.'

'Yes,' says Grace keeping her voice steady.

'That was before I left to come here. At first we wrote to each other regularly. I could think of nothing but going home to her. But now it is hard for me to remember what she looks like. And for the past year she has answered none of my letters. So that I know that she no longer remembers me . . .

Since you came I have been pleased that time has kept passing and no letter has come. Grace . . .'

But to Grace the betrothal is like a third person walking between them. Later Otto says, 'Grace, if I write to her and say that I know what her silence means? That it is better that we both be free. Then will you marry me?'

And the happiness Grace has been holding in check for months rushes over her.

But three days later when she saw him coming up the path towards her she knew what had happened. He was like a raincloud, she thought, shedding a livid light the moment before it breaks.

'She has been ill. That was why . . . She said it was the only thing – the thought of me – that kept her alive. I can't . . . '

'It's quite all right, Otto,' Grace said carefully, and went into her bedroom where she held a pillow in front of her face so that no one could hear the sounds she was making.

At the end of the school year she returned to Chefoo.

Michael and Humpty fell on each other with glad cries but I never really settled down in Chefoo again. Otto and I wrote to each other for months but what was the use?

After I'd been back for some while – I can't remember how long – I got offered a relieving job in a school at Shanghai and it seemed a good idea to have a change of scene so I took it. Humpty wanted to come with me so the three of us, Michael, Humpty, and I, set off together for Shanghai.

I never saw Chefoo again, but I know what happened to it. When the Second World War broke out the Japanese invaded the town. All the children from the mission schools and the foreigners living in the town were rounded up and marched to a concentration camp. They stayed out the war behind barbed wire. Food was poor and scarce and there was a lot of illness in the camp but the Japanese let the school go on operating there. It helped everyone, the teachers as well as the children, to stay sane and normal. The Japanese even let the papers for the Junior and Senior Oxford Exams to be sent out from England and the scripts be sent back. Every year except the last one – the year they were relieved – there was a 100 per cent pass.

It was the Americans who opened the camp at the end of the war. A plane flew in and landed on the camp ground. Out stepped the pilot, an old Chefoo boy. He'd specially asked for the assignment.

I've been told that the schools are all pulled down now. The boys' football field is a military parade ground. The gullies have been filled in so that the whole site is large and flat. And there's not a foreigner within miles of it.

The missionaries were scattered all over the world. They went to Japan, Thailand, Burma, Vietnam, Korea, Africa – all sorts of places. Wherever they went they started a school for the children of missionaries and each school was called the Chefoo School of the country where it was situated. The Chefoo School of Burma or the Chefoo School of Thailand . . . and so on. So the old original one cast its seeds far and wide.

∗   ∗   ∗   ∗

Shanghai used to be a fishing village on the banks of the Whangpoo River where the Soochow Creek flows into it. A few miles downstream their combined waters spill out into the great Yangtze, the ancient inland waterway of China.

It was a busy little place, well-situated, with the fertile Yangtze valley at its back door and the Pacific Ocean just down the garden path. For 700 years it grew at a steady sensible pace till by the early nineteenth century it was a small provincial town.

It was then that the barbarians from the west, randy with energy, set eyes on it. As part of the price of peace after the Opium War the port of Shanghai was opened to their thrust. That was in 1843. Ninety years later Shanghai was the sixth biggest city in the world. It was bigger than Paris or Vienna or Buenos Aires or Chicago. Four million people, banks and factories and warehouses, cinemas, brothels, churches, shipyards, beauty parlours, libraries, traffic cops, radio stations and money, money, money. It was a monument to the commercial passion of the west.

Britain was the first country to be in. Then came Austria, Brazil, Denmark, France, Germany, Italy, Japan, Mexico, the Nether-lands, Norway, Peru, Portugal, Russia, Spain, Sweden, and

Switzerland. They imported and exported, they manufactured, they built the sixth biggest city in the world. By and large the Chinese supplied the materials and the labour and the foreigners organized and made the profits.

The city was divided into three parts: an International Settlement dominated by Britain, a smaller French Concession and, with the biggest population of the three, a Chinese city. The geographical boundaries were rigid but the population blurred pleasantly across them. Shanghai bred its own *mores*. A Chinese bourgeoisie, wealthy and conservative, housed itself in the foreign concessions and thrived there and multiplied. If the foreigners should ever pack up and go home one might have expected that this would be the group who would take over.

But under the rich commercial growth different seeds were sprouting. Certain Chinese patriots looked at Shanghai and saw in it a working illustration of Marx's strictures on capitalism. In 1920 a secret handful of men met together in Shanghai and formed the first revolutionary Marxist cell of China. For safety and camouflage they moved to the French Concession. The movement grew. Labour unions, a strange phenomenon in China, sprang up and struck for higher wages and better conditions.

Seven years later Chiang Kai-shek, purging his way to power, found 300 communists and radicals to slaughter in Shanghai in a single night.

Grace arrived in Shanghai in 1931. That was a bad year throughout the world – depression, unemployment and despair. It was an especially bad year in China where as well as an internal war there was an attack by the Japanese and a vast natural disaster. The Yangtze River flooded in its middle basin destroying hundreds of thousands of acres of farmlands and crops. Villages were wiped out: two million people died. As the waters receded there were epidemics of dysentry, cholera and famine.

But Shanghai led its charmed life, unaware of disaster. It was certainly untouched by it. Money still poured satisfyingly into the commercial coffers.

Oh, it was a fascinating city. For a hundred miles out to sea you sailed in brown water, like strong milky tea. The Yangtze River. Shanghai had come out to meet you. A tide of foreigners, all sorts all nationalities, flowed through it continuously: a thousand a day, they said.

78

The French Concession and the International Settlement were divided by a very wide street, Avenue Edward the Seventh. In the International Settlement they had British laws and Indian policemen directing the traffic (India was part of the Empire then). Great big Sikhs they were, six feet tall. They wore huge turbans that made them even taller. On the other side of the avenue was French law and French policemen, little small-boned, delicate-looking men from French Indochina. They were Annamites, the same type as Vietnamese.

At first I worked for a Municipal Council school. Anyone could attend it and the people who did were mostly Eurasian girls. The Eurasians were a middle group between the Chinese and the foreigners. If they'd had a good education they could get jobs in shops and offices. A lot of them learned to be typists. They were nice enough people on the whole and some of them were stunningly beautiful but nobody really accepted them, neither the Chinese nor the Europeans. They were rather a sad lot and most of them were just longing to get away out of China. I knew one once who used to tell all the foreigners she met that she was Spanish. She hated being dismissed as just another 'little *chi-chi* girl'. Of course anyone who got to know her better would meet her mother sooner or later and discover the truth.

I took a flat and Humpty looked after me. I hadn't been very long in Shanghai when I was offered a job in the big French Municipal College. Even in those dark ages the French gave women the same pay as men. I became one of the five best paid women in Shanghai. And a *professeur* as well. If you taught in the upper school you were automatically a *professeur*. It was luxury teaching. Outside the classroom we had no duties. There were supervisors to look after the children in the playground, Chinese clerks to do the paper work, typists for the use of the staff, and of course coolies for all the odd jobs.

We worked from 8.30 to 1.30, six days a week. You taught for three-quarters of an hour, then there was a quarter of an hour's break with lovely French coffee served in the staff-room every time. I used to do most of my marking in the breaks so I had the afternoons and evenings free.

I was form mistress of a big mixed class – mainly eleven-year-olds, about a form one level. Once a clergyman came in to get statistics on all the children's religious affiliations.

'Stand up all the Catholics,' he said and about half of them stood up, mostly French.

'Stand up all the Buddhists.' It was mainly Chinese and Japanese this time. 'Protestants?' Most of the English and German children. 'Greek Orthodox?' – the White Russians. In the end he'd accounted for all of them except one little character, Bobby Verges, who'd fit into today's world really well.

'Bobby Verges! What is your religion?'

Bobby in his black overalls stood to attention. 'Moi, je suis paien!' (As for me, I'm a pagan!)

I taught the third and fourth form as well. The fourth form was the naughtiest as they always are. This one was appalling. Sometimes I could hear them way down the corridor, stamping their feet and yelling. And a teacher's voice rising frantically through the hullabulloo. 'Taisez-vous! Silence! Taisez-vous!'

The first time I ever went in there was pandemonium. I went to the desk and just stood there. None of them had ever seen me before and one or two glanced at me, puzzled. Gradually the noise began to die away till in the end there was silence, quite a tense silence. I said, 'Good morning pupils, I never teach till there's silence. Sit down!' I never had trouble with discipline: I never expected it, so I didn't get it. There are two tricks to discipline. One is to expect obedience. The other is to keep the children's attention once you've got it. Then they don't want to be naughty. I really enjoyed that class. You could still hear them from the corridor making a row with other teachers, especially the women. That sounds like boasting, but I couldn't help but know I was a good teacher.

The flat I had was a long way from the French College and Humpty was getting more and more homesick for his little boy so we decided that he would go back to Chefoo and I would move into a residential hotel up Nanking Road.

The back window of my new apartment looked across part of the Chinese sector of the city. Tiny flat-roofed houses all crowded together with no roads, just tracks and alleys between them. They said that five million people jostled round there. No foreigner dared go into it, not even the police.

Once a brash young American arrived in Shanghai and announced that he was going into the Chinese Quarter to take some photos.

He was told, 'Don't go alone. You'll never find your way out.' But he went in and was never heard of again. The police hunted but they found no trace of him. How could you find anyone in that maze? There were opium dens and any number of people who'd kill a foreigner for his money, knowing they couldn't be caught.

One day I went with two of the teachers from school, Mme Terzi and Mlle Lambertin, for a meal in a Japanese Sukiyaki place. We chose one over the Garden Bridge, just on the edge of the Chinese sector. How the rickshaw coolies ever found their way to it I don't know. We were sitting there eating a delicious meal when a thought suddenly struck me.

'Si on nous tuait ce soir, il n'y a pas personne au monde qui saurait ce qui etait arrivé.' (If we were killed tonight there's not a single person in the world who would know what had happened.)

Mme Terzi stared at me, then said, 'Mon dieu, c'est vrai!' And suddenly there was a strange little sinister thrill to the evening.

The school had its long holidays in the summer. The temperature started climbing in June: 90 degrees Fahrenheit – 95–100. Women began disappearing from the city. By August the temperature would be above 100 – I've known it go up to 105. It was a city of men and they went wild. The White Russians did a roaring trade. The first summer I hadn't got used to the high salary I was getting and I went down the coast to a sort of boarding-house place I'd seen advertised. It was run by two English women and was supposed to be very comfortable and just near the beach. Every guest, they said, had a private bath.

It wasn't a bad little place, I suppose. The bedrooms were very simply furnished and the swimming was only moderate.

'Where's my private bath?' I said.

'I'll show it to you,' the woman said. She took me down two passages to a place where there were a whole lot of baths in separate cubicles. 'This is yours.'

It was a Suchow tub – a great big urn of shiny pottery, big enough to get into, just like the pictures in Ali Baba. I could just sit in it with my knees right up to my chin and my head sticking out the top. My private bath! I was furious.

We were having breakfast on the veranda one day – all separate little tables – when suddenly a Chinese man brandishing a huge curved knife rushed in one door charged through the tables and out the other door. The owner of the hotel flopped down on the nearest chair and had hysterics. I thought it was time to go back to Shanghai. I packed up and told her I was leaving.

'I don't blame you,' she said morosely.

When I got back I found the garbage coolies had been on strike. They were employed by the French Municipal Council the same as we were. The council held out for a while but with the temperature above 100 they had to give in and the coolies got the 15 per cent they were asking for. The ludicrous thing was that we got it too. All council employees up 15 per cent. That 15 per cent rise alone yielded me more in a week than a poor old garbage coolie would earn all told in a month. About the same time someone told me that any teacher employed by the council who could speak Chinese was entitled to an extra ten dollars a month. I went and took the exam and got my ten dollars from then on. For no reason.

One day I came home at lunchtime and for some reason I had to go back to school in the afternoon. I was standing in my apartment when suddenly I was aware of a confused noise all round me – overhead and coming up from the street. I rushed to the window. Nanking Road was jammed tight with people, all milling about, some trying to push their way up the street and as many trying to force their way down. It was a real panic. People shouting and screaming. Above it I could catch the roar of an aeroplane flying low.

I rushed to the back window. And there they were! Planes turning low overhead then dipping away over the Chinese city. It was very old-fashioned like a slow motion film. There was a plane and hanging out of its underbelly a great silver bomb. Then I saw the bomb drop and heard the noise, the bang, and saw the smoke and flame leap up. I actually saw while I watched, one house up in the air still complete; and it disintegrated in the air and fell down. Fires began blooming all over the Chinese sector. I watched for about half an hour. By that time the crowd had drained away from Nanking Road and I could get across it to my car which was parked on the other side.

I drove back to school, in the French Concession, and they didn't know anything about it – hadn't heard a thing.

I said, 'I couldn't come back because there's bombing right over our heads!'

One of the men said, 'C'est possible!'

I was so angry. 'What do you mean "It's possible!" It's *true*! It's a fact!'

Of course the French say, 'C'est possible!' as we would say 'Really?' But I was too stirred up to think of that. I wouldn't speak to him for days.

I found out about the crowds in Nanking Road. There had been terrible flooding up the Yangtze and these people had been evacuated and brought down to a refugee camp just outside Shanghai. They'd never seen cars before, let alone planes, and suddenly they were getting killed from the sky. They panicked, thousands of them, just running madly through the streets of Shanghai.

The bombing went on intermittently for three or four days and the fires burned in the city for three weeks. One of them must have been a paper factory because for days burnt paper would fall on our heads in the streets.

It was the Japanese who had done the bombing and it was during that 1932 attack that the Chinese for the first time fought back. There was a battle at the Railway Station and the Chinese army actually stood their ground and repelled the Japanese. Foreigners went round saying to each other, 'Never thought the Chinks had it in them!'

After the bombing, my residential hotel, so close to the Chinese quarter, didn't look so nice, so I moved into the Cathay Mansions nearer the school in the French Concession. It was a tall building for those days, thirteen floors, and it belonged to the wealthy Sassoon family. Siegfried Sassoon, the poet, was one of that family. When I first moved in you had to step up two steps from the road to the lobby. When I moved out four years later you stepped down one step. Shanghai is built on a mud flat. To erect a building they have to sink sixty-foot poles then put concrete floats on them. The floats sink deep in the mud and the buildings are put up on them. They're quite safe but they just keep on sinking.

I always had rooms between the seventh and the tenth floors. That way I didn't have to have wire mesh on the windows or a mosquito net on my bed. The flying range of mosquitoes and flies only takes them to the fourth floor.

Oh, we were well looked after. They changed the sheets and pillowcases every day. Once there was a strike of laundry men and the hotel management apologized personally to all the guests because the sheets could only be changed every second day. If you came home at lunch-time and dried your hands on a towel, it had been removed like some filthy old rag and a new one put in its place by evening.

There were 200 suites in the building and 150 resident servants. For each wing of each floor there was a boy on duty all the time so that any hour of the twenty-four you could get tea or coffee or anything else that you fancied. After all these years when I wake up in the morning, I still sometimes find myself putting my hand out with the thumb down to press a bell for tea.

Those years at the Cathay mansions were the gayest of my life. I was never so light-hearted again. There were so many fascinating things to do and so many good friends to do them with. After I got home from school in the early afternoon, I'd have a rest, then get dressed and go out.

It might be to the French Club, just opposite the Cathay Mansions. I used to drive across the road in my car. We'd dance there and then perhaps go on to the Canidrome, an enormous night-club where a thousand couples could dance. Superb floor and wonderful orchestra. There was usually someone special to entertain in the intervals or else Teddy Wetherford, the resident pianist would play. He was a Negro from America – I can still see his black sausage fingers dancing on the keys.

When we wanted a rest from dancing we'd step through the glass doors at the side of the room onto a wide veranda that overlooked the greyhound racing track. The veranda was a partitioned-off part of the grandstand with its own place for betting. Over the partition was a different crowd – French, English, Russian and Chinese, in everything from sweaters to dinner jackets, all peering at their cards as though their whole future depended on it. The Chinese love betting and they'd spend thousands and thousands on it. I was always lucky with the dogs – I always seemed to pick one that came in for a place at least.

Down below in the glaring lights were the Russian men in white coats leading the dogs out. (They always had White Russians to look after them; they're much kinder to animals than the Chinese are.) The dogs themselves with their little saddles on, so pretty to watch and enjoying it too. I loved it!

The Canidrome closed at three in the morning. When they'd played 'Goodnight, sweetheart' and we'd waltzed the last waltz, often we didn't feel like going home and we'd go on and dance somewhere else and end up at Del Monte's having ham and eggs for breakfast at half past seven in the morning. I'd go home and wash and change and go straight to school and teach, then sleep all the afternoon.

We played a lot of bridge for cents or cash. You could win or lose a couple of thousand and feel like a millionaire or a bankrupt but in actual value it was negligible. Sometimes I'd give a bridge party in the big lounge at the Cathay Mansions. All you had to do was say, 'I'm having so many people for bridge today. Will you please serve tea at such-and-such a time,' and they'd prepare the tables and the food and wait on us. It would go down on my monthly account as an extra.

All sorts of entertainers used to come to Shanghai. Symphony orchestras from various parts of the world and individual artists too. Often they came, as they do to New Zealand, when they were just a bit *passé* but still worth seeing. I remember the Russian Ballet and Chaliapin, the operatic *basso*. We even had the Ziegfeld follies. They put on a spectacular show in the biggest theatre. For the big scene of the evening they'd built an enormous trellis right up to the top of the stage. When the curtain went up on this there were girls like flowers all the way up. All naked, or looking as if they were. It was a lovely sight but the police disapproved of so much nudity. 'Too navel,' they said. So all the girls had to put a jewel in the vital spot.

Some of the cast took one look at Shanghai, recognized its possibilities, and deserted. They set up in business in a house just across the Creek from where a friend of mine lived. We used to see them sitting on their balcony in dressing-gowns, taking a well-earned rest between customers.

We had some very plebeian amusements too. There was a Luna Park with switchback railways and coconut shies. I never went there – it wasn't my type of amusement – but from my seventh-floor window, all one summer, I saw the pole-sitter across the city in a sort of dentist's chair on the top of a sixty-foot pole. They sent food up to him on a pulley and I suppose he sent the other things down the same way. He sat there for sixty-three days.

Going round the bazaars and the curio shops was always a joy. Pedlars used to come to the hotel too with exquisite things to sell. One came with the most beautiful Chinese embroidery I've ever seen – a set of scrolls of the seasons. I bought two of them, the spring and summer ones. The delicacy of the colours! I used to gaze and gaze at them. Even when I went on holiday I took them with me and hung them on the walls.

What I liked best about Shanghai, what made it my spiritual home, was its tolerance. There wasn't a diplomatic set, or a business set, or a professional set. You could move and mix freely. Most people's lives are circumscribed by their backgrounds but in a way Shanghai was a city of people without background and they didn't judge or gossip. So your life could be as varied as you liked to make it.

I could spend the early evening visiting some of mother's ageing missionary friends and then go dancing for the rest of the night with the adviser to the Bank of China. I could spend an evening practising with the Shanghai Quintet, (I was their pianist) or listening to the Municipal Orchestra under the baton of a famous Italian conductor. I could go to the Chinese theatre or an American movie. I could sit quietly at home knitting and reading, or I could be out playing poker or bridge or betting on the dogs. There was so much to do and so many good friends to do it all with.

84

And they were real friends, not all out for themselves. If I were ill and couldn't go out with them, they wouldn't leave me to feel miserable alone, they would come and sit on the end of my bed and chat to me or play cards and cheer me up.

One of the 'backgroundless' people who turned up in Shanghai was Nancy Chan's son Edward. He was in a terrible state. Mr Chan had brought him up as his own son as he promised he would, but Nancy and her husband had grown apart as time passed. He became more and more Chinese as the memory of America faded and she became more American. She found it harder and harder to put up with the sort of restrictions that were imposed on a Chinese wife. Edward was about seventeen when he turned up in Shanghai. He'd only recently found that he wasn't Chinese. He'd always thought that Mr Chan was his father. He blamed his mother, the way adolescents will, and she left and went back to America.

Edward had taken some sort of apprentice job in Shanghai – the kind you'd expect a Eurasian to take. Most Eurasians would have thought it was a fairy-tale come true if they'd found they were pure 'foreigner', but to Edward it was a bit of a tragedy. He loved his father and his best friends were all Chinese. He didn't want to mix with foreigners; he felt confused and embarrassed by the whole business. He used to come and see me often to talk things over and I used to keep everything as ordinary and normal for him as I could.

I was often ill in Shanghai – it was the only drawback to living there. But if you had to be ill you couldn't be in a better place. In the first hotel I lived in I could lie in my bed and read the news – all the main headlines being spelled out in neon lights in the city. This was way back in the 1930s. The Cathay Mansions had a splendid library service. They had all the latest publications, fiction and non-fiction, sent out to them from England and America, and they always reserved for me the ones they knew I'd be interested in. I read the unexpurgated *Lady Chatterley's Lover* long before it was available in England. It bored me stiff.

The hotel gave excellent service and as well as that I had my own amah who came in to do my personal washing and ironing. Then there was the nail amah who came every Sunday morning to do my finger and toe nails. She was a lovely person, so pretty and nicely mannered, and she spoke English well. She had a marvellous way of taking every single hair off your legs with a piece of cotton. She'd twist it, put her hands in the loops and – whoovut! – up and down your leg it would go and every hair came off and never grew back again. See, I still have no hairs on my legs!

As well as that I had Fu-yen, a twelve-year-old boy who used to come after school each day and take Michael for a walk and generally care for him. He was a cheerful child. He only knew one English word and he used it for everything. When he came in he'd greet me, 'Goodbye! Goodbye!' Whatever he said to me in Chinese he'd begin with 'Goodbye! Goodbye!' He was so proud when he took Michael for walks that I asked him if he'd like a uniform. I had my tailor make him one, a sort of white pageboy outfit with a white pill-box hat and lots of gold buttons and scrolls of braid scattered over it. Everyone seeing this smart uniform would look to see what rare and valuable dog was being exercised. And there was little mongrel Mike.

Mind you, Mike had his own suit, tailor-made. My tailor made it from a picture in the Parisian Vogue, just as he did my own clothes. He took Mike's measurements and brought the coat along a few days later beautifully made. It buttoned up all along under Michael's chest and stomach – very cosy. *But* . . . I tried to explain. 'The coat is warm and well-made but it is not necessary for it to be as long underneath as above.'

'No,' agreed the tailor. 'I saw in the book that the coat was cut away but it is colder here so I have made it to fit more closely.'

'But I wish it to be shorter underneath. There is too much material here.'

The tailor looked hurt. 'If you think I have used too much material I will not charge you for that part.'

I felt so frustrated. 'You can just come along yourself,' I said, 'and undo those last buttons every time Michael comes to a lamppost.'

The tailor looked at me for a moment, then the penny dropped. He grinned. 'Ah!' and he pinned back the coat for alterations.

A lot of my friends found Shanghai more astounding than I did. There was Judy from Scotland who was horrified at me because I took it for granted that a rickshaw coolie would pull me along. And she thought I was rude because I said 'Hao' (Good) to the servants instead of 'Thank you'. 'Thank you' was an extravagant sort of thing to say, inappropriate for the ordinary little services the servants did. It is like saying, 'Thank you so much, Sir,' to a taxi driver.

The poor Americans, when they came out, got into terrible trouble with money. A rickshaw man would say to them 'One dollar' when he'd taken them somewhere and they'd say 'Chinese or American?' Of course the coolie would say, 'American,' – an American dollar was worth five Chinese ones.

One time I remember an American sailor and a rickshaw coolie were having a fearful argument as I passed. I went up and said, 'What's the matter?' The sailor said, 'I've given him six dollars already and he's still arguing and fighting.'

'Just leave it to me,' I said. And I turned to the coolie and said in Chinese, 'I know the custom.'

'Oh,' he said, 'You know the custom?' And he handed all the money back to me. I paid him the right amount and gave the rest back to the American. The coolies weren't dishonest but anyone who's a fool seemed fair game to them.

Once when I was in Chefoo I had some work done by a carpenter and he sent an enormous bill. I said, 'Rubbish' and we went through it item by item. What I really owed came to about two-thirds of the original amount. I paid him and he said, 'Oh, I like dealing with you! You know how to bargain!'

Once though a terrible thing happened and it's worried me all my life since. I'd been in a rickshaw and I gave the coolie a dollar – that was the right amount plus a tip. He followed me shouting and I said, 'I know what the fare is!' and went on. Still he followed right up the stairs shouting. And afterwards in my purse that night I found half an old dollar and I realized the dollar I'd given him had ripped and he only got half. I felt awful. I'd done something to give him a bad impression of foreigners. Because a lot of foreigners were rotten to the Chinese. I suppose that man must be dead by now—but it still worries me. I could never have found him again. You can't find one rickshaw coolie amongst thousands.

I didn't use rickshaws so much in Shanghai because I'd bought a car. I paid a coolie to bring it from the garage and park it in front of the hotel each morning and run it for a while so that it was nicely warmed up when I got there. Once I ran over two policemen in that car. I'd been out to dinner (I wasn't drunk, I don't drink). It was just beginning to get dark when I left the house where I'd been, but it wasn't dark enough to have my lights on. I drew out from the curb and turned a corner, slowly because it was quite close, into a wide road that had no pavements at all. There were trees down the sides so that people could walk on the left of the trees and the traffic go on the right. As I went round the corner I felt bump, bump, and I'd run over the two policemen one after the other. They were walking in the middle of the road with their backs to the oncoming traffic. There was no way of seeing them till you were on top of them.

I stopped. They were Chinese policemen and they were out cold. There was another policeman further down the road. I got hold of him and we managed to push and shove them into the back of my car. I drove straight to the police station and by that time they'd come round.

There was an Englishman in charge at the police station. I said, 'I'm terribly sorry but I've just run over two of your policemen.' He asked all about it and I told him. 'They were in the wrong,' I said, 'but if there're any hospital or doctors' fees or any other expenses, please charge them up to me.'

I turned to go. At the other end of the room the two policemen, quite recovered now, were talking to a third. I listened and by chance they were talking in Mandarin.

'We were walking along the pavement,' they were saying, 'and she came round the corner and ran straight over us.'

I went up to them and said in Chinese, '*Is* there a pavement where I ran over you?'

They looked at each other, then said, 'No, no pavement.' I never heard anything more about it. I don't think many women have run over two policemen at one go.

If you went outside the Concession of course it was a different story. You were immediately in Chinese territory and if you had a motor accident you'd be tried by a Chinese judge and that meant that the person who paid him the most won the case.

English people didn't have to pay any income tax in Shanghai – none at all. We were supposed to pay two dollars a year on our passports in lieu of tax. Once I realised that I'd forgotten to pay this for about four years. I went to the consular office and told them.

'Oh yes,' they said, 'you'll have to pay a fine for omitting to pay.' And they fined me two dollars. I didn't have to pay anything for the years I'd missed. Oh, it was an ideal place to live!

Sometimes though when I was ill I did get lonely and self-pitying. I thought, 'Here I am half way through my thirties and still an old maid. I'll marry the next man who asks me.' I really made up my mind to do that once. The next man who asked me was married already and I never did fancy marriage-breaking or bigamy. So I thought, the next one! When the next one came along he was five foot one, about as high as my nose. I couldn't face that so I decided it was fate and I'd better just get on with the job of enjoying myself.

There were a lot of radio stations in Shanghai. One of them, a private one, called R.U.O.K. was run by a woman. I was told to listen to her request session one morning. 'The next request is for Grace from Dickie,' I heard. The song was 'All of Me, Take All of Me'. While it was still being played I rang R.U.O.K. and said, 'This is the Grace that song is being played for. Will you thank Dickie for me and tell him I'll settle for half.'

'Why should I get married?' I thought. 'I'm having too good a time.'

Meantime the attitude of the Chinese to the Japanese was gradually getting more and more hostile, especially since the bombing. The first sign I saw of it was down near the French College. An innocent little Japanese was walking along the road and the Chinese began stoning him. It was horrible. He just walked on but some of the stones hit him. The flow of tourists from China to Japan began to fall off and Japanese travel and shipping firms offered special cheap rates. I thought, 'I may as well have a look at Japan too,' so one holiday off I went on a P. & O. Liner.

I'd booked in at the Myanoshita Hotel. It was world famous and terribly expensive but I was earning a fabulous salary and that was what I wanted. It was owned by a wonderful old man called Yamaguchi. He was president of the moustache club in Japan: his moustache measured eighteen inches from tip to tip.

In the lounge of the hotel there was a hot spring, right there, bubbling up and a tree growing beside it. You went to the desk and above it, about ten feet up from the floor, was a perch with a bird on it. It looked like an ordinary rooster but its tail was black and gold and huge. It fell to the ground and trailed several feet along it. The birds bred in only one island in challenge him. His years were spent in civil war trying to maintain an increasingly slippery position.

When Japan, the last and most ruthless foreign power to turn greedy eyes on China, demanded outrageous privileges and powers within the republic's borders, Yüan was unwilling or unable to resist. At the same time his veneer of republicanism had worn thin and the personal ambition was showing through very clearly. He wanted to be Emperor of China. There was a throne to let, he felt. He wanted to climb on it and found a dynasty.

A new dynasty was not what China wanted. Nor, it seemed, was Yüan. Region after region with its own military leader and its own army had risen against him. His death in 1916 came just in time to prevent his being forcibly deposed.

He bequeathed to his country a weakened central government at Peking and a vast confused dog-fight of a civil war. The warlords of the north, rampaging, were tearing each other to pieces.

Nor was that all. In the south at Canton disappointed revolutionaries had gathered to form the Kuomintang, the Nationalist movement, the people's party. Sun Yat-sen's battle cry – Nationalism, Democracy, People's Livelihood – sounded again. Throughout the 1920s the armies of Peking and Canton, the north and the south, struggled against each other for control of the country.

Armies, public and private and always on the move, lived parasitically on an impoverished countryside. Casually they stripped district after district bare, leaving hunger or outright starvation behind them. With their crops gone more and more peasants joined the armies themselves or turned bandit on their own account. Only the foreigners continued to flourish.

We were heading for Kuling, a mountain resort where a lot of foreigners, business people and missionaries, used to spend their furloughs. It was cool up there in summer and in winter there was tobogganing and other sports. A lovely place!

To get there you had to climb up a mountain – three thousand feet in a four-bearer chair. The path was narrow most of the way. The mountain rose sheer up on one side of the path and dropped sheer away on the other. I've known foreigners who walked it just for the exercise but most women didn't attempt to get out of the chairs. I certainly didn't. I've been carried up and down that mountain in every kind of weather. I've been down it in pouring rain when the path was so slippery that every now and then one of

Japan and out of 200 eggs there'd only be three or four that were long-tailed and only one that had a really long tail like this one – sixteen feet. It couldn't walk unaided for the weight of it. Once or twice a day a coolie would come and lift the bird from its perch. He rolled the tail up and held it, walking behind the bird while it strolled up and down.

The dining-room was huge with a wooden ceiling divided into squares and in each was a different Japanese flower exquisitely painted. They had a table that was always reserved for royalty. The Prince of Wales had used it when he stayed at Myanoshita and while I was there a Japanese princess dined at that table and later a Swedish prince.

The garden rose up a hill from the hotel to the swimming-pool at the top. You walked up through a greenhouse of beautiful flowers, or past the white peacocks on their special lawn, or beside the waterfall, any one of five different ways.

There were four choices of baths. I always chose the Roman one. When you had showered and washed yourself you went through to the huge twenty-foot square bath, fed by a natural spring always flowing. The whole ceiling was the bottom of a goldfish pond in the garden above. It was lovely to float there in the warm water and watch the goldfish darting about above you.

Yamaguchi had another hotel twenty miles away and always during the summer we drove there. The way was through an avenue of cryptomeria trees that were 400 years old. They're cypress trees something like the giant redwoods of America. This hotel was small but the lounge had huge plate glass windows. And there it was – nothing in front of you but water and Fujiyama. The perfect mountain perfectly repeated in the water.

The Japanese took such delight in their own lovely sights. Wherever we went there were lots and lots of Japanese sightseers, crossing the lakes; the boats were full of them. The women and the coolies were so friendly and nice, but oh, I didn't like the Japanese military at all.

I loved Myanoshita so much that I spent three beautiful summers there, in spite of the price.

I'd been in Shanghai four years by this time and my life was flowing happily along until the beginning of 1935. That was a momentous year for me. It started in the restaurant of a huge luxury hotel. Seven or eight of us were there in a party celebrating. At midnight with a great fanfare of trumpets, twelve Chinese cooks all in uniform with tall cooks' hats on came in one behind the other. Each one was wheeling a trolley and on each trolley there was an enormous block of ice, almost a yard high carved into one huge block letter, a Roman capital. They formed a line and the ice letters read – HAPPY NEW YEAR.

Under the coloured lights the ice gleamed and sparkled with colour as it melted and the droplets ran down. It was bitterly cold outside but the room was warm and glowing.

1935 was only a few weeks old when I received a disturbing letter from Olive in England. She wrote that Mother was ill and frail and failing fast.

The French College gave you a year's leave of absence on full pay and paid your fare home after you'd taught there for five years. I asked if I could take my leave ahead of time. They granted me seven months and arranged for me to travel by the Siberian railway so that I could get there as quickly as possible.

Just before I was due to leave there was an 'incident' on the Siberian border. What an 'incident' really is is a straight-out fight, in this case between the Russians and the Chinese. The border was closed and likely to stay that way for weeks. I tried to get a passage on a ship but before I managed it a cable came from Olive to say that Mother was dead.

I don't know quite what I felt. I hadn't seen her for a long time and I knew I couldn't have lived at home again because my ideas were so different. But we always wrote and it was lovely to have a mother. When she wasn't there – not anywhere – any more, I felt 'I'm really on my own now!' I had been on my own for years but somehow there'd always been a family in the back of my mind. Now there was only Olive and we didn't get on very well.

When Mark died, I'd been there and Olive and Mother hadn't. This time Olive was there and I wasn't. It sounds unfeeling, but in a way it was a relief not to be there when it happened. From a distance it was a sort of whoosh! – something gone out of the world that I wouldn't see again. I don't think I quite grasped it. I decided I would take my leave anyway.

※　※　※　※

U.S.A. – and the big-hearted days of ships and trains. First it's a banana boat, white and comely, ferrying fruit and a handful of passengers across the Pacific.

'Any time', says one of the passengers who is the owner of the Hawaiian Hotel, 'any time you're in Hawaii. You can stay as long as you want and it won't cost you a penny.'

I wonder if that invitation still stands.

And the girl from the Ask-Mr-Foster Travel Agency, who's trying out the trip firsthand. 'Just so that I know there's no hitches. It wouldn't be straight to recommend something I didn't believe in!'

San Francisco and a clutch of eager young reporters button-holing everyone on their way to fame and fortune. Three of them try to gobble Grace in her Shanghai-Parisian clothes.

'"Foreign government official"? There must be a story!'

'I'm only a teacher!'

'But it says right here "Foreign government official"!'

'It means I teach in a French school.'

Grace is booked at the St Francis Hotel because she likes service and is ready to pay for it. Before her suitcase is opened there is a call from the lobby.

'Please don't unpack, Miss Botham. We are giving you a different room. The Ask-Mr-Foster Travel Agency have recommended you. There'll be no extra charge.'

Grace is moved four floors up – four steps on the scale of luxury. *Everyone was so nice to me. In those days everyone was nice!*

A Marine officer phones, a friend of a friend. 'It would be a pleasure to show you the town, Ma'am.'

Chinatown is not like China. They eat chop suey there. That's not Chinese! It's what westerners think the Chinese ought to eat. Chinatown is fun – but it's not Chinese.

The American restaurant is more bizarre. Chairs edge-on to a forty-foot long revolving glass counter, rich with goodies. You pay for your meat course, a dollar fifty, and the rest is for free – soft drinks, fruit, ices, cakes. As the counter goes round you make your grab.

San Francisco, little wooden houses with coloured roofs against a green hill. Toy houses, ephemeral. *They looked so temporary. Pretty, but temporary. Like New Zealand houses. I never imagined I'd ever live in one like that.*

'Oh, look at that seagull! It's hurt! One of its legs is hanging down!'

'Why, that's a famous seagull, Ma'am! It had a little mishap with one leg so an old sailor here, he whittled a new one out of wood.'

Lunch at the Mark Hopkins Hotel. Down the centre, a long long table of high-pitched hilarity. A women's convention in the days when WASP meant a flying insect and liberation was something to do with darkies and the civil war. There are hundreds of these American Mothers with watches and floral sprays decorating the shelves of their bosoms, elaborate hats and many rings. And what a time they're having themselves! *They looked like a lot of fat fraus to me.*

The marine officer and his wife have a push-button bed in their living-room. Slowly, fatefully, half a wall descends with mattress and bedclothes ready to receive. You expect to see pyjamaed figures filed away on it.

There was a girl from the Chefoo schools, a friend of mine, Emily Horne. She married a man named Larsen and went to San Francisco. That's all I knew.

I thought, 'I'll ring her up.'

Three pages of Larsens in the telephone book. I read through the list and I hadn't any idea in the world which one it would be – if any. I thought, 'I may as well have a go. I'll try that one.'

I dialled. A woman answered in an American accent.

'Mrs Larsen? Were you once Emily Horne?'

'Why, ye-es,' she drawled. 'Who is this?'

'It's Grace Botham.'

'Why, Grace! What in the world! You come on over!'

I don't know how I knew. How could I know? But from three pages I picked the right one first go.

It was more than twenty years since we'd seen each other. We talked and talked. She had what they would call a simple house but it was centrally heated with a thermostat for every room.

'Why, what's this? This paper – it says 6 March! I should be on the train by now. I'm booked on the New York train for 6 March. Oh, how could I possibly have done anything so stupid!'

'Don't worry, Ma'am! It's an early edition. They got earlier and earlier trying to outsell each other. Now they're printing them the day before with tomorrow's date.'

Those American trains winding across the enormous landscape. Bathrooms with showers and real baths, beauty parlours, dining-cars, and bars, writing-rooms and reading-rooms; the huge American dailies and the glossy magazines – the *Saturday Evening Post* and *Variety*, *Colliers* and *Life*, the *Readers' Digest*, the *National Geographic*. The observation car, a glass bubble for sky and receding landscape, the friendly people.

During the night they pause near Reno to load a cargo of new divorcees. Drink and hilarity all night long. Five women celebrating like fun – freedom!

Great white plains of the Salt Lake district. The train is at ground level. As far the eye can see, white, white sand, not sand-coloured, pure white with here and there a stretch of water. Not a growing thing – not a tree or bush or blade of grass. So inhuman a landscape the mind cannot let it go. For years it comes back to embellish Grace's dreams.

Chicago where she is to change trains. She expects automobiles and dead bulls. But here on the platform to meet her is Danny, one of the Y.W.C.A. girls from Chefoo Days. And she is whisked away to a house by the lake which is as spacious and infinite as the sea.

I bought a hat in Chicago – a lovely hat like the ones Deanna Durbin used to wear. A green hat with a feather that stuck straight up in the air, all brown and gold. I thought I needed a hat to face New York. But I didn't wear it.

The train detours into Canada for half an hour so that, crowded in the observation car, they can all see the wonder of Niagara Falls.

Even Grace's pocket has quailed at the thought of staying at the Ritz or the Waldorf-Astoria. She has booked at the Roosevelt perched above Grand Central Station. She steps into a lift at the station and it deposits her in the lobby of the hotel.

Slim, superbly dressed, with money in her purse and a kind of infectious vitality, Grace expects the world to smile at her and it does, it does. Nevertheless on this journey she carries in her baggage a sense of loss. A pocket of loneliness for her mother who is dead. All the time she reaches out to renew old connections and make the legendary ones real.

The brothers of her father, that blank in her memory, came from the midlands of England to New York where the streets were paved with gold.

There was Uncle Harry the bachelor one who was a bit of an artist and Uncle Jack, who was the black sheep of his family as I was of mine. (Although I was as pure as the driven snow and I hadn't been driven very far either.) Uncle Edwin had died but his son, Cousin Arthur, was in New York.

I had a telephone call from the lobby. 'There's a gentleman to see you, a Mr Botham.' I said I'd be coming down and that I was wearing a brown fur coat. But there were several lifts – pardon me, elevators – discharging in the lobby and lots of old men standing about. I was afraid if I went up to too many of them I'd be had up for soliciting, but ultimately we got together. Uncle Harry was a nice old gentleman – tall and thin. I've been told that's what my father was like.

He told me that we were to go to Cousin Arthur's place. Arthur, he said, was an artist too but he had prostituted his art by using it to make money. He was a managing director of Coty, the cosmetics firm – in charge of all the American publicity.

We went to a high-rise apartment in a very fashionable part of New York. The maid ushered us into the drawing-room that was lit only by concealed lights above four masterpieces on the walls. Arthur was rolling in money. The centre-piece of the dining table was a great bunch of crystal grapes with the light shining through it. The dinner service was solid silver. You wouldn't think it would be nice eating from a silver dinnerplate but it was – very smooth plates with a light embossing round the edge.

I think they'd told the maid before I arrived how correct and careful everything must be because I was a missionary's daughter. Mabel, Arthur's wife, went out to the kitchen for something and she told me that the maid said, 'That's no missionary's daughter!' It was my Shanghai clothes, of course.

After dinner Arthur said, 'Would you like to see New York by night?' '*Rather!*' I said.

But first we had to listen to the Coty half-hour. Ray Noble and his orchestra were the resident musicians. There was no mention of Coty products. They were the sponsors, the music was their advertisement. We listened and Arthur said, 'Oh, Ray, I didn't mean you to do it that way!'

He phoned for his car and we went down, Uncle Harry, Mabel, Arthur, and I, and there at the door was the commissionaire to hand us into an enormous Cadillac. So comfortable – Uncle Arthur got in the back and immediately stretched out and went to sleep. The seats in the front were so low and roomy I was almost lying down too. What a wonderful way to see the lights of Broadway, the colour and dazzle! Yet all so clean and comfortable looking. I do love big cities!

The next day the lobby at the Roosevelt rang me to say there was a gentleman to see me, a Mr Botham. Down I went again. It wasn't Uncle Harry but Uncle Jack, the black sheep. I couldn't mistake him. Sitting on a sofa, a very dapper gentleman with a gold cane and a top hat on his lap.

'Sit down, Gracie,' he said. 'I wasn't going to come to see you. I didn't want to see any missionary type, but after what Harry told me last night I thought I'd come and by Jove, he was right!'

New York was full of the magic of gadgets and concrete. The tall buildings were like stone lace against the winter skies. Snow was falling on them in the upper atmosphere. Floodlights melted it from the balustrades in case it fell sixty storeys and killed poor earthlings underneath.

Grace goes to the theatre with Ruth, another Chefoo friend. They watch *Green Pastures*, the first play with a Negro cast ever to be seen on Broadway, and, more memorable for Grace, the mechanical high-jinks of the *Great Waltz* where chandeliers and dancing couples multiply, quadruple, bifurcate, foliate, till the stage is a whirling spectacular and the orchestra magically manifests itself now in the pit, now in the stage, now on a musicians' balcony, without ever seeming to move at all. Even the sophisticated New

Yorkers are impressed. 'I just don't believe it! I don't believe my eyes!' cries one of them next to Grace.

Radio City. A hundred strong orchestra plays Ravel's *Bolero* in colour as well as sound and a knowing little pageboy guide leans over the stairwell and cries, 'There he is! Look! There he is! The Old Man himself!'

It was Irving Berlin having his hair cut in the foyer below. He was so busy in those years that he didn't have time to go to the barber, so the barber came to him. I looked over the banisters but all I could see was the shadow of the barber's sheet round him.

New York is distracting, but whatever Grace is looking for will not be found in this clear light.

Mabel and Arthur sent flowers to her cabin, Ruth waves goodbye and a banana boat carries her off into the Atlantic.

It's a rough, rough passage all the way and the nearer they get to England the worse it is. The water in her morning bath rushes to the top of the tub, dashes Grace against the side and sucks abruptly away. Before she gets to England she is stiff with bruises. During the day she plays bridge with an adolescent American golf prodigy, his manager, and a returning Englishman. They lash her chair to the bar in the saloon. The other three players and the table lurch boisterously to and fro as the ship plunges. In a milder interval when other passengers have struggled to their feet Grace yields her place to another bridge player, an American woman, sixty, unmarried, whose capacity for emotional response is untarnished by time. As the ship rolls she lays down her cards and claps her hands in ecstasy. 'Won't the girls be thrilled when I tell them I played *with three men!*'

*   *   *   *

Olive lives in a cottage at Woking. At the sight of that dear, dowdy, moralistic woman, it seems to Grace, momentarily, that this indeed is what she has come half-way across the world to find. In all her life she had never known anyone else so well.

But although their mother's absence is a speaking fact, Olive and Grace do not speak of it. They are English, self-conscious, and their upper lips are stiff. Skirting this subject it is possible that conversation lagged. Grace phones the village and a car is bought for

95

£40, a baby Austin. Grace drives off unaccompanied, to pay a call on Cousin Alice Puckle of Langley Hall.

Cousin Alice, sixty-five, tall, slim, and upright, is one of those ageing eccentrics who flower so splendidly in England. Though she is dressed in unobtrusive contemporary clothes she carries so much sense of the past and continuity that memory clothes her in an Edwardian shirtwaist and a cameo brooch. If it's roots Grace is seeking, here they are in God's plenty.

Because she has been kind to Nellie Botham and to Olive, Grace has brought her a luncheon cloth and table-napkins hand-embroidered with her initials. Alice is delighted. 'Is it a wedding-present? Oh, yes, I'm getting married.' She shows a photograph of her fiancé, a vicar in London with two grown sons.

They go on a tour of the house. The nine bedrooms, all in a row upstairs, overlook the park. 'I can't decide which one my future husband will have.' The ninth has an extra room connected to it by three raised steps. 'I think perhaps I should settle on this one. He'll be in London all day and it would be rather nice to be near him at night. I don't know what to do about the wedding invitations. It is customary for the parents to write and invite the guests.' She turns to Grace innocently surprised by mortality. 'But our parents, you see, are all dead!' For the rest of her life, with tenderness, Grace carries the memory of Alice Puckle.

Olive has ordered a radio now Grace has come. 'I imagine *you'll* need some entertainment.' Her emphasis carries Grace back thirty years. She is the worldly, wilful, younger sister again, indulged because she lacks the moral fibre to suffer for Christ. Olive is steady and responsible. Everyone knows that Gracie (though there is no real harm in her – you have to laugh at her pranks) is a bit of a flibberty-gibbet who needs a steadying hand. ('Why can't you be like Olive?')

Grace goes upstairs to the attic bedroom they share. The single virginal beds are reminiscent of the Chefoo dormitories. She is a respected, skilful teacher, a *professeur*, one of the five best-paid women in Shanghai and one of the best-dressed. Her lovely clothes turn traitor on her before the solid righteousness of Olive's bedside Bible and lumpy slippers.

While they are having tea a young mechanic from the village arrives and installs the radio.

'Will it get New York?'

'Should do. On this band. Do you like listening in to America?'

'I've just come from there.'

Shyly he prods Grace with questions. Olive's world is so hedged round with prohibitions it has been difficult to talk. Now Grace's enthusiasm spills over. The young man is avid for what is beyond his village. As he listens Grace sees in his face that she is a bird of paradise blown by some absurd wind to the village pond and that he will remember this room and this hour for the rest of his life and date decisions or regrets by it.

Olive, knitting socks for poor people's children, jabs at the grey wool with steel needles. Is she back in Chefoo now, thinking, 'Gracie always gets the limelight!'

Later Grace feels ashamed of that small triumph and resolves to be good to Olive. And is, all the next day, under difficult circumstances.

We went for a picnic with some relations of Mark's Olive. She was away in Cairo or Jerusalem or somewhere founding a home for soldiers. But her relations had come out in force to meet me. There was an admiral's widow, and her daughter and a colonel's widow. All the husbands gone, they seemed to have a deadly effect on men.

We drove out to the Surrey Hills and settled down on a grassy slope among the bracken, overlooking a beautiful valley. It was a lovely warm day, the spring sun shining down. I was the only one without a hat and gloves on. They discussed whether that was the place where Wordsworth had sat when he wrote one of his poems. They went on and on about it. Surreptitiously the admiral's widow's daughter took off her hat and gloves. After a while Olive did too. They spread out the feast. The others took off their gloves. We picnicked sedately, then we drove sedately home.

Every day friends of Olive arrived, old school friends, all of them missionaries. 'We must do something to cheer Gracie up,' they'd say. I was always Gracie to them, the black sheep, the only non-mish. Little Gracie to be led back to the fold. They belonged to the Oxford Group. That was a very popular movement at the time. It was based on confession and restitution. Years later an old school friend of mine wrote to me saying she'd joined the Oxford Group.

'Dear Gracie,' she said, 'do you remember when we were at Prep. School you left a sweet on the table by your bed? I took it and ate it.'

It was so pathetic and I liked her so much that I didn't reply. I had a letter in my mind though. 'Thank you for the confession. Now how about the restitution?'

One day Olive and I were sitting over a fire in the cottage when one of her friends arrived. They'd arranged to have a breakfast for me, she said. They had most hilarious breakfasts, eating together, singing together, praying together. It didn't sound hilarious to me. I hate getting up in the morning. Just then the postman arrived with a letter for me.

'Go ahead and read it,' the visitor said. 'I don't mind.'

It was from a man in Shanghai in a very high position. Even now I wouldn't like to say what his job was because anyone still alive could recognize him. 'If you will give me three weeks of your life, just three weeks, that's not much to ask, I'll meet you anywhere in the world.' He was begging me to go to Honolulu with him.

I felt all stirred up inside. And there were the others still talking about this hilarious breakfast they were going to have on their knees. I wasn't tempted by his proposal. F— was a good friend of mine but I didn't want to go to bed with him – anyway he was married. But that letter gave me a real feeling and Olive and her friends seemed so false and critical of me and always trying to push me into their own narrow groove. I couldn't stand it.

As soon as the woman had gone, I said to Olive, 'I'm not going to that breakfast.'

'Oh, you've got to,' she told me, bossy as ever. 'You can't not go when they've invited you. It's all arranged.'

'I'm not going,' I said. 'Why are you always trying to push me!' I started waving the breadknife around. We had a real ding-dong row.

I couldn't stand it another minute. I went upstairs and got my things and flung them into the back of the car. And away I went to London, lock, stock, and barrel. No, I didn't take the barrel. I had a very large packing case with some things I'd brought across with me, a Chinese carpet and teak lampstands, and all the things my grandmother had left me that had been stored at Olive's. Her hand-painted bone china tea-set and other things. I thought, 'If I ever settle down anywhere, Olive can send them on to me.' I never saw those things again. Everything else I've had has been lost through wars but they were lost through sheer stupidity.

Off I went to London. I found an accommodation agency.

'I'll only be in England for another four months and I'll be going on some trips to see people I know but I want somewhere pleasant as headquarters,' I told the woman.

'I think Captain Morton might suit you,' she said. If I hadn't had that row with Olive, 200 people might have died in Hitler's gas ovens who lived out the rest of their lives.

Captain and Mrs Morton took only 'particular people', usually from overseas, the woman said. She picked up the phone and dialled.

'Oh no,' I heard her say, 'she's not Chinese, she's English.'

She gave me the address and I went along.

It was a big house in the West End. Four storeys with a portico. A lovely house. The servery in the dining-room was made from the posts of an antique bed, all elaborately carved.

I liked Mrs Morton right away. She was in her forties. Not exactly pretty – fine looking, I thought. Dark hair cut in an Eton crop and honest eyes. She had a calm and natural manner that put you at your ease. Captain Morton was tall, over six feet and big with it, a forty-four inch chest. When I first saw him there was something about him – what was it? Oh yes! He had a rash on his face. I thought, 'Blaah!'

There were a few other people staying. I didn't notice them much. I heard Captain Morton speaking Greek to one of them and German to another.

The Mortons took me under their wing right away. I suppose it was partly just good business but I think it was more than that. I felt they liked me. Captain Morton had been all over the world. He knew America and Shanghai. He spoke French as fluently as I did. It was like meeting someone of my own nationality in a foreign land. I was Grace to them almost immediately and they were Meggie and Guy. Guy and I were cosmopolitans but Meggie was pure sterling English.

When they had foreign visitors who didn't know London, Guy would act as a guide for them. He would take them wherever they wanted to go and they would pay the expenses. I'd been to the conventional places in London but I didn't really know it. I told them I'd like to be shown round. (The rash had cleared up by then.)

London is different from New York. You can't really see it by yourself. Guy loved it, every bit of it; it was a passion with him, and he was a marvellous guide. He took me up and down the river on boats and into such a strange variety of places. It all came alive for me. I remember an old, old churchyard tucked away right up near Fleet Street with the most fascinating epitaphs on the graves. And straight from there to the motor show. I would never have thought of going there, but he'd been a racing driver and he loved cars. We looked at the caravans and sat inside them and planned imaginary journeys.

Then to the Inns of Court and all sorts of places round Limehouse. I remember sitting in a sailors' pub with relics of wooden boats for hundreds of years back all around us. Guy had been a sailor too in his time.

One lovely day we drove down to Plymouth to the naval regatta. It was the King's Jubilee, George V's. There was a huge crowd and we didn't have seats. But Captain Guy Morton had a very commanding presence, and a public school accent. He expected to get what he asked for and he nearly always did. They gave us seats all right.

There were 150 ships in the harbour. It was all dark. Then suddenly at the same second all the ships sprang to light, just their outlines etched on the blackness. And the searchlights criss-crossing in patterns and probing so deep into the clouds. It was tremendously exciting. I felt so alive.

99

Guy was marvellous company and he was my nationality – 'foreigner'. His father had had something to do with shipping and had been stationed in Greece and Turkey. Guy had been delicate as a child (you would never have guessed it to see him as a man) and instead of being sent home to boarding-school in England his father had engaged a French tutor and he'd been taught while they cruised the Mediterranean. By the time he was seventeen, though he'd never been to school, he could speak Greek, Arabic, French, and German almost as fluently as English.

With his background he naturally went into the navy. King George V was Prince of Wales then and himself a sailor. Guy was chief cadet on his ship when they went all round the world showing the flag.

By 1914 Guy was a captain. He was attached to Admiral Limpus's squadron in the Dardanelles. They were sounding out the Turks to influence them to ally themselves with the English rather than the Germans. Before they'd finished the exercise war did break out and orders came for the squadron to return to Malta.

Admiral Limpus gathered his officers together. 'I need a volunteer,' he told them, 'to stay behind and keep us in touch with what is going on. Someone who has a thorough knowledge of the language.' He was asking for a spy, of course, and he might just as well have said, 'Captain Morton step forward please!' because no one else knew the language as he did.

Guy stayed alone. He was in his element, he loved excitement. He was on the top of a hill with his binoculars and a radio transmitter when the German fleet steamed through the Dardanelles. And the information was all sent out.

It wasn't long though before the Germans caught up with him. He was captured and convicted as a spy and that meant just one thing – execution. He was put in prison to await his end.

It was a Turkish prison because by now the Turks and the Germans were allies. Guy always got on well with the Turks – after all he'd been reared there. He became very popular in prison and he got to be great friends with the Turkish officer-in-charge. The Germans kept pressing for his execution but somehow the Turks just didn't get around to it. 'It's Ramadan,' they said, 'We can't go shooting anyone this month.' But in the end the excuses wore out and the officer-in-charge came to Guy.

'There is nothing more I can do. They insist we must execute you tomorrow. Goodbye my friend.' It was all very dramatic. They shook hands. Guy felt something cold in his palm and his fingers closed round a key.

He got away that night. He would never talk much about that part. I think something happened with the guards. I think he killed someone. But he managed to make his way to the coast and steal a little boat. He was alone on the sea for three weeks, but he knew that part of the world so well and he was a brilliant sailor. He landed just where he intended to at Malta.

He made his way to the Navy headquarters, a dirty, sunburnt figure with by that time a scruffy red beard.

He walked up the steps and the sentry challenged him. Guy told him he was Commander Morton.

'Oh yes?' said the sentry. 'I'm the Shah of Persia.'

While they were arguing an officer came down the steps and asked what was going on.

Guy spoke in his clear very English officer's voice. 'I am Commander Morton and I want to see Admiral Limpus.' I know just the way he would have said that with his eyes bluer than ever shining out of hair and sunburn.

The officer took him in. 'TOBY!' cried Admiral Limpus. 'Toby, we thought you were dead!'

He was always called Toby in the navy.

They sent him back to England. Because he was an escaped prisoner they wouldn't let him back on active service with the navy. He walked out of the Admiralty, down the road and enlisted in Whitehall. There was a shortage of officers then; the casualty rate was terribly high so in no time at all he was out in France as a captain in the army. He'd only been there a short time when he was hit in the leg. He passed out and when he woke up he was in a hospital bed and it was black night. He remembered what had happened and he felt nervously down the bed. His thighs were both there; so were his knees, and his calves, and his ankles. In the end he pin-pointed the damage – he was minus one toe. He felt round to find out where he was. His hand encountered what he thought was a wall. It was padded. He thought, 'They've no right to put me in a padded cell!' and he shouted as loudly as he could. A dark faceless face materialized above him all surrounded in white. He fainted away. When he woke again it was daylight and a lovely Maori girl, an army nurse, was looking after him.

He was decorated for what he did in Turkey and later when he left the army he was offered a pension. He refused it in his lordly way. 'Oh no, there are so many other people who need it more than I do!' But he didn't have any money and soon he was on the breadline. He couldn't go back and say he'd changed his mind. Not Guy Morton!

He got a job as a car salesman. Lots of ex-officers did in those days. And he did a lot of racing driving. He told me he drove at Brooklands when Malcolm Campbell was there. Guy got up to 99 m.p.h. which was very fast then, but not quite fast enough to win.

Once he was sent out by his firm to sell cars in the Middle East because he knew the languages. He demonstrated a car to the King of Greece, driving it straight at a big ditch. Up they went – whoops . . . and right over it. Then the King took the wheel, put the car in reverse and over the ditch they went again, backwards! The King decided on the spot that that car was just what he wanted, but it must have this and that modification. And it must be white. Pure white inside and out.

It was a special order worth thousands of pounds. Guy went back to

England, the pure white car was produced, and Guy as its guardian and protector was to deliver it to the King. He took it, cosseted like a baby, on a ship to the Mediterranean. They came to Piraeus, the port of Athens. Everywhere there were black flags and people in mourning. 'The King is dead!' He had died that morning from the bite of a pet monkey. Guy got the car off the ship and drove it in the funeral procession.

Oh, he was a romantic figure, was Guy Morton, even though he was fifty now, a husband and a father and a boarding-house keeper.

One morning Meggie brought my tea up to me and stayed to talk as she often did.

'I suppose you know,' she said, 'that Guy is in love with you!'

I didn't. I wasn't in love with him. I liked him a lot, he was a good companion but that was all. I was angry. I thought of F— in Honolulu and all the other married men who'd hung around me right back to Otto who was betrothed.

'I'll get out,' I said. 'I'll go somewhere else!' And I jumped out of bed.

Meggie said, 'Don't do that! He's fallen for people before but never like this. He'll follow you wherever you go. Right round the world. I know Guy!'

'That's what you think,' I thought. I got dressed and packed up. I paid Meggie and put my cases in my car and I shot off down the drive. As I slowed for the gate the door was wrenched open and Guy fell into the seat beside me.

I drove hell-for-leather, breaking every traffic rule. I got to St Albans and went round the roundabout. Then I stopped and I said, *'Get out and leave me alone!'*

He got out and collapsed on the road. Horror and shock I suppose that someone didn't want him. It was genuine though.

I had to stop. I got him into a road-house nearby. He looked awful, deadly pale. I ordered a brandy for him and a cup of coffee for myself. While he was sitting there drinking it he pointed to the menu. The name of the road-house was printed on it in fancy type. *The Spider's Web*.

After a while we began to talk. Already I was feeling a little different. If you like someone and they tell you how much they love you, you can't help but be moved by it.

I drove back and later I had a long talk with Meggie. I was still determined to go. 'This is ridiculous,' I said. 'I can go anywhere in the world (except Honolulu, I added to myself). Why shouldn't I be free to do as I like?

'Please don't go,' she said. 'He'll follow you unless you promise to marry him. If you do decide to marry him I'll divorce him. It's better to have one unhappy person and two happy ones than three unhappy people.' It was a very strange situation to have the man's own wife saying, 'Stay, for my sake!' I really blame Meggie quite a lot for all that happened. If it hadn't been for her I would have gone away even if it meant sneaking out at night.

Once she said to me, 'He has moods, he's very moody. But nobody's ever seen him in a mood but Mary and me.' Mary was the maid and she'd been with them for a very long time. I didn't know quite what she meant by moods then. I sometimes wonder whether Meggie's motives were mixed in all she said to me.

I said that I must get away by myself to think. You couldn't escape the situation in that house or see anything in proportion. I'd intended taking a trip up north to see various people I knew and to visit Edinburgh. Now I told them I would go up there and when I came back I would make some decision. Both Guy and Meggie made me promise to call in on a friend of theirs who was staying in Manchester at the moment. Guy had written to him telling him about the situation and they both had a lot of faith in his judgement and advice.

I went first to Cambridge. Do you remember Mr and Mrs Oswald Smith who were so good to us all during the war? Their house was always full of young people and laughter. They were living now in a nice little house in a crescent with trees all around it, but oh, the change! Uncle Oswald from being an up-and-coming man, marching along very quickly everywhere and full of life, was sitting in a chair all the time and shaking in every limb. He had Parkinson's disease and there was no cure. He would just get gradually worse and die.

They were still as pious as ever. Auntie Gertie took me proudly round the house and garden, saying, 'Isn't it wonderful what the Lord has done for us letting us get this lovely little house!'

I thought, 'My dear old lady, wouldn't it have been much more wonderful if he hadn't given Uncle Oswald this dreadful disease.' But of course I didn't say it. You can twist religion round to anything.

I drove on thinking about the Smiths and marriage and old age.

I went to Wells in Somerset and stayed with a friend. We were out driving one day and we came across a man with a very smart car stalled on a country road. I stopped to see if I could help. He had a tow-rope and my little Baby Austin towed this slick sports-car back to the garage. The driver was a city man, very smartly dressed and all the time he was thanking me I could see his eyes taking me in with appreciation. He asked for my name and address so that he could show his gratitude properly by taking me out to dinner in London. I drove away thinking there was something that didn't ring true about him – too effusive, too flirtatious. I was comparing him with Guy.

I went to the Midlands and visited Aunt Sarah whose hospital I'd fainted all over as a girl. She was upright as ever with her brisk matron's manner and her homely north country accent. She was seventy-seven and she shared a house with another old lady of seventy-four. 'That one always wants her own way,' she complained to me, 'I'm the older and she should do what I say.' I wondered if I would grow like that if I didn't marry. A spinster used to authority and unable to let go.

Wherever I went and whatever I saw my thoughts circled back to what they were trying to escape. It was a relief to get to Manchester even though I hated the thought of talking over my affairs with a complete stranger, no matter how good a friend he was to Guy and Meggie.

But oh, it was so easy. I met him in the Manchester Hotel, a naval officer, sturdy and reliable with a slight north-country accent. He wasn't my sort of man but you couldn't help respecting and liking him. It was so easy to tell him things. For three days we talked and talked and talked.

He told me he had had letters from both Meggie and Guy; he told me that Meggie never said things that she didn't mean; he said that as far as they were concerned all they could do was accept what had happened. But how did I feel, did I care at all for Guy?

'I'm beginning to,' I said. Because you can't feel a flow of love like that pouring out and not respond. 'I must go straight back to China or I'll be hooked!' He didn't try to advise me but what a relief it was to have talked about it.

I went to Edinburgh and the obsession had passed. I was seeing the country again. Edinburgh was lovely. I drove up and down Princes Street entranced by the view. Then I went out to the sister of a Shanghai friend whom I was to stay with. We had a really pleasant evening. I'd just got up in the morning when there was a knock at the door. 'A visitor for you.'

There on the doorstep was Guy. He'd been so desperate and worried about the whole business that he'd got on a cargo boat and followed me up. I was embarrassed and annoyed and touched.

We drove back to London together. There's a little signpost at the border with two arms pointing – SCOTLAND/ENGLAND. You can stand there with one foot in each kingdom. Guy got out of the car and kneeling down kissed the ground of England. It was a joke of course, but only partly. He did most passionately love England.

Those last few weeks in London were strange – the three of us together in the house and life going on with the thing unresolved between us.

An odd little incident happened then, one of those inexplicable ones. I was sitting in my room when I heard Olive's voice outside my door. 'Gracie!' she said in a sharp calling tone.

I went to the door and opened it and there, coming up the stairs, was Guy.

'Where's Olive?' I said.

'What do you mean? I've just taken a phone call from her. She's in such-and-such (he named a town twenty miles away) and she wants you to go and collect her because she's ill.'

I don't know if I heard something else and misinterpreted it. I only know that what I seemed to hear quite clearly was Olive's voice calling.

I don't know how I made up my mind. I suppose it happened imperceptibly. First of all it was 'if you get a divorce' and then it was 'when'.

Guy took me down to meet some relatives of his in Surrey, some cousins that he was very attached to. There was a photo there of Guy's mother taken a long time ago. It was funny to see that he had a family and a background of quiet people in a country house. I liked his cousins. They took him aside as we were leaving and said, 'You've done the right thing, old boy!'

It was a compliment to me of course, but I don't know that it was the right thing.

I was going back to Shanghai to wait until the divorce came through then Guy and I would get married. And Meggie was as friendly and nice to me as she'd been all along.

I had booked to fly back but Guy said, 'Please, darling, not by air. I'd be worried the whole time that something would happen.' Air travel wasn't thought of as being safe in those days. Like a silly mug I cancelled my bookings and went back the way I'd come.

Another banana boat. I loved them. Just a handful of passengers and so cosy and comfortable. I usually managed to get a cabin to myself but this time when I got on the purser came to me very apologetic – they'd had to put someone in with me.

I went to sleep in the bottom bunk – in the morning I could see the top one was full. We said good morning, chatted for a bit then she got up – I'm always the last. And her legs came over the side. And more and more and more leg. And finally she stood on the ground – six foot two inches. The tallest woman I ever saw, and so beautiful, dignified, and graceful with her hair plaited in a blond crown on top of her head. I liked sharing with her.

It was a memorable cabin. One day the steward told me that Sinclair Lewis, the American novelist, had had it before us.

'I helped him write his last novel,' he said.

'Oh, did you?'

'Yes! Every day he'd read me what he'd written and if I enjoyed it and laughed in the right places, that was the way it stayed!'

David Low, the New Zealand cartoonist, had travelled on that boat at one time and he'd painted a frieze round the saloon – all greens and browns on the creamy white walls. Monkeys in trees and as you sat in the saloon every one of the monkeys was looking at you with a different expression on its face.

I crossed America this time by the *Portland Rose*, New York to Portland, Oregon. Oh, what a delightful train! Grey carpet throughout, patterned here and there with a little pink rose emblem. All the stewards, most of them black in pale grey uniforms with a rose embroidered on their pockets. On every table in the saloon there was a silver vase with one beautiful Portland Rose in it just opening. The steward told me that they brought fresh roses aboard at Portland each time and put half of them on ice for the return journey.

Three days and four nights I think it was. I spent a lot of time in the observation car. Lots of people came and talked to me, so friendly. A lady said, 'This is the longest journey I've ever been on. How far are you going?' I told her. 'London to Shanghai.'

She found I knew no one in Portland. The boat didn't leave till the morning so she collected me in her automobile and showed me round.

Another banana boat. This time I had a drawing-room cabin, beds not bunks. Again an apologetic steward – 'I'm very sorry, Miss Botham . . .'. I knew what was coming. In the morning when I woke up there was someone in the other bed. We lay and looked at each other and began a conversation. Finally she said, 'Oh dear, I suppose I've got to get up first as you won't. I'm always frightened when people see me for the first time because I'm so little.' Out she got – four foot eleven.

Shanghai, my dear Shanghai. Cables and flowers from Guy, lots of good friends to meet me. F— was there, very disgusted with me, but he'd consoled himself with a White Russian lady so it didn't matter much.

I'd arrived just in time for the new term. I went up to the Principal's flat, an enormous luxury place above the school where he lived in great comfort and happiness with his grand piano and his Russian mistress. She played the piano, he was a violinist, an accomplished one of concert standard. He'd lost his right hand in the First World War. He had an artificial glove that he could wear most of the time so that you didn't really notice except when he was playing the violin. Then he had to use a hook that he fastened the bow to. He'd given up playing at concerts because, he said, people came to listen to the man with one hand playing and not to the music and he couldn't bear that.

I told him, in case he wanted to look around for someone else, that I probably would only be there for a few more months. That the old girl was going to get married at last!

Being in that flat with marriage in my mind made me suddenly realize that I hadn't seen Mme Terzi since I got back. She was a teacher on the staff, a Frenchwoman who had married an Italian. Her marriage was annulled by the Pope when her husband was caught *in flagrante delicto* with the houseboy. In reaction I think she'd fallen in love with the Principal but she kept her feelings to herself, only glowing quietly when he spoke to her. She was a sturdy little soul, undaunted. She lived in a flat up eight flights of stairs and I can still see those muscular shapely little legs running cheerfully up the stairs while I panted behind.

I asked in the staff-room where she was. 'Haven't you heard?' they said raising their hands and shoulders in surprise and pity.

'A stroke!' they said. 'Helpless. Utterly dependent on her amah!'

I raced round to see her. She'd been moved to a ground floor flat. There she sat, tiny in a big armchair, face and body all twisted and distorted. She couldn't speak any longer, only mumble indistinguishable sounds. She saw me and burst into tears. I wept too – there was nothing else to do.

Nothing could make me unhappy for long. Guy wrote to me every single day. Great big fat wads of letters every time the mail came in. You get to know a person a lot better that way, as though you're living in his mind. He lived in my mind too. Whatever I did or saw, I thought of as part of a letter to Guy. I saw my life through his eyes and feelings.

I read an item in the newspaper, that a detective had discovered how the brides in the bath were murdered. If you take someone's legs when they're in the bath and pull them up, they just slide quietly under the water and it's impossible to struggle. I was thinking about this in the bath and I didn't believe it. Experimentally I put both my legs up. Whooosh! down I went under the water and I couldn't get out. I did manage to hook my toe round the plug and pull it out, but while I believed I was drowning the thought that went through my mind was, 'If I die and Guy finds the seven love letters I've got from other people, he'll be upset!' So as soon as I'd stopped spluttering and was dry, I went and tore the letters up. I was so mad afterwards because I would have loved to have had them. I'd love to have them now. Love really makes you quite insane.

I thought before I left China I should see Hangchow – it's a famous resort – so one weekend three or four of us went up to stay at the Lake House. Four hours in a dirty jolting train – you should have seen the toilets! Then by rickshaw to the hotel. The road ran along the shore of the lake. It was sunset and the lake was coloured like a bubble all rosy and orange and mauve, reflecting the sky. There's an island in the middle and little semi-circular bridges connect it with the shore. We hired boats and floated there. The water was so still the bridges and their reflections made perfect circles that the boats seemed to pass through. And all the time in other boats Chinese girls were playing instruments, two-stringed ones, so that the lake was full of this weird music.

We stayed there till it was night-time with moonlight on the water. On the way back to the hotel we passed a little Chinese fortune-teller's shop. Behind the counter was an old man who was blind. He had thick cataracts over both eyes so that he looked uncanny – a blue-eyed oriental.

I said to the others: 'You go on. I'm going to have my fortune told.' I went in. Luckily he could speak Mandarin. 'Will you tell my fortune?' I said.

Immediately a crowd of Chinese began to gather, pressing against me. A female foreign devil who could speak the language of the Middle Kingdom. Foreigners didn't go to fortune-tellers, most of them because they couldn't speak the language, and the missionaries because they thought it was wrong.

He took a bamboo lacquered container with a lot of bamboo sticks in it. He told me to take one so I did. It had notches in it. He felt them. 'Take another!' He felt the notches on the second stick. Then he told me I could ask questions.

'Am I going to stay in this country?' I said.

'Why do you ask that when you have only just returned from a long journey?' I began to feel creepy – the moonlit lake and the weird music and the crowd pressing on me. How did he know I'd just come back?

'When am I going away?'

'You will leave this country in the first moon of the New Year.' I began to wonder if I was hearing all right or if it was somehow self-hypnosis. I looked round at this crowd of gaping yobs. 'Can anybody here write?' I said. One coolie type said he could. He scrabbled on the floor and found an old advertisement of some kind. He took the brush and ink that was on the fortune-teller's desk, and he wrote in Chinese characters on the back of the paper.

'Where will I go?' I asked.

'You will go the far eastern corner of a western country.'

The coolie gave me the paper. I can't read Chinese. I took it back to Shanghai with me and got Edward, Nancy's son, to translate it for me. It said exactly what I thought I had heard.

I got out a map and studied it. 'The far eastern corner of a western country.' The only one that seemed to me to have a far eastern corner was Czechoslovakia and that was nothing to me then but a funny sounding name.

About two weeks later I got a letter from Guy. It had been written about the same day as I saw the fortune-teller. 'I've got a job,' he said. 'I'm to lecture for the British Council in Uzhorod in Ruthenia'. Ruthenia used to be in the far east of Czechoslovakia. 'My divorce will be through by March so will you give notice so that you can come and join me in early March.'

The first moon of the Chinese New Year is from 15 February to 15 March. I left China on the 5th of March.

I have no explanation for the fortune-telling. It wasn't telepathy. I didn't know the answers when I asked the questions.

I began to collect the things I wanted to take with me. Everything was a rush as it always is for someone going away to be married. Oh, I had such lovely things! A set of blackwood furniture, a present from the school – tables and a long low opium bench (you'd call it a coffee table). A ten piece pure Chinese silver dressing-table set. Underwear, a dozen of everything, pure silk embroidered with chrysanthemums and hand-made lace on every piece. I had my tailor make lots of clothes. Whatever he made he always kept half a yard of cloth over. It was delivered to my shoemaker who had my last so I had shoes to match each dress and suit. The most expensive dress shop in Shanghai was Josephine C's. She had exclusive rights to certain patterns from the most famous designers in Paris. I bought from her a Maggie Rouff dress, flowing apple green crêpe de Chine with great bell sleeves. No embroidery or decoration of any kind. The shape was beauty enough.

I had sixteen evening dresses. I can still remember fourteen of them. The white and silver one, the black lace... They were so lovely.

A pedlar came to the Cathay Mansions with an exquisite hand-embroidered bedspread, completely covered with flowers, every inch of it, in pastel shades of every colour. He wanted $200 for it. That was a tremendous amount in those days. I thought about it.

'I'll tell you later. Come back.'

He came back a couple of days later. Yes, I said I'd have it. 'It's in the pawnshop,' he said. The pawnshop was the poor man's bank. 'It frightens me to carry anything so expensive. I'm afraid all the time I will be robbed.' He went off and brought it to me. I had hand-embroidered pillow slips, and sheets to match. I went with a royal dowry.

I was to go by Siberia but, as usual, there was an incident and the railway was closed. This was in 1936. Italy had invaded Ethiopia the year before and the war was still going on. There was an Italian ship in Shanghai waiting to return home and because of the war many people had cancelled their passages. There was a lot of feeling against Italy, but I'm not very interested in politics or other people's wars. When they advertised that they were selling first class tickets for second class prices along I went. A beautiful ship it was, the M.V. *Victoria*.

Just before I left Shanghai I had to do something terrible and sad. Michael was nine years old. He understood everything I said to him (well most things anyway) and I'm convinced that he knew that I was leaving. He fretted and fretted and got thin and sickly looking. I couldn't bear to have him growing old and ill and slowly dying without me there, so I had him painlessly killed. I wasn't sorry to leave Shanghai in the end, I felt so awful about Michael.

There were two Chinese ambassadors travelling on the *Victoria*. One of them was Dr Wellington Koo, China's most famous ambassador. He'd been ambassador to England and the United States, an acting Prime Minister and China's representative to the League of Nations. Now he was going to take up a position in France. His wife was as well known as he was. Madame Wellington Koo was photographed everywhere she went. She was one of the few really beautiful women in public life. Everyone said she was the most beautiful wife of a diplomat anywhere. Some people said she was the most beautiful woman in the world.

For the last two or three days before we left, the Koos stayed at the Cathay Mansions. Usually no hotels run by foreigners, and certainly neither of the Sassoon hotels, would have Chinese stay in them. It wasn't because of racism but because any Chinese person who was wealthy enough to stay in such a place would bring servants with them, dozens of them. And the servants brought fleas in. And foreigners wouldn't stay at a hotel that had fleas.

Dr Koo asked for a suite and was refused. So he said he would take a whole floor. He wasn't refused. I don't know whether the Sassoons thought they could confine the fleas to one floor or whether they couldn't resist the money. There were about twenty suites to a floor.

He and his wife and their three sons and their tutors and his secretary and her secretary and all their servants and their nine Pekinese dogs and the American girl who took care of them – they would have taken up quite a bit of space anyway. I went down in the lift one day with the American girl and the nine Pekinese dogs all on separate leads. But she wouldn't look at anyone or speak to anyone. Whether she was snooty or shy I don't know.

The ship was to go from Shanghai to Hong Kong then on to Colombo and by Suez to London. I went on board after a farewell dinner party and all the friends I'd dined with came along to say goodbye. A couple were boarding the ship at the same time, a handsome man in Italian uniform and a beautiful woman, – black, black hair and a long cardinal cape, glowing red, that swept the ground over her evening dress. Countess Edda and Count Giano, Mussolini's daughter and her husband. He was very powerful in the Fascist government and they were very, very attached to each other. Eight years later he was shot for high treason. They only stayed on the *Victoria* as far as Hong Kong.

It was a smooth, silent ship, sliding along with all this talent on board. The waiters were Italian and multi-lingual, speaking to all the passengers in their own languages. So handsome and slim they were and soft-voiced. Gino, Emilio, Tito, Nino – their names sounded like a song.

I shared a table with an Italian girl who'd been in Shanghai. You'll never guess what she'd been doing. She was a parachutist – way back in 1936 – sponsored to give exhibition jumps.

Another extraordinary pair on board were the Hungarian Count Palfy and his mistress. She was a priceless person, young and shapely. She went round most of the day in swimming togs with a cape over them that just reached to the top of her thighs. It always looked as if she were naked and had flung the cape round as a temporary cover. The only other things she wore were great bunches of artificial violets, a good six inches across. She'd have one round her neck and another drooping from an arm or an ankle or thigh.

I was seasick on that trip and I got the barber to come and massage me. It's a great help to have the back of your head massaged if you're seasick. He was a great talker, a great gossip – worse than Figaro. He told me he had just come from massaging Count Palfy's lady-friend 'And oh,' he cried, 'she has so many passion-scars! Never have I seen such passion scars. All over her!' I guess the cloak and the violets were to hide the love-bites.

Two or three times Count Palfy came and talked to me when she was otherwise occupied. He asked me where I was going.

110

I told him, 'A place called Uzhorod.'

'But that is Ungvar!' he cried (Ungvar is the Hungarian name for Uzhorod) 'You? Going to Ungvar? What is a person like you going to Ungvar for? It is an appalling place! It is in Czechoslovakia – in Ruthenia! In Podcarpatske Russ! Subcarpathian Russia!' Each name coming out in greater accents of horror. They were all words for Ruthenia. Ruthenia had once been part of Hungary and was now part of Czechoslovakia but even outraged patriotism wasn't enough to account for the horror in his voice. It wasn't encouraging.

He asked me which way I was going. I told him through Vienna where I was meeting my future husband.

'Oh ho! When you are in Vienna,' he said, 'You go to the *Drei Husaren* – the Three Hussars. That is mine, I own it!' He got out his card and wrote on it. 'You take this card and you show it. And you will take your fiancé with you. Be my guest for a meal!'

We came to Massawa, a port of Ethiopia where the war was going on. The little Italian boats came shooting out from the shore bringing refugees from the war. There were British newspapermen in shabby casual clothes – one of them had only a pair of white tennis shoes for his feet and he wore them throughout the rest of the voyage, first class. There were Italians in their smart fascist uniforms. While we were watching one whole launch full of people suddenly exploded with a bang and slowly, deliberately it sank. Just like that. It was nothing to do with the war, just spectacular engine trouble. Little boats scurried round picking up the passengers in the water.

On the last day of March we reached Genoa, and I got off the boat. Back in Europe.

(2)

CZECHOSLOVAKIA

1936. The decade of the dictators and the year Mussolini's Fascist army conquered Ethiopia. Bombs against spears; tanks to trample tribal villages. And nobody did anything to stop it, because nobody wanted war.

In Spain an ambitious general led a revolt against the elected Republican government. Hitler and Mussolini lent him assistance. The democracies held back. Nobody wanted war. Franco was on his way to becoming dictator of Spain.

1936 was the year of the Munich Olympics. In the sight of the beloved Führer, German athletes piled up gold medals for the fatherland. The four years of Nazi control was paying off. The Germans were happy, confident, and healthy, a rejuvenated people in a rejuvenated country. They heiled Hitler with enthusiasm. After the tragedy of defeat, the days of joblessness, starvation, and despair, he had brought back the sunshine, strength through joy.

Unless, of course, you happened to be a critic of the regime, a communist, or a Jew. In which case if you weren't already in a concentration camp you were headed that way, inevitably. You were arrested at night and imprisoned without trial. No one inquired what went on in the camps. Flogging and hanging were normal punishments.

If you were a German and had wrong thoughts about the Führer or the regime, you could, if you were quick and sensible, repent and throw yourself into patriotic and party activities, but if you were a Jew you were doomed. It was difficult for even fair-minded liberal Germans to keep on caring what happened to the Jews. There were anti-Jewish cartoons in the newspapers, a constant stream of them, anti-Jewish stories went the rounds, there were anti-Jewish songs and anti-Jewish plays. And there was Hitler's eloquent invective. Jews were beaten up in the streets; their shops and businesses were boycotted ('Whoever buys from a Jew is a traitor'); their passports bore the fatal *J* stamped in red. In 1935 the Nuremberg laws were enacted: only a person of German of kindred blood could be a citizen; marriage and sexual intercourse between German and Jew was forbidden. Jews must identify themselves by wearing the Star of David; they could only travel in special marked compartments.

When the M.V. *Victoria* was two days out of Shanghai, Hitler, loudly talking peace, had let his army flex its muscles by occupying the Rhineland, a demilitarized zone between France and Germany, guaranteed by pact and treaty. France protested, so did Britain. But nobody made a move. Nobody wanted war. Hitler's army, comfortably installed, fortified the Rhineland.

I can't speak Italian. I had some hours to fill in in Genoa before I got on the train for Venice. Most of the passengers I knew on the *Victoria* had left her at Naples. I wandered round Genoa by myself, not knowing what to do and unable to ask, and felt, for the first time in my life, like a tourist. I came to a cinema and went in. Inside it was made, of all gruesome things, of black marble. The film that was showing was Captain Blood, an English film with dubbed Italian dialogue. Here was this very Anglo-Saxon hero shouting away in Italian. But there was nobody to share the joke with.

At last it was train time. All the time I was getting closer and closer to Guy. There was an effervescent soda-water sensation in my stomach and my legs felt trembly. Overnight to Venice. In the morning a bath at the station; that's all I've ever seen of Venice, the inside of the station bathroom.

On to the Vienna train. I shared a compartment with an Austrian couple, nice, middle-aged, friendly people. I couldn't speak German in those days but their English was good.

'What! All the way from Shanghai! And right up to Vienna! Czechoslovakia? To Ruthenia! *To marry an Englishman!*' They looked at me so quizzically and laughed away.

It *was* a long way I'd come. And to change my life so radically. I'd had a birthday on the *Victoria* – thirty-nine. I'd been independent for a long time. My pulse was behaving oddly. Suppose he wasn't there to meet me! Three stations to go! Two stations to go!

And suddenly the door of the carriage was opened and there was a very large man looking in. Just for a second I didn't know him, couldn't believe it. Then I gave a shriek and he gave a shriek and we rushed at each other. The nice middle-aged couple said, 'Excuse us,' and tactfully went out into the corridor. Oh, I was so excited to see him, and so sure that I'd done the right thing. He'd travelled down and joined the train early to be with me.

Vienna! We went to the hotel where he'd booked in and then out to see the city. I suddenly remembered Count Palfy. 'I can treat you to a free meal here!' Off we went to find the *Drei Husaren*.

On the street, of all mad coincidences, we met a man who'd stayed at Guy's place in London the year before. He was a singer, big Laszi. He'd had an accompanist with him who was Laszi too, little Laszi. Big Laszi wanted to go back to England. 'Come and have lunch with us and we can talk about it,' we said.

The *Drei Husaren* was very exclusive. Dimly-lit luxury, with the tables in little pools of soft light. I showed my card and they gave us three free lunches. Very nice, too.

While we were sitting there talking, who should come in but Count Palfy. He saw me and came straight across and shook hands. I introduced him to Guy. He was most friendly and affable. Then he looked at Laszi. I introduced them. Count Palfy didn't say a word. He didn't even nod. His face set stiff. He turned and walked away.

We finished and went out. Laszi left us.

'Whatever happened?' I said to Guy. 'Why would Count Palfy go on like that? Just because I brought a third person!'

'Laszi is a Jew,' said Guy.

'Is he? I didn't know that. But how could Count Palfy possibly know?'

Guy said, 'They always know.'

We went back to the hotel. I was asking all about Uzhorod. Guy had written telling me he'd got a flat and he'd drawn a plan of it. For weeks I'd been thinking about how we'd furnish it and I'd worked out a lovely scheme for it.

'Where are we going to get married?' I said. 'Here? Or in Uzhorod?' I felt so excited. He'd written that we would be married as soon as I arrived.

It was then that he told me that the divorce hadn't come through. I just stared at him.

'What do you mean? What's happened to it?'

'I don't know.'

'But Guy . . . It'll be here tomorrow won't it? Or the next day?'

'I don't know.'

I couldn't understand what was going on. 'But you wrote and told me. You said we'd be able to get married as soon as I arrived. You said the divorce was through.'

'I thought you mightn't come if you knew it was delayed.'

I was shocked. 'I wish you'd told me the truth.'

'I wanted you to come.'

I felt awful. I'd told everyone I was getting married as soon as I arrived. I'd accepted wedding presents. He'd made a liar out of me. I never tell lies and I despise liars. Guy had lied. I'd thought he was free; I'd thought it would be he and I starting our lives together. But he was still Meggie's husband and as far as I could make out he might be for a long time.

I couldn't go back to China. It was too far away and I didn't have the money. Anyway my pride wouldn't let me. I had nobody in England except Olive and we weren't too friendly. Under the circumstances I could scarcely land on Meggie's doorstep. There wasn't anything else for it except to go on. In any case, though I would much rather have been married, I didn't really mind the thought of living in sin with Guy (as Olive would have said). What I minded was the fact that he'd lied to me.

We travelled on to Uzhorod. But for me some of the joy had drained away. Guy told me that the flat wasn't quite ready for us yet. We were to stay in the meantime at the Koruna Hotel.

'It's the best that Uzhorod can offer,' he said.

We arrived at night and went straight to the Koruna. The smell hit me as soon as we walked in – musty and stale as though there were dirt in the corners. We went into the dining-room. It was full of women's torsos, gilded over with paint, each of them holding a bronze lamp aloft with a naked bulb in it. They were jutting out from a row of imitation marble pillars right down the room. It was a ghastly sight.

The room was full of people; they were having a welcoming party for us. Guy had been in Uzhorod for some weeks and it was obvious he was very popular – there were lots of loud laughter and shouts of greeting – but I couldn't understand a word any one was saying, they were all talking in German or Czech. I was tired and depressed but I thought I'd better do the right thing so I went upstairs and put on my Maggie Rouff dress and joined in as best I could.

That evening was all confusion. Assertive, voluble people talking, talking. I got only one of them sorted out from the general blur. She was a rather stout little Jewish woman. Guy introduced her as the president of the English club. Wherever Guy was that evening she was at his side smirking up at him. At one point people rapped on the table and all the jollity stopped, and this woman, Gertie, made a presentation to us. It was a huge cake all iced in white, a wedding cake I suppose. They carried it up to our bedroom and put it on a table there with some other presents we'd been given. Finally all the people went away.

When I woke up in the morning it took me a second or two to remember where I was. There was something odd on the table, something big and black and somehow shimmering. Then I realized what it was and I yelled 'Guy!' and pointed at the cake. It was completely covered, every inch of it, with milling cockroaches. I never saw anything so obscene. 'Horrors!' I thought. 'What's happening to me?'

Czechoslovakia came into being as a separate nation at the end of the First World War. Ruthenia was a border province, Ukrainian territory that had been part of Hungary. Uzhorod was its largest town.

It was a town of about 26,000 people and completely multi-racial. There were Ukranians, Hungarians, Jews of all nationalities, Czechs, Slovaks, Russians, Poles, Germans, Romanians, Gipsies and probably five or six others that I've left out. There were supposed to be twenty-one different languages spoken there.

The awful dining-room at the Koruna operated like a café. All afternoon and evening there'd be groups of men in dark suits drinking coffee there, arguing, and picking up their fountain pens to jot things down in notebooks, all very important. They'd get up, join other groups, more coffee, more scribbling. I thought there was some sort of conference going on. But Guy told me no, it was the newspaper reporters at work.

'All those newspaper reporters for one little town?' After all most towns of 26,000 are lucky if they have one newspaper and a couple of reporters. Apparently Uzhorod had ever so many in all sorts of languages. They kept going financially on what they didn't print. Suppose someone were seen coming out of the doctor's. The reporters would write articles hinting that he had some appalling disease. They'd show it to him and he'd have to pay through the nose to get them to agree not to print it.

Oh, it was a corrupt little town! There were always lawsuits going on, civil ones. People used to make a living hiring themselves out as witnesses. Everyone took it for granted that you hired witnesses who'd swear to anything.

Yet with all this the people had such a conceit of themselves. I never met such a place for social pride. At the top were the Hungarian Aryans who considered themselves some kind of aristocracy, way above everyone else. The Magyar Jews felt superior to the Czech Jews. The Czechs felt superior to the Slovaks. And so on. The Magyar peasants for some odd reason seemed to be at the very bottom of the heap except for the Gipsies who just exploited everyone they could.

The day after we arrived Guy took me over to see the flat. It was in a block that had been built by an Italian insurance company – goodness knows why. It was lovely; light, fresh, and airy and so clean-smelling after the Koruna. The largest room had a big bay of windows and they looked straight down on the Uz River running almost past our door.

But the window bay was full of furniture. Horrible looking, lower-middle class, best-room furniture. An overstuffed settee up-holstered in blue satin with wooden arms painted a thick chocolate brown. And two chairs to match. On the seat of one of them there was a picture, waiting to be hung, of yachts in a harbour at sunset.

'Why, where on earth did all this come from?'

It was a present from Gertie. She'd taken Guy right under her pudgy little wing. I could have cried. Guy stood staring at the picture, then he shook his head in a puzzled way. He said the wind must have been blowing from every point in the compass at once for those sails to be like that.

The flat wouldn't be ready for a week or two and we couldn't face the Koruna cockroaches so Guy got us rooms with an aristocratic old Hungarian lady. She lived in her family's ancestral home, a great big old house (we called it the Baronial Hall) that used to be in Hungary until the end of the First World War. Then bang! – just like that – a line was drawn on paper, a new frontier, and she was living in Czechoslovakia. I think she must have been cut off from her family estates because she was quite poor now, letting rooms to people she approved of. We passed muster because we were Aryans not Jews. She still wore beautiful, shabby clothes that had been fashionable twenty or thirty years ago. Dark frocks with leg-of-mutton sleeves and lace tuckers.

Everywhere you saw evidence of the change of frontier. Ruthenia was a depressed area and the Czech government which was a very good one was trying to open it up. They'd built a superb highway into Uzhorod and very futuristic, clean-looking government offices. They had paternoster lifts in them, one going up all the time and one going down, each with an open door so that you just stepped into it as it passed. We were in one one day and Guy said, 'I'd love to know how this thing works!' He turned a knob, there was a clang and a banging and a whistling and everything ground to a halt. We hopped out and walked quickly away.

Just a stone's throw from these modern buildings was the market-place with little stalls kept by peasant women wearing ten or fifteen skirts all of different colours one on top of the other. When they bent over the skirts flared out like a flower. They all spoke the old Slav language and their roots were in the Ukraine.

Ruthenia was in an odd position. Though it was part of Czechoslovakia and governed from Prague it was an autonomous province with its own governor and officials. When there was an official function there'd be a dignitaries' table at the Koruna for the Governor and the Lord Chief Justice and the Polish Consul and his wife and the British Resident and his wife – that was Guy and me. It all had a comic opera flavour amongst the gilt torsos. There were only 500,000 people in the whole province.

Guy was employed by the English Club. Any club anywhere that could guarantee the wages could request the British Council to send a resident lecturer to them. His job, officially, was to spread knowledge and understanding of the British way of life. It sounded cultured and peaceful but it wasn't like that at all. Ruthenia was in the east of Czechoslovakia. The west bordered on to Germany with Hitler ranting against the Jews and his army, well-equipped and fanatical, camped just near the frontier. You only had to look at a map to see which way the wind was blowing. It smelt of concentration camps and pogroms.

118

The Jews, thousands of them, were thinking about leaving. But they couldn't just up and go. Even those with lots of money had to learn the language of the country they were aiming at. The others had to have a job to go to before they could be admitted as immigrants. So it was even more important for them to speak the language. The popular countries were England, Canada, U.S.A., and some of the South American countries. Everyone was wanting to learn English. Right from the beginning Guy was flat out teaching and for every person who wanted to leave there were dozens of forms to translate and fill in and letters to write. There wasn't a panic yet – that came later – but the pressure was mounting all the time. It wasn't long before I was involved too on the teaching side, more so as I began to pick up some German.

The English Club was composed almost entirely of Jews and to be honest I didn't like them much. They called themselves the intelligentsia and that word summed them up – pretentious people, social climbers. Anyone who had a degree of any kind they referred to as 'Doctor'; they never missed an opportunity to impress. Especially I didn't like Gertie. It was obvious she was madly in love with Guy. I was beginning to know him well enough to realize that he couldn't go long without a woman. I don't know what had happened before I arrived in Uzhorod and I didn't ask.

The club, like everything else, was held in one room of the Koruna. That was where people who wanted to learn English got in touch with us. Guy would give a talk on news from England or reading in English and then there'd be questions and discussion. After that people would make individual appointments with him and he'd find out what they wanted. The meetings always ended up with everyone going down to the horrible café part.

The weather was getting warmer and soon they abandoned the dining-room for the garden café. That was rather pleasant. On the opening day for the summer season they had a gala meal there with big menus written in three languages – Czech, Hungarian, and Slav. We didn't understand any of them.

'What's this thing?' I said. 'It's the same on all three lists'.

Guy spelt it out. 'HEMENEX. It looks interesting. Let's try it.'

So we did. How stupid we'd been! It was just what it said: Ham and Eggs. A special treat, you see, a foreign dish. In the winter in the café part, they often had an orchestra, usually a gipsy one. A man with a violin would come and play leaning over you with great googy eyes and your husband would have to pay him for the privilege. We did a lot of dancing. The favourite dance was the *Tsardas*, where the man puts his hands on the girl's hips and she puts hers on his shoulders and they wiggle-waggle slowly at first then faster and faster.

One day there was a Hungarian orchestra and the drummer was singing. We knew the tune well. As we danced past Guy leaned over and said,

'What language is that you're singing in?' The drummer was very indignant. 'It is English!'

Guy said, 'I might be able to help you with that.' When we got home we wrote out the words of the song in Hungarian phonetics.

> 'szouit hat, szouit hat, szouit hat,
> ouil ju law me ewa?'

and so on through the song. Guy sent him the paper.

The next time we came, as soon as he saw us the drummer signed to the orchestra to play the tune and he began singing:

> 'Sweetheart, sweetheart, sweetheart,
> Will you love me ever?'

You would have sworn it was an English person singing except that his pronunciation was so very correct. I've always found in teaching English to various nationalities that it's much easier, essential really, to know the grammar and phonetics of their native tongue.

I wasn't exactly getting to like Uzhorod but I was finding it interesting. Even the Koruna made a good joke when Guy and I were by ourselves. I was looking forward to moving into the flat and I was determined to make it as lovely as I could.

When it was time to move, my Chinese carpet and lampstands and my grandmother's hand-painted teaset – all in the big case that I'd left with Olive – still hadn't arrived. I'd written before I left Shanghai giving Olive the Uzhorod address and asking her to send the case on. Finally a letter came. She'd made a mistake, she said, and sent the case off to my old address in Shanghai. It didn't seem possible to me that anyone could make a mistake like that. But that was a minor matter.

She'd met Meggie in London (I'd introduced them before I left England) and she found out the dreadful truth. Guy wasn't divorced. He and I were living together unmarried. Olive had known for years that I played cards and loved dancing and went to the theatre. I think she even knew that I didn't believe in her particular kind of God. But this – her little sister deliberately embracing a life of sin.

The trouble was that she did love me and she cared what happened to me. Her missionary zeal sprang forward. She was determined to save this brand from the burning. Words didn't fail her, they flowed out all over the page. Fornicator! Adulteress!

I shouldn't have cared but I did.

I wasn't allowed to forget it either. More letters kept arriving. She told me no one in the family would have anything to do with me ever again. Then open postcards arrived every few days with the same words scrawled on them.

Guy wrote to the police in England. They called on Olive and warned her that it was an offence to send obscene matter through the post. At least that stopped the cards.

We were in the Koruna one night about this time when an Englishman who'd arrived in Uzhorod was brought across to our table and introduced. He was a tall, very handsome young man dressed in the English traveller's uniform – tweed jacket and grey slacks. His name was Christopher Sidgwick and he was writing a book about his journeys. He was the son of a publisher – the firm is Sidgwick and Jackson now – but he was determined not to publish the book with his father's firm because he didn't want people to think he had special privileges. He was a bit dumbfounded that first night because he'd just come across the Uzhorod way of doing business. When he'd arrived he'd booked a room at the Koruna and had paid for it for several weeks in advance. Then he'd gone away for a few days to see another part of the country. When he got back he found two other men installed in his room amongst his luggage. No one turned down the chance of making a bit on the side.

'We've got a spare bedroom,' we said. 'Come and stay with us!' So he did and we became great friends. Much later after the war Christopher's book was published and there were Guy and I in it. There was even a picture with Guy's face in the background.*

One day while he was staying with us, Christopher told us that another Englishman had turned up in the town, Henry Baerlein, a very well-known journalist from the *Manchester Guardian*. He had recently had a book published, *No Longer Poles Apart*. Now he was writing one about Czechoslovakia. Henry had a great sense of humour and a most extraordinary stammer. It sort of went 'bop-bop-bop-bop-BROP!' Whenever he told you anything you couldn't help laughing because of the comical stammer. Afterwards when you realized what he had said you were always glad you had laughed because it was genuinely funny.

Henry and Guy and I went together on one of the saddest journeys I've ever taken. There was an American woman in one of the outlying villages who was Ruthenian-born. She told us that a few years before she had come on a trip from America to see her birthplace, and she was so horrified by the poverty and despair that she found there that she had devoted her life since

* *The Feast of the Locusts* by Christopher Sidgwick Hutchinson & Co. Ltd. (no publication date given). Pages 136-7: 'Uzhorod itself was composed of seven different nationalities who shared some dozen different religions, many of them militant at that. Its staple industries, apart from commerce and slight professional practice, seemed when I was there to be bribery and blackmail. Large numbers of people made ends meet by fraud. It was an entertaining place.
It had, surprisingly, an English colony too: an amusing and amused couple who had gone there to earn a living and to escape from a sister-in-law who was a militant prude. Their living they earned together by teaching English to such professional society as the town could muster, and to ambitious Jews who had an eye on the American immigration regulations. This English couple had a fine new flat overlooking the river Uz, and treated me with the very greatest kindness. Guy was an ex-army officer who had done valuable (and highly dangerous) work inside Turkey in the 1914-18 war . . . His wife was equally high-humoured. They made an engaging couple, deriving much apparent amusement from an environment that must, to put it mildly, have had its limitations.'

to helping the people. Her village was in the district that had been Hungarian before the change of frontier. In the old days the people from the villages used to go down to the plains every year and work for the Hungarian farmers in the harvest season. Their payment was a wagon load of food to take back. With a few cows and pigs and the potatoes they grew in their tiny plots of land, they managed to subsist through the winter till harvest time came round again. Then came the war and after it the peace and the new line drawn on the map separated the villages from the farms on the plains.

There was no work, no means of subsistence. None at all. The cows were sold, the pigs eaten and not replaced. All the villagers' possessions were gradually sold. They were quietly starving to death. The American couldn't believe such things existed. These were her relations, cousins and uncles and aunts. She went back to the United States and raised money by a lecturing tour. Soon she had formed an organization that worked for her raising money in America while she ran an orphanage near her home village.

She told us some terrible things. Two of the children in the orphanage had been found being dragged along the riverbank by their mother. They were screaming and holding back and she was completely distraught.

'I can't stand it any longer. I've no food to give them, none at all. I can't stand their crying. I'm going to drown them!'

The worst of these dying villages were Volovec and Volové. We set off to see them in an enormous car driven by a Jewish chauffeur. Every time he spoke he lifted his hands off the wheel, gesticulating madly. It was quite unnerving.

At first there were villages every few miles and we kept having to manoeuvre our way past ox-wagons. But soon the road got rougher and narrower, there were no more wagons and the villages were farther apart. The country was hilly and covered in pine trees. After a long stretch of empty roads we drove into the village Volové – not really a village, just a single street of dingy huts. There were one or two people about who stared at us with a kind of dumb apathy.

The car stopped in front of one of these tiny huts and the driver honked. A middle-aged man came out in an old grey suit. As he got close we could see it was patched all over. He was the elder of the village, the rich man; he owned a cow! He took us on a guided tour. The people didn't mind; they were completely lethargic. We even went right into the houses and they barely stirred to look at us. Tiny one-roomed huts they were, each set on a plot of land not half as big as a suburban garden in New Zealand. In that bit of ground they grew potatoes. When those were eaten they starved.

The walls inside were made of packed mud, so was the floor. There was no furniture at all except a stove in one corner. The village was surrounded by forest so there was plenty of wood and cones to be picked up. The stoves were burning and the houses were warm. But there was no cooking being done – no food, and even if there had been all the utensils had been sold. In the middle of the floor of each hut was what looked like a wide empty coffin, just big enough for two people to lie down side by side. That was the bed. The elder told us that the 'wealthy' ones had straw for their bed boxes.

There were practically no men in the village. They'd all gone to different parts of Uzhorod to beg. That way they sometimes got a little money for food. In one or two houses there were icons on the wall. But most of them had sold even those – their dearest possessions.

As soon as the Czechs took over, Czechoslovakian law applied in Volové. The children had to go to school. But no one in the village owned two dresses or shirts so when their garments were being washed the children had to stay home. If parents kept their children from school the mother was arrested. They loved that. Three meals a day in prison. The Czechs in their kindly way managed to arrest people quite often so that everyone got a turn in prison.

I'd seen poverty in China but never anything like this. Everywhere else I've been there's been something to laugh at but there was nothing funny about Volovec and Volové.

On the way home we passed through another tiny village, the same kind of place, dingy, poverty-stricken and apathetic. The American woman said, 'That's where I was born.'

I was embarrassed and so was Guy. Neither of us could think of anything to say, but Henry Baerlein took off his hat and silently bowed to the village as though it were some kind of shrine.

Some very interesting people turned up in Uzhorod. One was Stuart Mann, a linguist married to a Czech girl. He was fluent in Czech, Slovak, German and Hungarian and his English was impeccable B.B.C. He told us he'd been reared in Yorkshire and he'd grown up speaking dialect. He had to teach himself proper English in the same way that he learned foreign languages. When we met him you would have sworn he was public school and county. He was supposed to be the only man in the world who'd turned Gipsy speech – Romany – into a written language. He listened and talked to gipsies till he understood the language perfectly. Then he translated some of the Bible for them. Stuart told us that the only gipsy village in the world with a gipsy school was in Czechoslovakia.

He, Christopher, Guy, and I went to visit it. 'Take plenty of sweets and small change,' Stuart warned us. 'You'll be mobbed.'

We were. There was a high fence right round the village. We left the car outside and as soon as we got through the gate it was locked behind us. Heaven knows what would have happened to the car otherwise. They were round us as soon as we were in, hundreds of half-naked brown little imps all grinning and shrieking and clawing at us and holding up their hands to beg. Their fathers were all professional beggars or musicians who played in the cafés in the towns. There was one woman with a baby on her hip, not more than five or six months old, and already it had its hand up in the begging position. We lobbed handfuls of sweets and copper *hellers* over the children's heads. They scampered after them and we got a few steps forward before they were back hanging on us again. That way we made our way to the school. As soon as we got through the door it was bolted from the inside.

It was holiday time. The school was empty but the teacher was there to talk to us. He enjoyed teaching there but he had his problems. There were forty desks for forty children but he never knew how many would come. Nobody knew how many there were in the village because the children never slept at the same house long enough to be counted. The end wall of the room was covered with little fiddles hanging from nails. The teacher tried to teach the three Rs but the children couldn't concentrate for more than ten minutes at a time. The noise would get wilder and wilder till there was pandemonium.

'All right! All right!' he'd shout. 'Get your fiddles!'

They'd storm the wall and begin to play – all by ear. They'd play and play till they'd calmed down and were dreamy little angels. Then he'd say, very quietly, 'Put your fiddles away. Come back to your desks!' and he'd get in another ten minutes' teaching.

Later the Gipsies, like the Jews, were rounded up for extermination. I wonder how many of those cheerful little imps ended up as skeletons in Hitler's mass graves.

It was all right when visitors were there but often in those first few months in Uzhorod I was very unhappy. The divorce still hadn't come through. Olive was bombarding me with accusations and it was six months before I could really understand German or talk to the people around me. I got depressed and I thought, 'I'd better do something. I'll do some writing.' So I bought a typewriter and I got the address of a literary agent in London. Guy used to laught at me when I was tapping away. 'Oh dear, the genius at work!' But when the first two or three articles that I wrote were accepted and I was paid for them – well, he never said anything to me but he started boasting about it to visitors.

The first article I wrote was about getting my licence in Uzhorod. I'd driven in England and Shanghai and Guy had an international driver's licence but that wasn't good enough for Ruthenia. You had to have a special test, no less! We took our oral exam with two Hungarian motor-cyclists, the four of us sitting in a straight line like good children in a classroom. The officer spoke Hungarian and German, none of my languages.

He started with the Hungarian boys. I could hear ominous words coming through – dynamo, magneto, technical talk. Guy whispered to me, 'When he starts on you even if you know what he's asking just keep on repeating, "I don't understand!"'

So I did. 'Werstehen nicht! Werstehen nicht!' The policeman was a great big fat man, very earnest and very worried. Guy kindly offered, in German, to act as interpreter. The policeman nodded approval and asked a long complicated question. Guy turned to me.

'It's no good telling you what he said because you wouldn't understand what he's talking about in any language. Just say something to me, anything.'

'Righto,' I said. 'Carry on, chum! Anything you say is all right by me.'

Guy turned and answered the officer.

'Sehr gut! Sehr gut!' he said, looking at me with surprised approval. I passed with honours.

For the practical test we all piled into the little Czech car we'd bought, Guy and I in front and the fat policeman jammed and squeezed into the back seat. The two Hungarian boys rode ahead. I drove, Guy drove. The policeman squeezed himself out again and leaning on the top of the car wrote out licences and handed them out all round. Guy and I leaned back and stretched with relief. He lit a cigarette and we drove off home.

A few days later when Guy was out the maid came in and told me that a policeman wanted to see me. In came a different policeman. He started telling me something I couldn't understand at all. Juji, the maid, tried to explain it to me but I couldn't understand her either. He walked over to a silver tray and picked it up.

'Hey! What are you up to?' I cried. Juji managed to get it across to me that we owed the police something. There was a fine. I said, 'Oh, well! Here, take this to settle it,' and I took down Gertie's sailing ship picture and offered it. But no, no, he waved it aside and clung to the silver tray. I managed to get Juji to tell him not to go away and I dialled the police station and asked for the doctor there who was a friend of ours and who spoke English. As soon as the policeman heard the doctor's name he put down the tray and started heel-clicking and bowing.

'Put him on the line,' the doctor said, 'and tell Guy to come and see me when he gets back.'

After he'd spoken to the doctor the policeman exited bowing and clicking quite frantically.

As soon as Guy got back he went to the police station. He'd been fined for driving with a lighted cigarette in his mouth.

I sold that story to *The Wide World*, a magazine with an enormous circulation. They illustrated it with a drawing of a tiny car and a huge policeman leaning over it and a little fat dumpling of a woman inside. Libellous! I was really slim.

Shortly after I began writing, an Irish couple was brought across to our table at the Koruna. The man was editor of the *Irish Times* in Dublin, a paper that had a strong British bias. He saw some of the things I'd written and sent me a very formal letter on his paper's letterhead, appointing me Central European correspondent to the *Irish Times*. I had a press pass and free railway travel all over Czechoslovakia. I did write some articles for them later but I never used the railway pass.

All this gave me a boost but there was still a sort of despair just below the surface. What was I doing here – I, Grace Botham, a kept woman in this corrupt little town?

And there was another thing. I never told anyone about it; no one knew it was going on. On the surface Guy and I must have looked like an ideal couple. I know lots of women envied me, he was so charming and loving and protective. Women were always saying to me, 'I wish my husband were like that!'

Well, it was true seven-eighths of the time, twenty-one days out of twenty-four. The other three days were sheer hell.

He'd wake in a mood – do you remember how Meggie had said, 'He has moods'? Oh, I knew what she meant! He was like someone possessed – in a furious blinding rage for three days and violent with it. I was afraid of him then and I had good cause. He often hit me and threatened to kill me. I used to think, 'This is not happening. I'm dreaming it.' Or if I couldn't believe it was a dream I'd think, 'This'll pass. I'll live through it.' Then after three days he'd wake up looking quite different; loving, normal Guy again. The storm had blown itself out. I don't think he could help it, but it was hard to live with. Yet always in the good times I'd forget how bad the bad times were or I'd persuade myself that it wouldn't happen again. But it always did.

At first it shocked me dreadfully. I packed a suitcase. I don't think even at the time I was clear in my own mind whether I was leaving him or going to England to see about the divorce. I don't know what I thought I was doing. I just wanted to get away. I couldn't take much money with me because there were legal limits to what you could take out. I remember sitting in the train and thinking, 'I'll find out about the divorce. If it's quite near I'll stay in England till it comes through. Then I can go back and get married and maybe, at least, I can be friendly with my family again.'

I got to Prague where I had to spend one night in a hotel. I went out in the evening and sat in a café not far away. Once, quite a while back in Shanghai, I'd been taken to a film by one of my friends – a ghastly picture about a wax museum and a murderer with a dreadful face who killed people by dipping them into wax and then set up their corpses as a display. It was so horrible I wanted to walk out but this wretched escort of mine wanted to see it so I just sat through the whole thing with my eyes shut. Just occasionally I'd open them to see if it was still awful and each time I did, what I saw was this dreadful face. I'll never forget it.

Well believe it or not, in this café where I had the cup of coffee, I looked up and there at the next table was this face. It looked exactly the same. I got the creeps. Where am I? Am I in Shanghai? Am I dreaming? But I was in Prague and all alone. Guy was at the other end of the country.

126

I went to the hotel and spent a very disturbed night. The International train passed through Prague at midday. I went down to the station and got a porter. I showed him my luggage and told him in German to put it on the International train. I gave him my seat and carriage number. He listened and answered in Czech, nodding every now and then. 'Ano, ano', which means 'yes, yes.'

The train came in. I got aboard and waited for my luggage. No porter! I waited and waited. The train started. There I was with no luggage. I panicked. There was such a nice German man just across from me. I told him what had happened. He kept cooing, 'Arme Liebe, arme Liebe!' (Poor darling, poor darling!) In a comforting tone.

He told me I should get out at the next station and take the local train back because once the train had passed the two Prague stations I would be carried right across Europe.

I did that and found my luggage sitting there on the station where I'd left it. I suppose the porter hadn't understood a word I said.

I had twenty-four hours to fill in and I wasn't in the mood to be happy with my own company. I mooched around, went back to the hotel for the night and finally got myself and my luggage on to the train the next day. I arrived in London in rather a weird state of mind.

I took a room in a West End bed-and-breakfast place and decided I'd better find a job. I was a member of the N.U.T., the National Union of Teachers, so I went there with my certificates and references (I had some very good ones) and told them that I wanted a job teaching English, if possible on the continent. I didn't want to stay in England, with Olive and the rest of the family feeling about me as they did.

I hung around, not knowing what to do with myself, waiting for letters. I got two. The first offered me a job teaching geography in Durham, the second teaching algebra in the south of England. Nothing to do with what my qualifications were! I was so annoyed I wrote to the N.U.T. saying it might be a joke to them but it was serious for me.

I went out and posted the letter, got home and there was a letter from the N.U.T. telling me of a vacancy for a teacher of English in Sweden. Just what I wanted. I sat straight down and wrote an application. A few days later I had another letter from the N.U.T. They told me that the advertiser had rung them to ask if I were a suitable person. They had replied that after the letter they'd received from me they couldn't recommend me for any position. So that was that. Teaching was out.

I had heard of a place in London where they specialize in finding positions for ladies. It was called the Universal Aunts. Being myself an 'Indigent Lady', or 'Decayed Gentlewoman', I thought I'd try it. I had trouble finding the place so I asked a policeman.

'Are you looking for a governess?' he said.

'No, I'm looking for a job!'

He looked me up and down. It was winter and I had a beautiful fur coat on. 'You don't look as if you ever worked in your life,' he said.

The Universal Aunts were very nice to me. They were Indigent Ladies themselves. I told them that I only wanted something temporary so they found an address of an American lady whose husband was away on business. She wanted a companion till he got back. I thought I'd make quite a good companion. They phoned and off I went. It was very pleasant; the maid showed me in, the lady from America was charming, and we had plenty to talk about. She had a lovely dog who made friends with me right away. She felt like a friend too. 'This is going to be all right!' I thought.

Then she said, 'Now on the maid's day off you'll be able to get breakfast, won't you?'

'I've never been in a kitchen,' I said. 'I've never done anything like that!'

'Oh, but you'd be able to boil an egg, wouldn't you?'

'No,' I said. 'I wouldn't have a clue how to boil an egg.'

She was horrified and shocked and I didn't get that job. That's hopeless, I thought. I'm not cut out to be an Indigent Gentlewoman.

I know it sounds ridiculous that I couldn't even boil an egg but after all if you took most New Zealand housewives, put them on a platform and told them to teach forty children the uses of the partitive article in French they'd be flummoxed. And to me that's the simplest thing in the world, as easy as boiling an egg.

I felt despairing. I was running out of money and Guy either couldn't or wouldn't send me any. He kept writing and begging me to go back. I thought, 'I'll go to the Inns of Court and find out exactly what the situation is.'

I'd been there with Guy light-heartedly sight-seeing not so many months before. It's a beautiful place, old, old buildings all covered with ivy. After some trouble I found the right lawyer.

'But this divorce has barely been started,' he said. 'It'll be a long time. Months, perhaps longer. There's nothing moving at all yet.'

I was horrified. The shock was that Guy had been lying to me all the time, making a fool of me. He must have known the truth. And what was I to do? What was I to do?

There was a teashop on the other side of the road. I'd noticed it when I was going in. Somehow or other I got there, found myself there. Someone must have brought me a cup of tea. I don't remember. I just sat there and the tears poured down from my eyes. They were not tears, it was a flood. Shakespeare says it somewhere – 'Hot salt flooded.' I didn't even use a handkerchief. It was like being behind a waterfall.

I have no idea how long I stayed. My mind was blank. I didn't know where I was or what was happening. Until finally I put out my hand and there was a cup of tea beside me. I suppose I paid for it. I don't know. When I came to myself I knew I was going back to Czechoslovakia.

On the way home I sent a telegram to Guy. SEND TICKETS. I went back to where I was staying and in that long night I thought it out. There was Guy and me. And there were those people in Uzhorod. I didn't like them, some of them I disliked intensely. But that didn't matter. You don't ask a nurse if she likes a patient before she preserves his life. We were the lifeline. Guy and I. The Jews were beginning to be hunted. It wasn't hard to see what was coming, all the signs were there. We knew what was going on in Germany.

I could teach English, I was good at it. And I was beginning to get a foot in the writing world. I could tell people what was going on (or so I thought).

Guy knew the necessary languages and he had the military bearing – a sort of habit of authority – that made him able to deal with frontier people and officials. He could bluff his way through anything. And now I knew the other thing – he had the gift of lying. That's what you need when you're dealing with the Gestapo. Between us we had all the qualifications and fate or chance, a hundred accidents, had brought us to that place at that time.

It was as well I went back when I did. If the divorce had been near and I'd waited a lot of people would not have got away.

The tickets arrived and, when I was leaving, there at the boat train to see me off was Christopher Sidgwick. Guy had sent him a telegram. Oh, it was lovely to see him looking so gorgeous in his London clothes, Savile Row. And he was so nice and kind. He put me in a corner seat that he'd reserved for me and bought me magazines. I felt loved and appreciated again.

✻   ✻   ✻   ✻

Back to Uzhorod, to our lovely flat overlooking the river, to Guy at his most loving, and to Juji. She was our maid and one of the two really good friends I made while I was living there.

She was a plump Czech girl in her early twenties and she had a great sense of humour. They still used the dowry system for marriages in Ruthenia, but if a girl who was poor could prove that she could run a home efficiently and make it a comfortable place, why, that was as good as any dowry and she could marry well on her reputation. Juji could make a home a very comfortable place.

When visitors came for dinner with us they'd never thank me for the meal. Out they'd pop to the kitchen and thank Juji and leave a tip for her on the table.

I don't know how I would have survived without her. Do you remember how Meggie said her maid was the only person beside her who knew about Guy's moods? Maids live in the same house, they always know those things. On the difficult days Juji never said anything but she'd be specially nice and thoughtful to me. And in the ordinary course of living when Guy said things that were stupidly masculine, Juji would quietly twinkle at me. We understood each other.

She was a wonderful cook. We went out once and came home earlier than we intended. Juji opened the door and looked taken aback. 'Oh, I didn't think you'd be back so soon!'

We wondered what she'd been up to. In the dining-room was an oval table and it was completely covered with what looked like a cream plastic cloth. Do you know what it was? Strudel dough! Rolled and stretched paper thin. Then she covered it with sliced apples and sugar and spices, rolled it up, cut it into lengths and baked it! It was delicious!

She knew I knew nothing about cooking but she backed me up in everything. It was the custom, when visitors came, for the lady of the house – anyone who was anyone, any member of the intelligentsia – to serve their own speciality made with their own two hands. Just the one dish; the servants did all the rest.

Shame on me! I didn't have a speciality. One day I said to Juji, 'Make me some jelly!'

'No!' she said, horrified. 'That's made of deadmen's bones!'

'That's all right,' I said. 'That's what English people live on.' She gave me a look!

Guy was always going off to England, helping people out or checking on refugee places. 'Next time you go bring me back some jellies,' I told him.

When he came back he had jellies packed in all over his suitcase. Fourpenny ones they were in those days. Juji had never seen fruit jellies. 'Bring me some boiling water,' I said and I made one. She loved it.

The next time I had visitors she made a lot of jellies, various colours, set in champagne glasses, and offered them round. 'The Gracious Lady made them herself!' she said reverently.

Afterwards she told me that the ladies kept coming to her on the sly and asking for the recipe. Juji said, solemnly, 'Oh, no, I couldn't tell you. Even I do not know it. It is the Gracious Lady's family secret!'

So I, who couldn't boil an egg, got the reputation of being an accomplished cook.

Every morning Juji used to take the carpets out to the *klopfbalcon* – a special carpet-beating balcony, every flat had one. There she'd fling the carpets over the rail and beat them with a flail. Then she'd polish the parquet floor, put the carpets back and comb out their fringes with a special comb. When it was all clean and neat she'd bring in our coffee and wake us. She must have been working since about five o'clock.

She spoke Czech and Hungarian and some German. I tried to teach her some English. When we had time we'd sit down with some books I'd bought and I'd try to get her to read them working out the meaning by the German she already knew. One of the sentences was 'You must speak distinctly!' Juji laughed and laughed. She got to the 'stinct' and read it from the German as 'it stinks'. She laughed so much we could never take English lessons seriously again.

Washday was a big event in Ruthenia. It only came round about every six weeks and the whole day was given over to it. Juji fetched our meals from the Koruna and spent the day in the basement where there were washing-machines, electric dryers, automatic irons, everything. She was so proud of my Shanghai underclothes and so careful of them. She used to boast to the other maids down there, 'These are like Baroness's clothes, these are!'

Most people's washing was done simply on the river bank. In midwinter when the river was all frozen over you'd see the washerwomen come down with their baskets full of washed laundry to rinse. They'd walk out, in their bare feet, on to the ice and they'd cut out a wedge of ice, the way you do when you're cutting up a melon. Then they'd kneel down and plunge their bare arms in to above the elbow rinsing the clothes. It made the washing beautiful, spotless and so white, but just to watch them gave me the shivers in my centrally heated flat.

My other friend in Uzhorod was the Polish Consul's wife. Guy had been taken to their house for dinner before ever I arrived. When he got there he asked Madame if he could wash his hands. 'Oh yes, of course!' She fetched a towel, took him to the bathroom and stood chatting politely while he did just that. Guy was suffering deep torment before the evening was over.

She was a person I felt really at home with. She talked my languages, English and French, and she'd studied art in Paris. Whenever I had time I'd spend an afternoon chatting to her. She wanted to paint a portrait of me and often she'd be standing there painting away while we were talking, but she could never get it right. One day she exclaimed, 'Les traits sont durs mais les couleurs tellement delicates.' (The features are strong but the colours are so very delicate.) She never did produce anything I wanted to show anyone. I've never been beautiful.

One day when Juji was out, there was a ring at our doorbell and there was the Polish Consul's chauffeur in uniform with an enormous hunk of bloody meat in his hand. He held it out to me saying something I couldn't understand at all. He spoke only Hungarian and Polish. I was having the same problem with my dog who could only speak Hungarian. I'd learned enough to have satisfactory conversation with her. I could say 'aloudni' (lie down), 'nem sobot' (not allowed), and 'dragam' (darling). It was an interesting vocabulary but not altogether suitable for dealing with male chauffeurs.

I took the meat very gingerly and put it in the kitchen. When Juji came back I made the same sounds at her that the chauffeur had made to me. She laughed. 'You're saying, "It has been hung". It must be venison!'

When the dignitaries' table was set up at the Koruna for special functions, along with the governor, the Lord Chief Justice, the Polish consul, the British resident and all their wives, there was often another couple – the Russian general and his wife. Both of them were elderly and they looked like the walking dead. He was tall, thin, deadly serious, and unapproachable. She was a pathetic little creature who always wore the same moth-eaten close-fitting felt hat with a bunch of absurdly girlish-looking curls on either side. He was horrible to her, either ignoring her or, on the rare occasions when she spoke, listening without ever looking at her, his features screwed up into a look of aristocratic distaste. He must have unbent at times though, because everyone knew he had at least one mistress in town.

I couldn't speak to the General's wife; Russian was her only language. But once I asked my Polish friend about her and she told me a story that has haunted me ever since. The General, she said, was in the Czarist army at the time of the revolution. When the Czar and his family were executed all his senior officers were rounded up too and taken to face the firing squad, row after row of them. Most of the wives and families fled, but our general's wife went to the authorities to beg for her husband's body for decent burial. Somehow she got permission.

She went with her maid to where the bodies were piled up. Can you imagine it? Those two women manhandling that heap of corpses. At last they found him. His eyes were shut and his mouth compressed as though he had died in great agony. Neither of the women was big and they had trouble pulling the body free. At the first tug his eyes opened and looked at them with a terrible reproach.

Somehow they got him away across the frontier into Ruthenia – it was Hungary then. He recovered but always with this bloodless look about him. She became ill, all her hair fell out: she was totally bald. 'She's a bit touched,' people said. I think it was the right way to put it. She'd come too close to something you shouldn't know about, not if you want to stay ordinarily sane.

There was another Russian couple whom we knew who'd escaped from the revolution but they were quite different, a nice, jolly, cheerful couple. They were just children when they'd been brought out. George was a naval officer and Sonja a countess, but she never used the title. Lots of White Russians claimed to be countesses but Sonja really was.

The other people we knew and mingled with were 'the intelligentsia', the members of the English club who were mainly Jewish. For me that just meant Gertie – she overshadowed everyone else. She and her husband would come to dinner with us sometimes. He was a dear little man, a plump little dentist who'd been learning English for seventeen years. So far there was really only one word that he felt at home with and that was 'Yes'. (Maybe it was all he needed – Gertie really henpecked him.) But oh, to hear the subtle variations of Laszi's yes. He could ask questions with it 'Is that so?' 'What happened next?' He could make it apologize – 'I'm afraid I don't quite understand.' He could sympathize with you, cooing it like a kindly dove, or lend enthusiastic support 'Yess! Yess!' so brisk and cheerful.

But Gertie; once she was in your house she'd take it over. I had to snub her once or twice. When we'd finished dinner she would stand up, indicating that it was time to move into the other room. I would just sit there and so would everyone else until she had to sit down again. Then immediately I would stand up and the others would follow me out. I said to her once, 'Since you're learning English you should learn the customs of the country too. The lady of the house is the one to stand after a meal to give the signal to leave.' I was a cat to her really.

Once I did something worse. Guy and I were going to drive out to the Tisza, a tributary of the Danube. We could both read maps perfectly well but Gertie insisted on coming with us to show us the way. If ever Guy was anywhere she had to be there too. We drove quite a distance and there was an open piece of grass and a lovely swift-flowing river. So pretty – the sound of the water rushing past. We decided to bathe. Gertie got into her togs; she was short, plump and bulgy. I was very slim. I was never proud of my face but I did have a good figure. I wasn't in the least ashamed of what could be seen. So meanly I went in naked. Guy had no eyes for Gertie that day however much she made up to him. What made it better was that Gertie and Guy, both having some weight, could sit in the rushing water and keep there but I was swept away by it and Guy had to rescue me. I didn't plan that either.

There was getting to be less and less time for trips and social life. Hitler's campaign against the Jews was in full swing in Germany. You could tell from the newspapers and word-of-mouth stories that he was gaining a lot of support in Austria too. Czechoslovakia is an inland country with no access to the sea. Germany and Austria were just across the frontier of western Czechoslovakia. There was beginning to be a real fear of being surrounded, taken over. The Czechs themselves were friendly people, peaceable and sane. So were the Slavs. They were the real natives of the country. But there were a lot of German Czechs. They were only too ready to stir up trouble and most of those people would have welcomed the Germans. Already a lot of the Aryans hated the Jews and, though they didn't dare openly attack them in sane and sensible Czechoslovakia, all the time the feeling was getting worse. I remember once at a dance at the Koruna one man leaned over to Guy and said, 'You and I, Morton, are the only whole men in this room.' It wasn't anything, but that sort of remark was getting more and more common.

Guy was busy all the time writing letters. For every person who wanted to emigrate he had to get a permit from the country they were going to and letters of recommendation from Czechoslovakia. None of this was straightforward and all the correspondence had to be in English. For every person there was a wad of letters to be written and replied to.

133

A woman couldn't go to England unless she could prove that she had a job to go to. Some of the very wealthy people went off to England to be housemaids, cooks, charwomen. To get men away was really difficult. Older men weren't wanted much in other countries and the Germans made all sorts of difficulties for young men of military age who tried to cross to the coast that way – even when they had all the right documents.

Children could get into other countries only if they were being adopted. Guy had met a woman in England, Mrs Roger Smith, who ran a refugee organization and we worked closely with her. Parents who despaired of arranging emigration for themselves, or who had no money, would sometimes beg for their children to be adopted. Photographs would be taken and sent to England and Mrs Roger Smith would show them to parents that she'd found who were willing to adopt. They'd look at the photos and say, 'That's a good one! I'll have that one!' Of course we sent information about the child too, but it was a terribly haphazard system all the same. But when we thought of the danger they might soon be in, it didn't seem important how they got away, just so long as they did.

I remember one man – they called him 'Baci', Uncle. He was a wealthy Jew from New York and he came across to try and get his family out. They were preparing a party to welcome him and the little boy of the family was learning a speech of greeting. We used to hear this little chap rehearsing over and over again, 'Servus, Baci (Greetings Uncle) . . .'. His mother kept him at it till he was word-perfect. Guy helped them in some way and Uncle was so grateful he gave me something I prized very much, a movie camera. Later it was confiscated by the Germans.

The English Club was changing. When I first arrived it was mainly middle-aged people who went there but now young people were flooding into it. And not just from Uzhorod. Someone would appear at a meeting and would tell Guy that they wanted help. All their papers and documents were at home, they'd say. Would he come out to such-and-such a town or village and see them?

So he would fix a date and some time in the next week or two we would drive out there. But we would find not one person waiting to see us but a whole roomful and as soon as it was known that we'd arrived more and more people would crowd to the house.

I shall never forget driving out to those villages. Every few kilometres along the road you'd see a shrine, either with a crucifix in it or a Madonna. Very often at the foot of it there'd be an enormous many-coloured flower – the skirts of a peasant woman who was kneeling there in prayer. All you could see of her was the rose of her skirts and a pair of little bare feet poking out.

In the villages there were storks' nests – great big things on the roof of every house, like untidy baskets of twigs near the chimney for warmth. Once one of these huge storks flew across the road so low that its long trailing legs were hit by the windshield of our car. But it just pulled them up a bit and went on flying to its nest on the next roof.

In the villages there were really orthodox Jews wearing caftans and their hair in ear-locks. They never approached us to get them out. I think they accepted the idea of suffering. But others who were almost as strict did come to us. Once we were visiting two girls in an outlying village, and a young man heard we were there and came as fast as he could to see if we could help him get away. He caught us on the footpath outside the house. It was a Saturday and as we stood there talking a storm that had been threatening all day broke and the rain teemed down. Guy said, 'Get into the car and we'll talk about it there.' But no, it was the Sabbath. He was afraid someone might see him and think that he'd been travelling. So while we crouched in the car he stood there drenched to the skin, the rain pouring down his face.

Almost everyone in that eastern part of Czechoslovakia could speak German: it was the common language as French is in western Europe. But often now if we approached anyone with questions they would be suspicious of us thinking we might be German agents. We learned not to open conversations in German.

'Mluviti anglice?' we'd ask in Czech. (Do you speak English?)

Then if the answer was no, 'Est-ce que vous parlez français?' Maybe they would answer, 'Un peu.'

Then we'd risk saying, 'Perhaps you speak a little German?' and the conversation would be launched.

Everyone was getting very jumpy. Once when Guy was away one of the local papers was delivered and there was a big heading in it in German. ENGLAND DECLARES WAR.

I was terrified. What were we to do? We were enemy aliens. I couldn't get in touch with Guy. I rang the paper office. I knew the editor well because he was a pupil of mine. 'What am I going to do?' I said.

He laughed. 'Don't worry. We're going to contradict that headline in the next edition. You've got to have something to print!'

Well, it was a typical Uzhorod trick, but the thing was that I'd been prepared to believe it. Our nerves, everyone's nerves were on edge expecting disaster.

The days went by and it was winter again. The winters were very hard in Uzhorod. The Uz froze over and people walked across it to visit their friends on the other side. I remember one evening at the Koruna. We'd all been dancing after a meeting of the English Club. It was snowing, too cold to walk home even the little distance we had to go. The wheels had all been taken off the carts and replaced with sleds weeks before. We rode home in a sleigh. The horses had bells on them like Santa's reindeer. It was a lovely ride. But it was the first time I had been involved in a traffic collision. At the corner there was a sleigh coming the other way and it didn't have bells on.

This was our second winter in Uzhorod. We were waiting for the ice to crack on the frozen river outside our window. The previous spring it had been so exciting! Juji had come into our bedroom one morning and called us. We had run out to the balcony and spent the whole day just watching. Never mind lessons or anything else! We stayed there all day. Just twenty-four hours it took to turn from solid ice to a flowing river. First there were just the cracks and we watched them get bigger. Then there were pieces breaking away, great big pieces at first, then smaller ones till there were just little pieces of ice floating by on a full flowing river.

This spring, before the ice cracked, the pattern of our lives broke up. A letter came from England with a cutting from the paper. The divorce was through. The next day we were married. Sonja and George were the witnesses so I can honestly say that I had a countess as matron of honour. We were married by the registrar who was also the mayor of Uzhorod. He could speak Czech and Hungarian. The police doctor stood by him and translated the questions for us and our responses for him. In ten minutes it was all over and we went home.

We took the others back to our flat to have a drink. We were laughing and excited the way you are after a wedding. Guy turned on the radio for some background music and almost immediately the programme was interrupted for a news flash. It had happened. The German army had invaded Austria. They were entering Vienna. It was the 12th of March 1938. The Anschluss. It was also my birthday. I was forty-one.

We'd all known it was coming of course, that invasion. There had been a lot of disruptive Nazi activity there, street-fighting, explosions, demonstrations. And Hitler had been putting pressure on the Austrian government too. The shock was that it came when it did. The Chancellor of Austria had decided there should be a plebiscite to find out whether the majority of Austrians wanted to join Germany or remain independent. The plebiscite was to be held on 13th March. But that wasn't good enough for Hitler. He called a meeting with the Austrian Chancellor and bullied him till he agreed to resign. The German troops entered Austria the next day before there was a chance to hold the plebiscite. The message was clear. Hitler was going to get his way no matter what the people of the country wanted.

Ruthenia was in an odd position. It was only loosely part of Czechoslovakia. We all felt that it might be the next place that Hitler had his eye on.

'We won't be able to help anyone if we're behind the Nazi lines ourselves,' Guy said. 'It's time we left.' We decided that he should go over to the west of Czechoslovakia and find somewhere for us to live and work. I was to follow as soon as he sent for me.

In the meantime Juji and I packed up our furniture and sent it to the station so that I could go at a moment's notice if I needed to. I gave the dog and the cat away to good homes and moved into the Koruna Hotel. Yuck!

136

I didn't have much time to think about how awful it was. When Guy had gone I had to open the mail that came. What a shock I got! Dozens of unpaid bills! It wasn't really any of my business I suppose but I was too proud not to pay them. I settled down to teaching at the Koruna.

No trouble about pupils of course. After the Anschluss the pace was really on. They didn't care what they paid. I didn't have a minute free from breakfast till late in the evening. I got all the bills paid. Just as I was about to pay the last one the toilet on the floor where I was living stopped working. Of course at the Koruna they didn't bother with a little thing like getting it mended. It was the last straw. Everything was filthy anyway and now it smelt as well.

I sent Guy a telegram. GET ME OUT OF THIS HOLE. Unfortunately for some strange reason the people in the Post Office sent for somebody to translate it. The manager of the hotel heard about it and was terribly hurt. 'Oh, you don't know what you've done to me, talking about my hotel like that!' he cried. I didn't care.

Guy sent a letter saying 'Come to Pardubice.' Among the people who'd passed through Uzhorod there was an uncle and niece, from the north of England – worthy provincial people who for some unknown reason were very interested in Czechoslovakia. They'd been coming here for holidays in the summer for two or three years. Guy had come across them again in a tiny two-roomed flat in Pardubice. Like most people they were unnerved by the Anschluss and were off home again in a hurry. The flat was too small for two of us but it would do for me till we were settled.

I arrived there – it's a town about 100 miles from Prague – just before they left. Niece showed me how to wash a milk bottle and put it out – that was my first introduction to housework. I had all my meals at a nearby café, but I taught myself to wash the tea-towel and hang it over the towel rack till it dried!

Niece had found herself forced into teaching English when she was living there and her pupils came straight to me bringing others with them. 'I'm only here for a week or two,' I said. 'It's not worthwhile.' But they wouldn't take no for an answer. Just another lesson, they begged, just a few more words! As though their lives depended on it; which of course they did.

I hadn't had time to feel lonely before I got a telegram from Guy, BRING THE FURNITURE AND COME. He'd got a flat in Teplice Schönau, a provincial town in the west, right near the German-Czech frontier.

I came, but the furniture didn't. That very day the frontier had been closed and they refused to send the stuff out of Ruthenia. I don't know why. It was just another of those mysteries of other people's wars. I was thrilled to see the end of Gertie's blue satin suite, but oh, my Shanghai blackwood tables!

The train pulled in to Teplice Schönau. There on the station to meet me was Guy. And – oh, heavens! – guess who else? Gertie! I knew she and Laczi had left Ruthenia when things got dangerous. Gertie was quite well-off. Half of the trouble I think was that she held the purse-strings. She was trying to get to South America. I suppose Guy was the lifeline to her as he was to all the others. Maybe it was all innocent. I don't know how long she'd been there – I didn't inquire. She stayed only a day or two after I arrived but it was two days too long for me.

'What would you like to do now you're here, darling?' said Guy, very loving and pleased to see me again.

'Oh, more than anything else in the world, I want to go to the opera!' Teplice was right on the German border. Lovely Dresden with its fabulous opera-house was just a short drive away, and Guy and I had British passports that would take us across the frontier with no trouble.

'Oh, but we've arranged a welcome party for you!' said Gertie, all gush and hypocrisy. As soon as I got Guy alone I told him I wasn't going. But he talked me round. 'They mean well,' he said. 'Don't hurt their feelings!'

It was horrible. A gang of Gertie's friends talking away at the top of their strident voices in German and Hungarian and making jokes and references that I didn't understand. I was completely left out. The next day, thank God, she left and we were able to get on with living again.

Teplice Schönau was in a district called Sudetenland. If you told people in those days that you were living in Sudetenland they said, 'Where's that?' A year later the whole world was talking about it and we two were almost the only people there to tell the truth about it.

It was a cheerful little place in those early days. Oh, there was tension, where wasn't there tension in Europe? But what you noticed was the sweet normality of it. Right on the frontier was a big pine forest, the Zinnwald, and people used to drive out there in hundreds to picnic on Sunday. They'd leave their cars and wander through the beautiful forest walks and eat at the little cafés. Our favourite one had windows that looked on one side into Czechoslovakia and on the other into Germany. Sometimes German holiday-makers would come up and eat there too.

We did go to Dresden, several times. That lovely opera-house, all white and gold with crimson carpets and curtains. And the singing was beautiful. The *prima donna* was a bit on the large side but it didn't matter. We saw *Tannhäuser* there. There were six circles and for each of them there was a circular balcony that went all the way round the outside of the building. In the intervals you could step out and stroll round and round. Those were lovely nights – the excitement of the music and the fine drive back and Guy in a marvellous mood.

Sometimes we stayed overnight at the Bellevue Hotel right on the riverbank. Near it was the Zwinger with its great stretches of formal gardens and paths. Beautiful statues here and there and bronze dolphins with fountains coming out of their mouths. It was there in the Zwinger art

138

gallery that I saw, really saw, my first original masterpiece. Raphael's Sistine *Madonna*. It must have been ten feet high, at the end of a gallery, and you could have sworn it was real. You felt you must touch the blue velvet of the gown. We went several times to gaze at it and always there were silent people just standing there staring, rapt. I never understood until I saw that, what pictures could really mean. Later when I saw a reproduction I didn't recognize it as the same picture.

There was something about Dresden, especially the Zwinger, that gave me the same feeling I'd had in King's College Chapel. They were the parts of the world that seemed to me pure beauty. I used to think, 'So long as there's that in the world there's something that man has made that's purely beautiful.' It wasn't till long after the war that I learned that Dresden had been bombed and utterly destroyed. And by, of all people, the Allies.

By the time I arrived in Teplice Schönau Guy was already in touch with a lot of people who needed help. The Jewish population here was completely different from the Ruthenian one. In eastern Czechoslovakia they always seemed to be saying, 'We are the intelligentsia. We may be Jewish but we have more money and brains than you have so it is your duty to help us.' But here in the west they were gentle, educated people and we wanted to help them not out of pity but because we liked them and they became our friends. I felt as if I had come out of an unhealthy, nasty type of world into clean civilization.

One of the first friends we made was a German non-Nazi, not a Jew, I think. He was an elderly man, a judge, who lived with his daughter-in-law, and her family. We used to go and play bridge with them quite often. They were delightful people and they simply did not believe that there was going to be war. What they said about Hitler was exactly what we thought; but they couldn't believe that the things that were being reported as being done by the Germans were true. I think they were typical of a lot of decent Germans. It's always hard to know what to believe of all you hear – what's true and what's propaganda. A lot of honest Germans didn't know till much later how evil the Nazi regime was.

Three of my pupils I remember very clearly. There was Zimmer, a little man, manager of a ceramic factory. We were very fond of him, he was delightful. He said he felt secure even though he was a Jew. Because if the worst came to the worst and the Germans came, they'd still want the ceramics factory to go on operating because it was so profitable and he would be essential because he was the only person who really understood the business. All the same he must have had some doubts because he was busy learning English.

Mr Hammer was tall and thin, a bachelor with a quiet sense of humour and a deprecating air. He owned a linoleum factory, a very flourishing business. He had excellent machinery that he'd imported from Scotland, and he took a lot of quiet pride in the quality of his product. Like Zimmer he felt safe because no one would be silly enough to expel or imprison him.

139

He was improving his English as much for business reasons as from fear. Both of them began as pupils and ended up coming to see us as friends.

Then there was Robert, sixteen, and in his last year at high school – Czech by nationality, German by race. Robert wanted to learn English, or rather improve his English, only for educational purposes. He had a good mind and was ambitious and energetic. He wanted to go to a German university, a particular one (I've forgotten which) where just the courses he wanted were taught by the best possible people. He hoped the Germans would come and take over. He admired Nazi efficiency and all they'd done for Germany and he felt sure that if they took over Sudetenland he'd have no trouble getting into the university he'd set his heart on. I used to encourage him to come and see us often. He was the only pro-Nazi we knew and it kept us in touch with what was being thought and said.

We lived in a flat on the ground floor of a big old house. There was a large mosaic entrance hall with a staircase rising from it and our flat to the right. It had a funny basic sort of plan, a passage down the middle ending in a lavatory and three rooms off it on each side. Each room had a door into the passage and a door into each of the rooms adjoining it. It was the sort of plan a child might have thought up for hide-and-seek or chasing.

Upstairs were three characters who might have stepped out of a book, two sisters and a brother who had inherited a large drapery shop in the town. I forget their real name; we always thought of them as the Drapers. They were all spinsters, the brother as much as his sisters; kind, gentle people who lived to a quiet routine. They never made a noise or spoke a harsh word about anyone. They belonged in an orderly stable nineteenth-century world.

We hadn't been long in Teplice when the atmosphere began to change. Odd stories began appearing in the English papers we got, about Germans being attacked and ill-treated by the Czechs. We became suspicious because we saw no evidence of this and it was impossible to imagine the sane, friendly Czechs ill-treating anyone. So we decided to investigate three reports that were supposed to have originated in Teplice. The first story reported that if a child arrived at school in a Nazi uniform the Czech teachers would strip him naked and thrust him out the gate. Then there were reports that German children were being discriminated against and weren't allowed on railway stations. And there was also a story that the Czechs had ganged up on a German and killed him.

Guy started off with the story of the German killing. He asked various German Czechs about it. They said that it had happened all right, but not in Teplice but in Ausberg, a town a little further along the frontier. He drove to Ausberg and inquired of all the officials there. They told him, 'Oh yes, it happened! But it was in Eger.' Eger was another frontier town. Off he went to Eger and the pro-Germans told him that they knew there had been such an incident but that it had happened in Teplice Schönau. So that seemed to prove conclusively that it hadn't happened at all.

Meanwhile we'd discovered the origin of the story of German boys having the clothes torn off them at school. The rule of the particular school was that the children were to wear school uniforms, not Nazi ones. One boy went to school with his Nazi uniform under his school shirt. In class he opened up his school shirt and was displaying the uniform to his friends. The teacher saw him and said, 'You're not to wear that here. Take if off and put your school shirt back on.' He took off both shirts then ran away out of the school gate. You can see how wildly distorted the report was.

We went to the railway station. A guard was quite open about what had happened there. He'd been walking along the railway platform signalling and blowing his whistle and a gang of these pro-German boys were marching up and down behind him imitating his walk and whistling when he did. Every time he turned round they whizzed round behind him. At last he jumped round suddenly and shooed them away. 'Get out of here, you little brats! And don't let me see you down here again!'

There were lots of other instances too. It was obvious that there was a propaganda campaign going on to influence the English against the Czechs and to make them think that the Germans in Sudetenland were a persecuted minority. Nothing could have been further from the truth.

I gathered up all the material and wrote it into a long article for the *Daily Telegraph* in London. Guy made frequent trips to England. A lot of the wealthier Jews wanted to send their children to boarding-schools in England so that they could learn the language and the way of life and if the worst came to the worst they would be out of the country. Guy had found a school in the south of England where the headmaster was sympathetic and made the boys welcome. Guy used to take the boys across himself and at the same time see Mrs Roger Smith – they worked together on adoptions and getting jobs for women in England.

On his next trip I went with him. We took my article in person to the editor of the *Daily Telegraph* and left it with him. Later they rang us at the Cumberland Hotel and asked me to call. I saw the editor of the Sunday paper that was linked with the *Daily Telegraph*, the *Sunday Express*.

He said, 'Now I am very interested. I would like to print it. But we are not allowed in England to print anti-German material!' That was before Munich. So much for freedom of the press! 'But it should be printed', he said. 'If you are willing to forgo payment for the article I think we can manage it. If you'll write the whole thing out in the form of a letter, I'll undertake that it'll be printed in full.' So that's what I did. A column and a half in a London paper! The point was, of course, that the editor has no responsibility for the views of the correspondents.

There was a lot of uncertainty in England about what was going on in Czechoslovakia. With all this propaganda everything seemed to be pointing to Sudetenland as the place that Hitler had marked down for his

141

next *coup*. Everyone was uneasy at the way Hitler was just swelling and swelling in power. The English decided to send a fact-finding mission out to Czechoslovakia.

It was headed by Lord Runciman. What made them think he'd be a good person to judge, I can't imagine. He arrived in Sudetenland and he conferred with all sorts of people but everyone that he went to visit was a pro-Nazi. For quite a lot of the time he was there he stayed in Count Clary's castle and Count Clary was a notorious Nazi sympathizer. Guy wrote to Lord Runciman explaining that he was a resident in Teplice and that he had a lot of information he could give and the snooty reply he got back was, 'I have all my own advisers, thank you.'

One day Guy was driving along not far from Count Clary's castle and he saw a very large car with a British flag on it drive up and park. As well as the flag there was a big swastika painted on the car. Guy stopped and went up to it. There sitting in the front was Unity Mitford with a friend. She was the sister of Nancy and Jessica Mitford, the writers. Much to the embarrassment of the rest of the family, Unity was a very outspoken Nazi supporter. She was a personal friend of Hitler and often used to visit him.

There she was with a very sleek, well-dressed, young Englishman beside her. Guy put his head in the window and said, 'Don't you think you're rather letting your country down?'

She turned to the young man and they looked at each other then both looked away into the distance. Neither of them spoke. Much later Unity Mitford committed suicide.

One of the odd results of all this tension building up about Sudetenland was that we began to have quite a lot of money. I was teaching and writing for the papers, and that was bringing in a small steady income. But people who wanted to get out of the country or to get their savings or valuables out of the country would pay Guy commission for doing all the business for them. Usually they paid him when it was all completed and often in English money. All the time Czech currency was dropping in value and English currency was rising. Ten English pounds were worth the equivalent of a hundred in Czech money, so that quite trivial sums of English money would keep us for weeks in Czechoslovakia. That was how Guy paid for the trips to England.

The Czechs themselves weren't green. They could see better than anyone what was happening. All round the border between Sudetenland and Germany they had hidden fortifications. High in hills they had hangars dug with aeroplanes in them facing out towards Germany so that they could take off at a moment's notice. Everywhere they were preparing to fight and they were desperately patriotic.

One day we were asked to go up to a place called the Panorama Café. It was right on the hills close to the frontier. We had been there some months before and had had a meal. There had been cars all around and a cheerful crowd. Now it was completely deserted. The woman who ran the shop took Guy into a private room to talk with him and I was left alone. Guy would never let me know anything about the dangerous illegal escapes he planned. He felt that it would be some sort of defence for me if we were caught that I just didn't know what was going on.

I stood there in the empty café looking out. I knew this much, that all the young boys of the district had got together and gone out into the mountains. They were living there training themselves to be guerrillas so that they'd be ready for anything that happened. This woman's sons were amongst them. I stood at the window and I had the most awful feeling. Everything that had been spick and span and busy was bleak and neglected. Right in front of me there was a little ornamental plant growing. No one had watered it, and the leaves were all drooping and dying. I picked off the dead leaves and I watered it with a cup. It was dreadful, the feeling of hopelessness there.

We never heard what happened to those people. Most of the stories we played a brief part in had no ending. The people just disappeared – dissolved into war. However fond we were of people, we scarcely ever heard what happened to them afterwards.

One evening after we'd been teaching and working all day we went across to have a game of bridge with the judge and his family. When we got back the maid had gone to bed – she was a capable girl but I was never close to her as I was to Juji. We turned on the radio while we drank a cup of tea before going to bed.

Guy twiddled the dial and got the B.B.C. We were just in time for an announcement: ALL BRITISH RESIDENTS OF CZECHOSLOVAKIA ARE TO BE EVACUATED IMMEDIATELY.

We looked at each other. We didn't know what was going on. The train to Prague left Teplice at midnight. It was about a quarter to.

We raced round and threw clothes into suitcases – I found out afterwards I'd packed table-napkins instead of handkerchiefs. Guy ran down the corridor and woke the maid and left the radio with her so that she could find out what was happening. We threw our suitcases into the car and I grabbed my little dog Dizzie. We lived on Station Road. We made it to the train.

We reached Prague in the early hours of the morning. We still didn't know what was going on. Guy parked me at a hotel and rushed off to see the British Consul. We had to have visas for whatever countries we were to pass through but we didn't know which they would be. We had no idea which frontiers were open and which were closed. I had a rest and a meal. Guy picked me up late in the morning. He didn't even have time for a cup of coffee. Straight down to the railway station. There was a train leaving at noon. He'd got all our papers in order.

The station was packed. Czechoslovakia was mobilising, soldiers everywhere. The train was crammed with Czech boys, all so excited and thrilled. There was going to be resistance to the Germans. They were going to have the chance to fight.

There were forty-four British residents on the train, and twenty-two of them were journalists. Some of them were from Berlin. They'd moved to Prague because things were getting exciting there and they'd all been staying at the Embassy Hotel. But they didn't *know* anything. It was all rumour and speculation. They kept saying things like, 'Can I quote you?'

Knickerbocker, the famous columnist, was amongst the journalists. And our old friend Stuart Mann, the linguist, appeared. There was a Chinese musician from Hong Kong who held a British passport. He was playing in a band in Prague and he was terribly upset because he'd had to abandon his cello. There was an extraordinary middle-aged English spinster who complained all the way because she'd packed anchovy paste instead of toothpaste. There was a Czech girl who was a British citizen because she was married to an Englishman.

We were pushed into three compartments that were meant to hold a third of that number. It couldn't be helped: the whole train was bursting at the seams. We were jammed in so that you couldn't move either way. I had Dizzie on my knee. We set off eastward right across Czechoslovakia. The Czech-German frontier was closed. The Czech-Polish one was open.

Just as we pulled out, a mass of German planes roared over us. We could see the swastikas on their wings. We all thought 'This is when the bombing starts,' but they passed on overhead. Nobody knew if it was going to be war. It seemed that in twenty-four hours we'd know whether or not. Hitler was due to make an announcement. It was the day of the Munich crisis. I remember thinking as the planes passed, 'What's the good of being frightened, we're all in the same boat.' If you're alone it's very easy to be frightened but if everyone who's with you is in the same danger, the fear is sort of shared out and your share is less.

We moved on, stopping again and again at little stations. At each stop somehow someone would pass Dizzie along and out the window so she could relieve herself. She never made a mess all day.

There was nothing to eat or drink. Most of us had had a meal in Prague but Guy had had nothing to eat since dinner the day before. By eight o'clock at night he was ravenous.

'Hasn't anyone got anything to eat?' he said. 'Anything at all?' Stuart Mann was perched on the seat opposite, his knees bumping against ours.

He said in the very English B.B.C. voice that he'd cultivated, 'Well, I do have some bread in my suitcase up there, but it's rather stale!'

Guy cried, 'My God, man, I don't care how stale it is! Give it to me!'

So Stuart wriggled and managed to stand up and all the other bottoms immediately flowed together like water, filling up the gap. He got his case off the rack and he wriggled and pushed his way back onto the seat. He opened the case and got out a knife and a loaf of bread and started sawing a

144

piece off. He stopped in the middle and said apologetically, 'I'm afraid I'm not cutting it very well!'

Guy yelled at him. 'I don't care how you cut it! Give it to me!'

Finally he got a hunk of dry bread and my poor old man just gobbled it. Then Stuart had to put the suitcase back up again with all the fuss of easing himself out from other people's sit-upons and pushing his way back in again.

After hours and hours of travelling I was desperately anxious to go to the lavatory. I said to Guy, 'I've got to go!' but I didn't have a show of getting through the corridor.

Finally Guy said, 'Right! We'll go.' We both stood up and everything fell into place, and the part where we'd been sitting wasn't there anymore the moment we'd evacuated it. Guy went in front. He was fifteen stone with a forty-four inch chest. The corridors were absolutely jammed but he barged his way through inch by inch and I kept close in his wake and at last he got me through to the lavatory.

In the little cubicle were five Czech soldiers. They were lovely boys, so kind. How they got out of there I don't know, but they did, and they managed to hold the door open for me to get in and to keep it shut till I'd finished. Then, as I came out, they just spilled back in again. One on the seat, another on his lap and another on his lap and the other two wedged into the floor space.

When we got back Guy forced his way on to the seat, compressing the other bodies, and then forced a space for me, and there we were, mission accomplished, a bit more comfortable but not much. The Czech girl looked at me and said sadly, 'Well, if anything happens at least you're with your man. Mine isn't here!'

It was true. Guy was in a marvellous mood, loving, kind, and cheerful. So to me it wasn't a nasty time but a lovely one.

When night came all Czechoslovakia was blacked out. We travelled on hour after hour in pitch darkness. It was a weird feeling, as though all the cities and towns had died. We might have been travelling forever through this dead landscape. And then suddenly we realized we were there. Moravska Ostrava, the Czech town on the Polish frontier that we were headed for. We were piling out when word came down the train: the frontier was closed. We piled in again and the train went on. The next stop was another border town, Cesky Tesin. There across the river were lights cheerfully beaming out from Poland. We could see cafés still open for business. It was three o'clock in the morning. And the frontier was open!

The bridge was no-man's-land. Czech officials at one end of it and Polish at the other. Nobody bothered about our leaving Czechoslovakia but the Czech guards told us, 'Go through if you want to, but go at your own risk. There's been shooting across this bridge every night for the last week.'

We had to go across. A number of men formed up in front in a line with

145

their arms above their heads. 'Wir sind Engländer!' they shouted again and again. And in Polish 'Anglitzki! Anglitzki!'

We were all carrying our luggage, some people had their cases up on their shoulders. The old anchovy paste woman was kicking hers along. I had Dizzie on the lead; she was prancing with delight. It seemed a very long bridge, a long time crossing it.

No one shot at us. We stepped off the bridge and had our papers inspected and stamped and then, oh, what a pleasure it was, we were sitting in a warm lighted café with coffee and food, recovering our senses a bit.

Guy put through a call to the British consul in Warsaw. He must have spread the news because when we arrived there, about midday the next day, there was a group of people to meet us and we had become 'a party of British refugees'. They had prepared a large room in a hotel and got blankets and mattresses and food waiting for us. All the traditional bit. It was the first time I'd ever been a refugee and I felt like a fraud.

Among the people welcoming us was the British correspondent of the London *Times*. His son was training to be a journalist too and he was there on vacation from Oxford. They invited Guy and me to go over to their flat and spend the night there instead of being wrapped up in the refugee blankets.

The father and Guy sat up nearly all night talking. The boy spent his time phoning London and that night he got his first story onto the B.B.C. news. It came over at nine o'clock when we were tuned in. Whatever else was happening in those days you never missed the nine o'clock B.B.C. news.

'Forty-four British residents of Czechoslovakia who escaped under the charge of Captain Guy Morton arrived safely in Warsaw this afternoon,' it said. Or words to that effect. It wasn't strictly true because Guy wasn't really the leader – he just sometimes got pushed to the fore. I'm not sure that escape was exactly the right word either.

From Poland there were two routes back to England. One was safe but long: through Sweden or some Scandinavian country avoiding Germany altogether. The quick route was to go down again through Germany. It was possible because the German-Polish frontier was still open. We didn't know whether it was going to be war, or not, but we'd found out that according to the Geneva Agreement foreign nationals have to be given twenty-four hours to leave an enemy country after a declaration of war.

The party split up. Stuart Mann was in the group that went up through Scandinavia. We never saw him again. Guy and I and eight or nine others travelled down again to Germany. I can't remember that journey at all – we must have slept all the way. We arrived at Friedrichstrasse, one of the two big stations in Berlin, about noon next day. Two and a half days travelling and we were only a few hundred miles from the place we set out from.

We went into the railway café to have a meal while we waited for the next train out. The café was divided into two classes with a door between. We'd just started our meal when a goup of S.S. officers armed with rifles marched in. They stood to attention across the door of the first-class café and across the door of the second-class café and in the doorway in between. We were in the first-class one, right near the door. It was the hour at which Hitler was to make his speech. Was it war or peace?

They turned on the radio and the loudspeakers full-blast. The noise was appalling, a frantic distorted voice. All the Germans at the tables leapt to their feet and stood at attention. We sat still, feeling conspicuous. It was so loud that we couldn't hear a word.

Guy leaned back in his chair and said over his shoulder to the guard, 'Turn it a bit lower, old man. Then we can hear what he's saying!'

The guard shouted, 'Nicht erlaubt!' (Not allowed.)

We shrugged our shoulders and went on eating. It was a dreadful noise, a dreadful atmosphere. The speech went on and on. When it was finished they played the Horst Wessel song and the distortions were worse than ever. All the Germans sprang to the Nazi salute. 'Heil Hitler!' they shouted. It was a horribly menacing moment but exciting too and tense.

When it was finished the S.S. men saluted too and then turned and marched away. We'd heard enough to gather that it wasn't war, not yet anyway. We finished our meal and got ourselves on to the train.

We crossed the Channel from Holland – Flushing to Folkestone. It's longer than the Calais-Dover crossing and they served a meal on board. By this time almost all of us had run out of ready money, and we were hungry again. Guy went off and presented himself to the Captain and the purser. He told them he would take full responsibility and would sign a receipt for dinner for us on behalf of the Foreign Office. So the ten of us had a jolly good meal. Guy was never at a loss.

When we arrived in England one of the first visits we made was to the Foreign Office. In Downing Street across the road and a little along from No. 10.

'I have signed on your behalf,' said Guy, and presented the bill.

'That's quite all right, Captain Morton!'

We had got safely to England, but poor Dizzie wasn't allowed to land. Telegrams flew from Folkestone to London – surely she was a special case. But no, the regulations were adamant. The kindly Captain took charge of her and carried her back with him to Holland.

       ✲   ✲   ✲   ✲

That was a strange week in London. The streets were full of refugees, nervous, furtive-looking people who ducked their heads or turned aside whenever a policeman was passing. They couldn't get over the dread they felt when they saw a uniform, or grasp the fact that the English police were friendly and helpful.

We went to Cook's International Bank to change some money. Guy asked them if they would take in some German marks.

'Marks? Nobody wants them,' they said. 'They're 300 to the pound!'

Chamberlain went to Munich, clutching his umbrella and made his shameful agreement with Hitler. Sudetenland was handed over to Germany. 'Peace in our time,' Chamberlain proclaimed, and the crowds cheered him. For the first time in my life I was ashamed to be British.

Teplice Schönau was now in Nazi territory. We talked over what we should do but I think we both knew from the beginning. We were going back. People depended on us there, all our possessions were there, we made our living there, but those weren't the real reasons. Everyone said we were mad to go, and in a way we were and we knew it. But the thing was it was exciting, it was living. You may as well live while you can.

We went back to Cook's. 'Are marks still 300 to the pound?'

'They are,' said the teller. 'Nobody wants German marks!'

Guy passed him a £5 note. 'Change this for us into marks.'

Flushing. On the wharf to meet us was an enormous Dutch policeman attached by a lead to minute Dizzie, hysterically happy.

We went through Nazi Germany in fine style. We didn't know what might be waiting for us at the other end. Danger can make you gay and reckless. On our £5 of marks we spent money like water staying in the Royal suites of the best hotels.

We went by train through Germany to what had been the Sudetenland frontier of Czechoslovakia. There the train stopped and it seemed as if everything else had stopped there too. There was no one in the German passport-check office. We walked over the 100 yards that used to be no-man's-land to the Czech office. There was one young boy there, bleary-eyed, with a five day growth of beard. All by himself and looking utterly miserable.

We put our passports on the counter. He pushed them back, unopened, unstamped. 'You can do what you like,' he said. 'I don't care. It's not my country any more.' He told us he hadn't had any sleep for five nights.

There was no transport. Sudetenland had been given to Germany but it hadn't yet been occupied. This was no-man's-time – the gap between the old regime and the new. We picked up our suitcases and began to walk. The road was empty. Then we heard the sound of traffic coming and we stepped to the side. It came past us in a steady stream as though it would go on for ever – tanks, lorries – every type of military equipment, being driven away from Czechoslovakia into Germany. Enough equipment, Guy said, for six divisions. I remembered the excitement and joy of the Czech boys on the mobilization train when they believed they were going to have a chance to fight for their country. And the trained hidden companies in the hills in the west, and those aeroplanes all facing Germany. Nothing had come of it all.

The German boys driving the machines looked so pleased with themselves. They looked the way the Czech boys had looked on the train.

You couldn't blame them. *Deutschland Über Alles*! It was their country and they felt about it as the Czechs did about theirs and we did about ours.

Oh, war's a ridiculous human thing!

We turned off into the road through the forest where families and lovers used to picnic on Sundays. The road was barricaded. Large trees from both sides of the road had been cut down alternately so that they lay more than half-way across the road from the left and then more than half-way across the road from the right. No vehicle could have got through. I suppose the Czechs had done it before Sudetenland was signed away.

We gave up the attempt to zig-zag our way through and walked in the forest itself. It was deathly silent. No noise anywhere, not even a bird singing. Only the tiny, fluttery noise of Dizzie dancing along on the pine needles, so happy to be with us again. It was like being in the middle ages all of a sudden. No traffic, no human noise. For two hours we walked on. It was uncanny. But enjoyable too. There was no past and no future. Only the present. And that was silence and emptiness.

After about two hours we suddenly heard *ting-ting-ting*. Just for a moment we didn't know what it was. Then we recognized it. A tram bell! We came out into the road just at the place where we used to enter the forest on the other side on Sundays. And there was one lone tram going right to the station of Teplice Schönau.

We got on it, still with the dog and the one suitcase each that we'd left with. Still with the table-napkins carefully packed instead of handkerchiefs.

Guy handed our money to the conductor. 'Station Road.' He looked us up and down. 'There is no Station Road. There is Hermann Goering Road.' Guy said, curtly, 'Station Road.' The conductor clipped the tickets furiously. 'Hermann Goering Road!' and he thrust them into our hands.

We arrived at the flat. There was my knitting lying on the couch just where I'd put it down in the middle of a row when we heard the broadcast ten days before. The maid was so excited to see us. Her friends had been gathering there at nights, she said, so that they could all listen to the B.B.C. on our radio.

It was a few days before the actual occupation was to take place and they were extraordinary days. It was a different town, utterly different. More than half the shops were closed. The town was like a toothless old man. You'd see one shop open then three gaps. Half of them had *JUDEN* in great big letters splashed crudely across their windows in red paint. Other owners who were Aryan Czechs had just closed up their doors and gone.

All day along Station Road people passed. Cars, carts, wheelbarrows, all laden with luggage, people leaving, walking away. You felt there couldn't be anyone left.

Robert came to see me, terribly excited. He just couldn't wait for the Germans to come. He'd filled in his application form for the German

149

university he wanted to go to and posted it off. Any day he expected to hear he'd been accepted.

I asked him what he thought about the persecution of the Jews. Oh, he had nothing against the Jews, he said. He had quite a lot of friends who were Jews. But when you were all in a crowd it was great fun baiting Jews. You couldn't help but get caught up in the excitement.

The night before the Germans finally came, the stream of wheelbarrow pushers and carts dwindled and dried up. All who were going had gone.

Robert came in glowing. 'I can't stay long. We're going to be out tonight changing all the street names. The new signs are ready! Everything will be in German from now on.'

In the morning flags went up everywhere: German flags, Nazi flags, ordinary, decorative pennants just to look gay and greet the Germans.

'We'll jolly well show them that we're British,' Guy said and we put a Union Jack outside our flat.

'We may as well see what happens!' We went out into the street with the crowd. The Germans were not anti-British at this stage, especially in view of the Munich agreement. Hitler was anxious that nothing should happen to antagonize the British. So in a way we were in a better position than anyone else.

Late in the morning we walked down into Market Square where the crowd was massed. I had Dizzie with me, on a lead. There was a silly idiot of a woman beside me, very, very pro-Nazi. She had a dog with her too and the two dogs sniffed and nuzzled each other and made friends.

'Oh, look,' she cried, 'even the dogs are happy now that our Führer is coming!' That's the sort of hypnotized state the people were in. So stupid!

At about eleven o'clock the planes roared overhead. Then we heard the motor bikes coming and the people were all throwing flowers and waving. The motor-cyclists had wreaths of flowers round their necks and everyone was shouting and cheering. Then came the tanks and the military equipment.

We didn't stay to the end. It was horrible. It just went on and on.

In the afternoon there was great excitement. A procession with Henlein in it, the new Commissar of the new province of Germany, Sudetenland. He went right past down Station Road – Hermann Goering Road. He was standing up in a car acknowledging all the waving and the shouting. He looked up and saw our flag and jerked his head round as he passed, still staring. I hope he didn't think we were greeting him.

We heard a lot of noise going on in the evening but we didn't go out, we'd had enough. The next day Robert called in. He was hilariously happy. He told us that in the evening German military vehicles had drawn up in Market Square with great loads of food on board and they were handing it out to anyone who wanted it.

'I'd had a great big dinner at home,' he told us, 'but I went round and collected three more, anyway.'

Later on we saw in an English paper a photograph of people in Teplice Market Square reaching their hands out for the food the Germans were passing out of their truck. It was published under the captions, 'Germans feeding the starving Czechs'. What rubbish! Czechoslovakia was far better fed than Germany. Any crowd of young people will hold their hands up for free food – it's all part of the fun. Another time I saw the same picture with a caption saying that it was the Czechs welcoming German liberators with a Nazi salute!

That second day of the occupation the papers were taken over by the Nazis and Gestapo-run. Instructions were issued that everyone must read both the morning and the evening papers to see what their orders for the day were. There was a timetable published every day. It might go something like this. 'Men between the ages of 20–25 years inclusive to report for military parade and training at such-and-such a place at 8 a.m. Men between 25 and 30 at 10 a.m. Women aged 15–18 to report at some other place at 8.30 a.m.' And so on. One husband and wife we knew said they had to make appointments to see each other because they were always parading. They were still half laughing about it. They hadn't got to the non-laughing stage yet.

Down Station Road we would hear the awful tramp, tramp, tramp, as this or that group passed singing German songs. The main emphasis was on the young: the Hitler Youth was being pressure-cooked. They had all sorts of activities but the emphasis was always on marching; all working up to an atmosphere of war.

We didn't see Robert for a while. When he did drop in, he looked quite different. He was miserable. He'd found out that his hopes were all astray. He'd received instructions to attend a particular university, not the one of his choice and, he said, he had no time to study and prepare himself for it because the parades took up so much time. He had to give up his English lessons altogether. There was no time for private interests. Once or twice more he came to see me but all his sparkle had gone. He had idolized Hitler. The reality of a dictatorship was far more of a shock to him than it was to those who knew what to expect.

We didn't stay long after the occupation. The town had changed completely. It was as uncanny as that walk through the forest. From being a cheerful, bustling little place where people like the judge and his family were leading happy civilized lives there was now all this marching and parade times and windows smashed all over town where Jews lived or worked, the papers controlled and people disappearing and everyone afraid to say a word. The slightest criticism, the most casual word, could be reported back and you'd be in the Gestapo's clutches. No trial of course. Just the shattering thump, thump, thump on your door in the middle of the night and you disappeared – sometimes forever.

Our pupils stopped coming to the flat – they were afraid that that would

151

rouse suspicions. Guy met people secretly or in apparently casual encounters. I didn't know much of what was going on because it was all illegal now and for my own safety I was kept in the dark.

Of our old friends, the Drapers had gone. A day or so before the occupation we saw them struggling down to the station each lugging a suitcase – no taxis for Jews! The flat upstairs was empty though their furniture was all still there. They hadn't been able to get it moved. They had left a key to the flat with Guy.

Mr Hammer of the linoleum factory had realized that he must get out. The Germans had put a Nazi party-member into the factory. Hammer knew that once he had learned the business it would be taken over. We looked for a place for him to go. We combed the encyclopaedias and found that New Zealand imported all its linoleum at this time though it had all the resources that Hammer told us were necessary for manufacture.

Guy wrote to the New Zealand government explaining that here was a man with the technical knowledge and all the necessary machinery who could give occupation to a hundred men if he were allowed to immigrate and start up a business there. We waited and waited but for a long time no answer came.

In the meantime little Zimmer was in the same position. At first he felt safe. He wasn't exactly popular with the Germans but they needed him, he was an expert on ceramics. But soon after the occupation he realized that there was a German stooge in the factory who was learning – and in the fast efficient German way – exactly how to manage the factory. Something happened one day that convinced Zimmer that his time was running out. He managed to contact Guy and they had lunch together, apparently casually, at a café. They came back to the flat still working out what could be done. I was out at the time – thank goodness!

Suddenly there was a loud knocking on the door. Guy opened it. Two Gestapo men were there.

'Do you know a man called Zimmer?' they asked.

'Zimmer? Zimmer? Yes, I've had two pupils of that name,' Guy said affably. 'But let's not stand here talking about it. Do come in and sit down.'

He led them into a room next to the one where Zimmer was hiding.

'The Zimmer we are enquiring for owns a ceramics factory and he was seen in your company today.'

'Oh, *that* Zimmer!' Guy said. 'Yes, he is doing very well. He tries hard but he is still apt to place the verb at the end of the sentence. It's a common fault – German syntax you know. Still I was able to tell him today – I ran into him at lunch you know – that he is definitely improving.'

'He is wanted for questioning,' the Gestapo man said. 'We believe he is in this flat. If you attempt to conceal his presence you are guilty of conspiracy against the Reich.'

'Oh, my dear fellows', Guy said, all concern and amazement, 'I wouldn't dream of such a thing. If he is here, he's here without my knowledge, but I'm sure you must be mistaken. Still, let's have a good look. Surely he wouldn't break into my flat. He seems such a pleasant little fellow! Still you never know, do you?'

He led them into the passage talking loudly all the way and opened the door of the room where he'd left Zimmer. You remember how our flat was all connected with interior doors? Zimmer of course had nipped through to the room they'd just come out of. They went all over the flat that way and then back to the original room. Zimmer wasn't there either of course.

All the Germans were being very nice to the English at this stage. They'd been told to do nothing to antagonize us. The Gestapo men actually apologized when they went away. Guy had enjoyed himself immensely. It was just the sort of situation he loved.

We had a tense evening. Just before midnight Guy went out with a suitcase. The flat didn't seem to be being watched. Zimmer followed him and they went together to the station. Guy bought a ticket and got on the train to Prague. He stood on the train platform while Zimmer waved and called out various goodbyes. Just as the train began to move Guy hopped off and Zimmer jumped on.

We'd just got to bed when the thunderous knocking came again on the door. Guy went to the door in his dressing-gown pretending he was terribly sleepy.

The S.S. men pushed in aggressively this time. 'We know that the man Zimmer is here!' they said.

Guy said, 'Not again.' He told them he admired their devotion to duty – at one o'clock in the morning. They shoved past him and began searching. This time they realized that all the rooms were connected. They consulted together and tried to make a plan but they ended up dashing in and out of rooms like an old-time comedy film. When they'd finally convinced themselves that Zimmer wasn't there they began to question Guy. 'We believe you have knowledge of his whereabouts.'

Thank goodness we were English. If we'd been Czech, or German even, Guy would have been taken to headquarters and beaten up.

Guy was still pretending to be helpful but with an air of injured innocence. 'I can't think of anything he said at lunch that would help you. Or did he? Let's all have a cup of coffee – it'll wake me up.'

They didn't want coffee. 'Are you sure? Perhaps you'd prefer a drink. No? You won't mind if I make myself a cup will you? I really am a bit confused by all this.'

He made himself coffee and began recalling ponderously a fictitious conversation he'd had with Zimmer at lunch, all about obscure points of syntax and grammar and the meaning of words. They must have felt ready to murder him. All the time he was surreptitiously keeping an eye on the clock. When it was well after two, he suddenly struck his forehead and cried, 'Of course, I remember! He said he would buy the book tomorrow.' This was a book on English grammar that Guy pretended he'd

153

recommended to him. 'He couldn't get that in Teplice. He must be going to Prague. What time does the train leave? Oh, my dear fellows, what a shame! You've missed him. He'll be there by now!'

Prague was beyond the new frontier, still Czech and free.

*　　*　　*　　*

A week or so later we were woken again by the knocking in the night. It's a shocking way to wake up. You've no idea how frightening that thunderous banging is. I daren't think what it must have been like for people who were really in the Gestapo's power.

It wasn't at our door.

'Guy', I said, 'listen! It's upstairs at the Drapers' flat.' We got into our dressing-gowns and went into the big hall that the stairs led out of. The elder Draper sister was coming downstairs with one Gestapo man in front of her and another behind. She was walking very erect, her head held high.

Guy stepped forward to speak to her but she turned her head away, the complete snub, and walked on with her escort. After they'd all gone Guy went up to the flat, we had a key to it. There were clothes laid out on the bed and an open suitcase. We realized that she must have sneaked back to try to retrieve some of the things they'd abandoned. Winter was closing in; they probably needed warmer clothes.

Later we got a letter from the Drapers. They were all in Prague. The Gestapo had released the elder sister after questioning. They were trying to get to South America, they said, and as it was now clear that they could not avail themselves of any of the furniture or possessions in the flat they would be delighted if we would help ourselves to anything we liked. They would like us to regard it as a gift of appreciation for past kindnesses. The elder sister, in her gentle way, apologized for her rudeness in not acknowledging Guy on the night of her arrest. She had not wanted to involve us in any unpleasantness.

By this time we had realized that it was hopeless trying to work in Teplice. You can't help people escape when you're in prison yourself. And that's what Teplice was like – a prison. We were conspicuous too in a town of that size. We'd made up our minds to go to Prague.

Guy said, 'Let's take the Drapers' furniture with us. If they do get away to South America at least they can sell it before they go, and get the value of it.' As English people we had no trouble getting a Gestapo permit to leave Sudetenland.

We packed up the flat and booked a furniture van to take our furniture across the new frontier of Czechoslovakia and into Prague. It was supposed to arrive at seven o'clock in the morning. It didn't. At nine o'clock the driver arrived to tell us that he hadn't been able to get a permit to take our stuff across the frontier, but they had told him to call again the next day at the Gestapo office. But the next day the same thing happened.

We tried a different removal firm. The same thing over again – come back tomorrow.

It was fairly obvious what was happening. Ever since the Zimmer episode the Gestapo had wanted to get us. I don't think they had proper evidence that we'd broken the law of the country and without that evidence they couldn't attack English people or deny us a permit to leave but they could prevent us taking our possessions and maybe while we waited for the permit we'd give ourselves away. They may even have guessed that we'd take the Draper furniture with us.

Guy was a stubborn man. 'I'm not going without the furniture,' he said. 'I'll sit them out.'

It was then that I had a brainwave – one of the two good ones I've had in my life. 'Suppose I go to Prague,' I said, 'and hire a furniture van there. I'll get the Czech permits and it can go into Teplice as though it's delivering some stuff there. Then surely the Gestapo won't question its coming out again.'

It seemed a good idea. Guy saw me off at the frontier. It was terrible. There were people with all their possessions tied up in bundles with shawls, people with sacks over their shoulders, with old shabby suitcases and smart new leather ones. There were Gestapo people with swastikas on their arms, women with tiny babies, old people, children. I was jammed in, I couldn't get through the crowd, and Guy as usual with his big shoulders made a passage for me.

I had to travel by bus. Armed German guards were at the barrier going through everyone's possessions – bundles, suitcases, purses. People kept being turned back by the guards and arguing with them or beginning to cry. If you were a Jew it was just death to be turned back because you couldn't get a job in German territory – it was forbidden to employ Jews and you couldn't get charity, even apply for it. That was forbidden too. And what money you had would sooner or later be confiscated. I got through easily enough of course with a British passport.

On the bus there were two young Nazis wearing swastikas on their lapels. Just before we got into Prague they took them off and pinned them underneath the lapels. The Fifth Column moving in. There were a lot of spies around at that time.

A lot of people we knew were already sheltering in Prague by this time, so I had no trouble getting a bed for a few nights and somehow or other, by sheer luck, I managed to find a flat, a little one, about three rooms and kitchen and maid's quarters. I got hold of a Czech furniture removal company, got permits from Prague to go to Teplice, paid them for the return journey and with no hold-ups they collected our furniture and most of the Drapers', and Guy himself, and dropped everything off at our new flat. Mission accomplished.

We went to visit the Drapers. They were in a part of Prague we hadn't seen. A big four-storeyed building with doors right on the pavement in a

155

street of such buildings. We went up three flights of stairs and into a room. It was like an old-fashioned hospital ward but dirty and messy. Rows of beds with tiny tables beside them with cooking stoves on them. Clothes all hanging from nails in the walls. There was an old man in one bed coughing and coughing, as sick as could be. Children, young girls, families. Little bits of food being cooked up all over the room.

We went through that to another room the same, and then another and another. In the fourth room we found the Drapers. These lovely people from their lovely, orderly, gentle home, living in that dreadful place. They hadn't changed at all. They welcomed us graciously and were so nice to us and to each other. And very grateful to us for what we'd done.

Of course the furniture was no use to them. I hope they were able to sell it and get some money. I hope they got away. I think they were still there when we left Prague. I can't bear to think of it, what might have happened to those gentle people.

We'd been busy in Uzhorod and in Teplice but it was nothing like Prague. Right from the beginning people swarmed to us. Half my time was spent fixing appointments for them to see Guy. I couldn't teach language in the proper way any longer – meaning, syntax, grammar. It was just words and phrases all the time, learned by heart, parrot-fashion. The exact words you needed at a frontier, to identify yourself, to ask directions, to buy food.

A woman came in and tried to give me a six-month-old baby. 'Take her!' she said. 'Have her as yours. Take her to England!' What could I do? How could I take over a six-month-old baby? Once we took one we would have been inundated. It was the most terrible refusal I ever had to give.

A lot of people were anxious to go to America. Guy called on the American ambassador and we were both invited to have afternoon tea there and tell them about our work. We went through nine reception rooms each leading out of the next. For entertaining ambassadorial style. In the ninth were the ambassador and his wife and a secretary and his wife and child. They wanted to know everything and all the time they were asking what could they do to help.

The British consul was quite different. A very cautious gentleman indeed.

It was about this time that Guy managed a very stylish Pimpernel-type rescue. When we were in Sudetenland we'd been in touch with a Jewish family who had a little daughter, Julie. There wasn't much chance of the parents getting out, so with much heart-break they had put Julie up for adoption. We sent her photograph to Mrs Roger Smith and in due course she found adoptive parents willing to take her. Then came the Munich agreement and the part of Czechoslovakia where Julie lived became a province of Germany. It seemed impossible now to get her away. When we were in Prague we got a telegram from the family, 'Julie arrested.' She was five years old!

156

Guy decided he'd go down and see what could be done. He knew he might be involved in something illegal so it wouldn't be wise to use his own identity. A travelling brush salesman had left a handful of leaflets and price lists at our flat and they happened to be from an English firm. Guy posed as the firm's overseas representative, dressing himself up very correctly in a dark grey three-piece suit, and carrying a leather brief case with the pamphlets in it. Off he went on the train. He had no trouble getting across the Czech frontier but when a few minutes later the train had crossed no-man's-land and the German guard came in checking passes and passports, it was a different story.

Guy produced his travelling permit but not his passport. He pretended that he couldn't speak a word of German. He told the guard in English that he was such-and-such a firm's overseas representative and whatever the guard said he kept waving his bundle of leaflets and his travel permit under his nose. The guard couldn't get it through to him at all that he wanted his passport. Finally Guy heard him mutter, 'Verdammter Engländer!' and he stamped his permit letting him into the occupied zone.

When he got to the house where Julie lived he found she'd been returned to her family. The story was this. When Sudetenland was given away the new frontier ran through this particular town dividing the house where Julie lived from her uncle's house that was in the Czech zone. The family had a very good maid, a Czech girl, intelligent, and full of character. She began taking Julie for a walk every day. She chatted up the German guards who were watching the frontier. One day she said to them, 'Couldn't I take the little girl across to see her uncle! She's that fond of him! I'll be back, you know me!'

'Mind you are!' they said and let her through.

She did this to or three times. When she'd got them used to the routine she came back one day a little later than usual. It was getting dark. 'It's me!' she called out to the guards.

'Where's the child?' they said.

'Oh well,' she said, 'she's scared of the dark. You know what kids are! Such a performance! So I had to leave her there for the night. I'll fetch her in the morning.'

'Verboten,' said the guard.

They didn't arrest the girl but they went into the Czech zone and arrested Julie. Illegal exit and entry! After a while she was returned, very frightened but unharmed. The family were threatened with the most dire consequences if they ever tried a trick like that again. And they were watched from then on.

Guy stayed with them all day talking. When the time came for him to go back in the evening the whole family came to the station to see him off except Julie and the maid. The trains there were corridor trains. They had doors into little compartments, with seats on each side facing each other, and a hook in each corner where passengers could hang their coats.

Guy leaned out of the window, his big shoulders filling the frame, and said enthusiastic and individual goodbyes to father, mother, grandfather – all of them. Then the whistle blew and the train started and after a few minutes the German frontier guard came through.

Guy went through the same routine – an Englishman, no German, couldn't understand a word the guard said to him and the brush pamphlets waved about. This guard too cursed the English and finally took himself off muttering. A few minutes across no man's land then the Czech guard made his rounds and Guy produced his passport and had it stamped. They were safely in Czechoslovakia.

'Come on, Julie, you can come out now,' he said. The maid had gone round the back of the train over the rails while they were all saying goodbye and had managed to stow her under Guy's hanging overcoat and to get off the train herself.

That five-year-old child had stood for a quarter of an hour completely hidden without making one sound. She lay on his knee and slept all the way to Prague and within a few days she was on her way to England. All that part was legal, her adoption papers were signed.

When we were in that flat Guy was very busy one day in one room taking details from a lot of people and I was working in another, when the maid came in and said there were two women to see me. She brought them in and one was – guess who – Gertie! Dressed up to the nines, if you please! The friend who was with her I'd met before: she was rather nice.

Gertie asked me in English if she could see Guy.

'He's busy at the moment,' I said. 'He can't see anyone.'

She turned to the other woman and said in German. 'She doesn't understand a word I'm saying, so I may as well tell you that he . . .'.

I interrupted. 'Excuse me, I understand very well what you are saying. You are not welcome in my house.' I said it in German. I was fluent and correct.

I turned to the other woman and said, 'If you would care to wait I'll take you in to see my husband as soon as he is free.'

I rang for the maid and when she came I said, still in German, 'This lady is just leaving. Will you show her out?'

Gertie's face was a reward for all that I'd suffered from her. I never saw her again but quite a lot of telephone calls came. If I answered the phone it would be slammed down; if Guy answered there'd be a long conversation and I could tell from his voice that he was talking to Gertie. Often after such conversations Guy would go out for a while. I think he was helping her. Gertie did get out of the country in the end to South America. I never asked any questions.

About this time another character came strolling into our lives. Have you ever had a strange cat wander in the door and sit down by the fireplace as cosy as you please and then later just get up and stroll away again? That's what it was like with Freddie. He was an English chap, plump, unmarried, about twenty-five or so, and the quaintest soul you ever met. He was living in a village somewhere out of Prague teaching English to little boys.

We were the only English people that he knew around Prague, and once a fortnight or so he'd come wandering in to visit us. Once we said, 'Stay the weekend, Freddie,' and he did. The next morning he came strolling through to our bedroom to see if we were awake. We were and he hopped into bed between us, and told us the story of his life.

His father was a master baker in England and Freddie was brought up to take over the business. His father wanted him to know every facet of the trade so he sent him to Canada to study wheat growing. Freddie wasn't much interested in the baking trade and he wasn't much interested in wheat growing in Canada but he did meet a girl there that he rather liked.

When he went home again his father put him into another branch of the trade to get to know it but he still wasn't much interested so he wandered off to the Continent. All day we struggled with the dreadful tragedies of refugees from concentration camps and pogroms. And here in bed between us was this plump and mild refugee from the bakery business. He'd drifted into Czechoslovakia and there he'd found people came to him and said, 'Teach me English.' So he'd just stayed there and taught. And there he'd found his vocation. What he was interested in was teaching children.

One evening when Guy was out Freddie was sitting talking to me. 'You know that girl I met in Canada?' Mary her name was and he hadn't seen her for two years or written to her at all. 'I think I'd rather like to marry her.'

Perhaps seeing us married had given him ideas. Maybe he thought it would be rather nice to have a bed of his own instead of being the one in the middle.

'Do you think that would be a good idea?' he said.

'Yes, it'd be fine. Company for you.'

'That's what I thought,' he said, nodding very sagely. 'I'll write to her and ask her.' And he strolled mildly away to do that.

We were so busy now with the real refugees that we couldn't keep up with the demand. We had the offer of another flat, a big very modern luxurious one on the banks of the river Moldau near the Charles bridge. We grabbed it and got an option on the flat next door.

The next time Guy went to England he advertised for two secretaries there and out of the rush of applicants he picked two to help us. Nowell had just come down from Oxford; Roy hadn't long left school but he had a respectable knowledge of German. They were thrilled of course – off on a real live adventure. We installed them in the flat next door and got two maids to run the double household.

Anna, the older one, was a dear. A Czech peasant woman of about fifty, a steady, hard-working, grandmotherly person and a wonderful cook. Much of her day was spent showing people in and out. She was appalled at the people who came and the stories they had to tell.

'Jesus Maria!' she'd say in pity and horror, 'Jesus Maria!' And if it were very, very bad, 'Jesus Maria and Joseph!' We all got in the habit of saying that partly in fun and partly in despair.

The other maid was Maria. She was much younger and none of us trusted her entirely, Anna least of all.

Our days fell into a pattern. The four of us – Nowell, Roy, Guy, and I – would have breakfast together in the morning, then at nine o'clock, we'd open our doors for business. People poured in all day. The three men each had a room to work in. I went to and fro amongst them, deciding which were the difficult cases, where maybe we'd have to do something risky, and referring them to Guy. I kept an eye on the boys, translating for them when their German failed them, and checking over the records to see that all the details were there. Guy kept no records of the difficult cases – too dangerous. He had a wonderful memory and he stored all the details there. That's one of the reasons why there was so much went on that I don't know about. It was never written down at all.

We never paused all day. Sometimes someone would grab a moment between writing and interviewing and would dash out for something. Or Anna or Maria would bring a tray of coffee and sandwiches. It was terribly exhausting but you didn't think of that. All you felt was this terrible urgency.

That winter they held the world skating championships on the frozen River Moldau, not far from our flat. The tune that was popular was the 'Donkey Serenade'. There was a lot of noise and that tinkly tune would sound over and over again. Even now I can't hear it without a rush of the old feeling – the desperation and the comradeship.

At nine o'clock sharp we shut up shop and listened to the B.B.C. news. We never let Anna and Maria cook a meal for us at night – they were working so hard all day. As soon as the news was over we'd go into town and have a meal, a different place each night – wonderful food and gay surroundings. We'd go to cabarets or nightclubs or sometimes to the films or the theatre. Anything to let tension go completely out of your mind. We couldn't have kept going otherwise. Wonderful cabarets they had in Prague that year and people flocked to them just to be able to forget for an hour or two.

It was a race against time. Everyone knew that Hitler was going to take over the rest of Czechoslovakia. After Sudetenland the message was clear. Nothing and no-one was going to stop him. It wasn't just people we were getting out but their valuables as well, gold and jewels, anything people could live on in a new land. Every time Guy went to England he'd smuggle stuff through with him. He never wrote down any names and if the things were found by customs officers – well, Guy could always spin a good story. When he got to England he deposited each piece in Cook's Bank in the name of the owner. He never made a single mistake.

160

It was mainly the rich who got away, wealthy people who'd stashed away funds in foreign banks. Often we'd say to them, 'Yes, we'll help you provided you pay for one other person who hasn't any money.' Usually they did but there was one man, fabulously wealthy, who refused to pay for anyone who wasn't a relative. I was disgusted with him.

Ourselves, we were showered with presents. When people were leaving they would come and say, 'I can never use this again and I can't take it with me. Please accept it with my gratitude.' We had suites of furniture given us, exquisite Lalique glass, Meissen and Dresden china, all sorts of things. Someone gave us a Ford V8 de luxe, almost new. And the boxes of chocolates and flowers that came my way almost every day! People imagined that by making up to Guy's wife they'd get more help. It was rubbish. We were giving all we were capable of.

One man owned a clothing factory and the four-storeyed building that housed it. He was a Jew and he knew when the Nazis came it would be taken from him. He got it all transferred to Guy, registered in his name. Why should the Nazis have it! And he was worried about the jobs of the people who worked for him. He was a wealthy man and we got him out quite easily.

The factory brought in £100 cash profit a day. Every week someone would arrive with the takings. Guy used to shove the money into a safe we had there and we drew on it for getting people away who couldn't pay for themselves. Once Nowell and Roy decided to count the money in the safe. It took them three hours. There were 3,000,000 Czech crowns.

It was no good accumulating money. Guy knew that none of us would be able to take that with us when we went. When the safe got too full, or the flat too cluttered with gifts, he'd make a clearance and go out and buy a genuine Persian carpet. He said they'd hold their value anywhere in the world. The flats had lovely parquet floors but we covered them with Persian carpets, two deep in some rooms, and we hung them from the walls. In the end we had twenty-two of them – fabulously beautiful and expensive.

We owned seven cars. Three belonged to the factory, Guy had an air-cooled Tatra that he used when he had to drive children across Europe; there was the V8 and one that Nowell used that we'd acquired somewhere or other, and for my birthday that year Guy gave me a Jaguar. They were a new type then. I had a Standard Swallow – the S.S. Jaguar. It was white with green leather upholstery. I had a loose driving coat made to match. The last thing I did in Prague was pay the dressmaker's bill for that coat as I was leaving.

We lost one of the cars – a sacrifice to friendship but an accidental one. Freddie still wandered in regularly. Nowell and Roy accepted him as we did as a sort of household pet. He always got a welcome and if we were all too busy to talk he settled down just as happily in the kitchen with Anna and Maria and they chatted to him and fed him tea and cakes.

161

One day he came and said, 'You know that girl in Canada? She says she'll marry me. Now I can't remember what she looks like. What'll I do?' He pondered the problem for a minute or two, then he brightened up. 'I know, I'll ask her to send me a photo.'

In due course the photo came and a sweet little face it was. So he wrote and told her to get on the boat and he'd meet her in France at Cherbourg. Then he looked thoughtful and asked us, 'How will I get her from Cherbourg?'

'Well, take one of the cars if you like,' Guy said. Freddie could drive, he'd driven quite a lot in London.

In due course she arrived and they got married right away. Freddie had a one-roomed flat. Now he rented the one next door as well and set up house keeping. It was quite cosy and nice. Mary was a quiet little Canadian girl – very shy and very unsophisticated.

A little while after they were married Freddie came to see me alone. He said he wasn't quite sure about things.

'What things?' I said.

'Women,' he said and, as an afterthought, 'and marriage.'

'Let's go down to a café,' I said, 'and I'll fill in some of the details.' So we had a cup of coffee right away from everyone else and I told him what he should know. Later he told me that had made all the difference.

But he never did bring the car back. He obviously thought that Guy had given it to him outright and nobody had the heart to disillusion him. In a way it was just as well because before he had a car of his own one or other of us would quite often drive Freddie home when he'd been to see us. And that was rather a trying business. Freddie had one flaw – a very weak bladder. He'd only got to look at a bush and we had to stop. 'I've gone all Freddie,' was our euphemism for wanting to go to the lavatory.

Freddie was a homely sort of light relief and we loved him for it. There were times when you had to get away – when one or other of us would rush out and go to the pictures, do something silly, anything to let the tension go.

Guy was constantly on the move, collecting people, transporting them, organizing, planning. I didn't know half of what was going on. Sometimes he took Nowell with him, sometimes me. Once I went with him on a very routine trip to Brno to contact someone who needed help. We drove there calmly and peacefully and did the job. Outside our hotel there were some German soldiers marching about doing the goose step. That was an unusual sight to see in unoccupied Czechoslovakia. I had my movie camera with me and I took some shots of them. They came up to me and confiscated the camera and I never got it back – camera, film or anything.

In the hotel we went into the lift. 'Heil Hitler!' said the liftman, giving the Nazi salute. When we were between floors Guy said, 'You're a Czech aren't you? What on earth are you heiling Hitler for?'

'Sh . . . sh!' he said. 'You have to now!'

162

'Well, heil George the Sixth!' said Guy.

The next morning we started driving back to Prague and on the way there were six new road blocks where we had to present our passports and have them checked and stamped, frontier style. The day before it had just been an ordinary winding road. Now it seemed they had drawn a straight line across the map and said, 'This is the new frontier!' The Germans were just doing anything they liked – there was no one to protest. There were no foreigners or newsmen about and Czechoslovakia had been so weakened and betrayed. As we got near Prague it was evening.

'What's the matter with Prague?' I said. 'It looks different.' There was a sort of red glow about it that wasn't the sunset. We looked and looked and finally Guy said, 'My God, they're Nazi flags!' They were hanging from the tops of some of the buildings – great strips of red, four or five yards wide with swastikas on them. Hanging down five, six, seven storeys.

'What's happened?' we said to each other. 'Whatever's happened?'

We drove on in and it seemed, apart from the flags, everything was just the same. When we got home the boys could tell us nothing so we went to bed still wondering.

I dreamed that two women were standing by our bed pulling off their rings and bracelets and earrings and throwing them down on to the eiderdown.

I woke up and it was true. They were the Jewish women from the flat upstairs.

'Please take them!' they were saying. 'Please rescue them!'

Guy grunted sleepily, 'Go away! We don't start work till nine.'

'But they're here!' they cried, 'they're here! They're here! They're here!'

'Oh, go away! Don't be so silly,' Guy said getting irritated.

'Look out of the window!' they cried. 'They're here! They've come!'

We hauled ourselves awake and stumbled across to the window. Planes were roaring overhead. On the road across the river the motorbikes were passing. Behind them came the military cars and then the tanks. As far as you could see they were streaming endlessly straight into Prague. It was half-past six in the morning.

We didn't go out to watch them come in. There was nothing to do or say. We knew it would happen. It had happened.

We heard afterwards that Hitler had sent for President Hacha, that they had bullied and threatened him all night; they would utterly destroy Czechoslovakia if he didn't sign a document inviting the Germans to come in and 'protect' the country. Hacha held out. Some people say he was tortured and drugged. Ultimately he signed. I've read some history books where it says he signed the document at eight o'clock in the morning and that then Hitler's massed army poured over the frontier. Either he signed earlier than that or the army was sent in before he signed. I know what time I saw them coming into Prague.

Hitler arrived that day to enter the city in a ceremonial way. He went straight up to Wenceslaus Palace. The people were stunned. They just stood in the streets and looked. It was such an unwelcoming welcome, so different from Sudetenland that he went away again after a couple of days.

That day, the day of the occupation, Dizzie went missing. I was terribly worried; it seemed part of the sinister atmosphere. Guy looked at his watch and said, 'They'll still be accepting advertisements for tonight's evening paper. Let's put in an advertisement right away. If we offer a substantial reward we'll be sure to get her back.'

We drove straight down to the newspaper office, wrote out the advertisement and handed it in.

'I'm sorry, this cannot be inserted today,' said the man in the office. We were indignant – weren't we in time?

The man looked embarrassed. 'The paper has already been read and passed for publication. No change at all is possible now.'

'Who has passed it for publication?' Guy asked.

'The German authorities. It is the law now.'

I said, 'Suppose Hitler died right now? Could you print that?'

He looked round him, horrified, then he twinkled at us but he didn't say a word.

We went straight to a printing office, had a hundred posters printed immediately, describing Dizzie and offering a hundred crowns reward. We paid a man to distribute them all over the part of Prague where we lived. Dizzie was returned that night.

The occupation didn't make much difference to our lives. We were busier than ever. There was always a queue of people waiting before we opened our doors in the morning and it was a dreadful business sending people away so that we could close at night. More of the escapes we engineered were illegal, but the routine was just the same.

Do you remember how, when we were in Warsaw, Guy sat up all night, nearly, talking with the correspondent of *The Times*? I think it was then that he laid the foundation of an underground route out across the Polish frontier. He used it for some people if all else had failed. It was a dangerous business for the people who made the crossing and everyone who helped them. It involved passwords, forged documents, illegal entry – the lot.

Before Guy would even whisper a word of that way out he had to make sure that the person wanting help was genuine. After the occupation Nazi spies swarmed round us like house flies. If they once found us doing anything illegal they could have had us in a concentration camp before you could turn round. It was illegal to help any man of military age to leave the country, so when a young man came we had to be extra careful – if he was a Nazi spy and we didn't spot it and agreed to help him out, we were done for.

Guy had a friend, the Baron, who was useful that way. He was a genuine baron and a very nice person who hated the Nazis. He was pure Aryan, but he was tall and dark with a big nose and you would have sworn he was a Jew. If someone came in for help, a young man of military age, I would make an appointment for him to see Guy later on and we'd make sure that the Baron was around when he came. While Guy was conducting the interview he would press a buzzer under the desk and the Baron would come in wearing a chauffeur's uniform. The Baron had an infallible instinct. He could always tell Nazi sympathizers by the way they reacted to him, thinking he was a Jew. No matter how they tried to disguise it, he said, their contempt and disgust showed through.

He and Guy had worked out a system of communication. Guy would ask him if the car was available. If the Baron said yes, it meant that the person Guy was interviewing was genuine. If he said, 'I'm sorry sir, it's not back from the garage yet,' Guy would dismiss him and say to the young man, 'But my dear fellow, it's impossible to help you. Don't you know it's against the law?'

As well as having to be genuine, people had to be fit and young to try the Polish route. It was over rough, hilly country and they had to go on a dark night.

Once we broke that rule. A middle-aged Jew came in, rather overweight from a sedentary job. He was in desperate danger. The Gestapo were on to him and he knew he was headed for the concentration camp. There was no way of getting him out except by the illegal frontier crossing. I was in Guy's study the day he left. He took my hand and said, 'Madam, I thank you. Whatever happens, I thank you for all you have done and have tried to do for me. Please accept this as a token of my gratitude.' And he gave me his fountain pen. It was pure gold, eighteen carat. Only last year I gave it to my son as one of the only valuables I possess – a kind of heirloom.

That man didn't get through. He was to attempt the crossing with a party of young people. We found out later that they all got over the frontier. Then the moon came out and the Germans saw them. They all ran, but it was straight up hill and he was too fat to keep up. He was shot. I suppose there was nothing anyone could do to go back and save him. It's a bad memory to have – that we sent him to his death. But I think it might have been better to die that way than in a concentration camp. A quicker death.

Sometimes it seemed so unfair. We all liked that man and he died. There was another that we saved about the same time. His name was Braun and he was really well off. He had enough money to live in England – or anywhere else – without working. He'd been stashing money away in a Swiss bank for ages. The only problem was how to get him out because he was a Jew and couldn't travel. Guy bought a ticket and booked a seat on a plane, had his passport checked and went and sat in the plane. Braun wandered out across the tarmac (they weren't so strict in those days), ostensibly seeing him off. Just before they took the steps away Guy strolled down and spoke to him. Then Braun went up and Guy walked away. It was surprising how often it was possible to use that simple trick.

165

Some time later his mother old Mrs Braun arrived at the flat lugging a great big suitcase. We were frantically busy with all sorts of desperate, urgent people. Mrs Braun came to me and said, 'Here ·- my family silver. Please send it to England for me.'

I said, 'We can't possibly do that.' It was such a bulky great suitcase we wouldn't have had a chance. 'We'll be lucky,' I told her, 'if we manage to get any of our own stuff out.'

The old lady went straight through the flat and walked into Guy's study in the middle of an interview.

'Oh, all right! Leave it there,' Guy said when she asked him. He knew we couldn't do anything with it, but it was easier to agree than to argue. When we closed for the day there was this great elephant of a suitcase standing there. There was a high cupboard in the passage over the kitchen door. Guy just shoved the case in there and we forgot about it. It might be there to this day.

Months later, after we were in New Zealand, a policeman called on us. He said they had had a letter from England and they had to investigate. A man named Braun alleged that he had given property to a man named Morton who had refused to return it. I told them the whole story and I wrote a letter to Mr Braun – they had his address.

I said, 'If only we could put you right back where we rescued you from and take someone else instead. Someone who wouldn't turn like that and accuse those who saved him.'

The person I had most in mind when I wrote that was our friend Mr Hammer, the owner of the linoleum factory in Teplice. We had moved to Prague before we got a reply back from the New Zealand government to our suggestion that he be allowed to set up a factory there. It was uncompromising. No, they didn't want him. We wrote again just the same – what else was there for him? By this time we knew he wouldn't be able to get his machines out: the Nazis were obviously preparing to take over his factory. But he might still be able to get away himself if he were sponsored by a country willing to receive him. We were sure he would be an asset to any country. The answer came just one day before Hammer came to see us in Prague. Again he was refused.

We didn't tell him what was in that letter because it no longer mattered. He looked terrible. He was very pale but he still had an awkward smile on his face. He was a very brave man. He told us that the Germans had sent for him – called him into his own office where he was manager and owner. A young Nazi was sitting in his chair and Hammer stood in front of him.

He was told, 'We have decided that we will buy your factory.' Hammer waited cautiously.

'We will pay you three million Czech crowns.'

Hammer couldn't believe his ears. That was just about what the factory was worth. With that amount of money he would be sure to be able to get away.

'There is just one thing.'

'Yes?'

The young Nazi stood up and yelled. 'This factory has been owned by a filthy Jew. We will have to clean every inch of it before decent people can work here. And that is going to cost you three million crowns.'

Hammer told us that and he laughed. 'So here I am you see with nothing. I have come to say goodbye and thanks for what you have tried to do for me.' He shook hands with us and left.

We knew what it meant. Suicide. He was not allowed to work and earn money – he was a Jew. He was not allowed to receive charity – he was a Jew. We didn't tell him he'd been refused entry into New Zealand.

Luckily he had no family.

It wasn't only Jews that we helped. The strangest case we dealt with I suppose was the case of sixty-three. Before the occupation Czechoslovakia had managed to make an agreement with Hitler. One train every week was allowed to travel through Germany sealed. People got on to it in Prague and their papers were checked there. Before it drew out the doors were locked. They weren't unlocked till it had reached France – nobody got on or off the train while it passed through Germany. What it meant was that each week a small handful of Czechs could travel to the coast without Nazi interference.

A group of sixty-three people had fled from Germany to Czechoslovakia before the occupation. They all hated Nazism and had said so. In Czechoslovakia they had got themselves organized to travel on this train. They were going as a group out to Canada where they had bought a farm. They had been planning the enterprise for a long time and at last they were ready to go. All that was still needed was the signature of the British Consul on their visas, since they were going via England.

The leaders of the party, a young married couple, had gathered up all the papers and passed them into the consulate one afternoon. They were to collect them again in the morning. The train was due to leave that day.

They woke up in the morning to find Prague occupied. The leaders rushed round to the consulate but what a timid man the British consul was! He would not sign their visas until he had assured himself that the new government, the Nazis, approved of what was going on. Without papers they couldn't get on the train. The leaders went again and again to the consulate but always there was an excuse – the papers weren't ready for them.

Imagine what it was like for them. Sixty-three of them, no papers, no money (they'd spent all they had on their passages and buying land in Canada), and all of them known enemies of the Reich. There were a lot of children in the party too.

Well, it was an Englishman that had let them down but the leaders took a chance and came to us. Where else could they go? Money was no problem of course. Guy just dug into the safe. But every hotel and boarding-house in Prague was visited daily by the Gestapo checking on the papers of the guests. It wasn't quite so bad on the outskirts of the city. The police were a bit lax there and only turned up to take a list of guests every second day.

The sixty-three scattered to the villages round Prague going off in twos and threes and never staying more than one night at any place. They spent most of their days sitting in cafés trying to make one cup of coffee spin out for hours.

They were terribly conscientious. Every time the married couple had to come for more money they gave Guy an exact account of how every penny had been spent. We didn't care, it wasn't money that was the trouble.

Guy ran round like a maniac but he couldn't get any joy from the consul – I don't think the consul liked us much, we were an embarrassment. But gradually in dribs and drabs the group was dispersed. One or two would go over the Polish frontier. One or two would sneak away trying to make their way through Germany to Switzerland. Some were arrested. Some managed to get new papers. In the end there was only a handful left including the married couple.

We knew of a group about to attempt the crossing over the Polish frontier. 'Why don't you go with them?' Guy said. 'It's about your only chance. Give it a go!'

'How can we?' the woman said. And she looked down at their six year old child, little Boris.

I happened to be in the room at the time. 'Let me look after Boris,' I said. 'I'll take him to England with us and pretend he's my child.' Guy was going across to England in a few days anyway.

'Do you really mean that?' they said.

Guy said, 'Jolly good idea. We've got to take someone else across anyway.'

The next day he arrived at our flat, this little dot of a child with a tiny case that should have held play-lunch and an infant reader instead of all his worldly possessions. He talked German with a Berlin accent. A little Berlin sparrow, he seemed. I really took to him.

The other person we were to take with us was Gigi – George was his real name. He was eighteen, the brother of two women we'd helped in Ruthenia. He'd made his way to Prague to find us and see if we could help him get away too. He didn't look Jewish at all. He would have passed for an English boy anywhere. And that was what we were relying on.

Children are entered on their parents' passports. Guy and I both had British passports but with, of course, no mention of any children on them. But we got a visa for Captain Morton and his wife and two sons and we hoped that with good luck that would get us through the frontier.

The car was loaded with valuables that we were trying to smuggle to England for various people. There were great hunks of gold in the tool box – six or seven inches across – smoked so that they looked like dirty putty, the sort of thing you might carry for makeshift repairs. I was decked out like a Christmas tree – necklaces, bracelets, earrings, brooches, rings. I've never been so over-dressed in my life. I had a five pound box of chocolates in my lap and every piece of silver paper had been taken off. The chocolates were wrapped in sheer platinum. Guy had all our papers in his attache case. International drivers' licences, papers for the car, passports, visas. They were in the top compartment. Below it was full of gold and jewels.

We set off so merrily. That's the thing about danger. It makes your adrenalin flow. You can't help being excited and thrilled. We were to drive straight through Germany and across Belgium to get these two to England. We were hoping to arrive before Boris's parents – if indeed they managed to get there at all.   Little Boris chattered all the way. He kept telling me long stories about what they had done in Berlin and other places. He'd start off each time in his piping little voice, 'Weisst du was?' (Do you know what?) But when we got to the frontiers all you had to say was 'Boris, Gestapo! Nicht sprechen!' and he would sit absolutely silent. Poor little fellow, he had experience enough in his young life to know what that meant.

We were going down a long road not very far from Frankfurt near a place called Aschaffenburg when suddenly – it was horrible – a German army lorry coming towards us deliberately swerved across the road and bashed into us. It scraped right down the side of our car, ripping off the door handle beside me, and shot past. Guy pulled into the side of the road. None of us was hurt but we'd all been flung about and shaken. He got out to inspect the damage. It was the wrong moment to have an accident.

The lorry swung round and came back towards us. I thought it was going to have another go at us but it stopped and two very apologetic soldiers got out. 'We thought you were Czechs,' they said. We had a Czech numberplate in front and a British one behind. After they passed they'd looked back and seen the British plate. They seemed to think that if we'd been Czechs it wouldn't have mattered. The only bad thing about it was that they'd made a mistake.

'Please don't report us!' they begged. If only they'd known! Imagine us driving into a police station with what we had on board.

Guy was furious. If he hadn't been he would have pretended to be, but it came naturally at that moment. And Guy furious was very frightening. He took down the driver's name and number and the number of the truck. I've still got the piece of paper with those numbers written on it. The soldiers kept on pleading with him. 'We'll get into terrible trouble. Please don't report us! We thought you were Czechs!'

They went off in the end looking very depressed and we limped into Aschaffenburg. The gloss was off the adventure; it felt like a bad omen. We had to take the car to a garage. Suppose they found the gold in the back? We had to stay at a hotel for the night. Suppose someone wondered how two English parents came to have German speaking sons! And there was such

169

suspicion everywhere in those days. People would report anything to keep in well with the Gestapo.

Gigi looked pale and sick. He was the one in real danger.

'Can we order a meal in the bedroom for Boris and me? You can't have him chattering Berlin German all over the dining-room.'

We got to bed in the end, all still shaken except Boris who slept like an angel all night.

In the morning Guy woke up in one of his rages. What an awkward time to have one! I don't know what I was supposed to have done but he wouldn't speak a word to me.

Late in the morning he went round to the garage. The car was ready. We were all waiting outside the hotel when he brought it round. Gigi got in the front beside Guy. Boris clambered into the back. Before I could follow Guy leaned over, slammed the door, and drove off. I was left standing on the pavement.

I was in Nazi Germany, I didn't have my passport, I didn't know a soul in the town and all the money I had with me was a few loose coins in my purse. I thought, as I always did, 'I'm in a dream and I'll wake up. It's not happening.'

I counted out the money in my purse. Just enough for a cup of coffee. I went back into the hotel and ordered one and I sat and drank it very slowly trying to think what to do. But I couldn't think of anything. I just sat there blankly while an hour crawled past.

Then the swing doors opened and Guy came in and called me. I went out and got into the car. We drove on and for the first time since I'd known him, the one and only time, Guy got over his temper quickly. It didn't take three days; it didn't take much more than three hours. It was a miracle.

On we went right across Germany. We reached the Belgium frontier – in a few minutes we would be safe. I thought we looked like an English family. Boris was asleep on my knee. With tension and fear, Gigi looked sulky the way lots of adolescent boys do when they're travelling with their parents. Guy picked up his case and strolled into the frontier guardhouse. We three stayed in the car. Through the open door we could see Guy toss the briefcase onto the small counter and draw out the papers from the top compartment. A couple of minutes, then he and the guard strolled together across to the car. Guy was talking – something about the weather or the roads – and the guard nodded in agreement, smiling.

His face came to the window and he gave a quick routine glance at us. All in order. His mind was on the conversation with Guy. It was going to be all right. I nearly offered him a chocolate.

'The best stretch,' he said to Guy in German, 'is . . .'.

His voice, so close to the window, woke Boris. As always he woke up talking.

'Weisst du was?' he said in his clear treble. 'Ich habe . . .'.

The guard swung round. 'One moment! That is no English child!' His face in the window was quite different now – sharp and professional. 'You!' he said, nodding at Gigi, 'you! Show me your papers!'

It was all happening too quickly. Even Guy couldn't bluff. We'd been caught out. Gigi produced his passport. Stamped across the full page was that awful bright red *J. Jude*. Jew.

'You know the Führer's orders. Get out! Get back where you came from!' He was angry. I thought for a moment he was going to take Boris too. But apparently he was too young to bother about. He jerked his head at Guy to carry on.

Gigi just stood there on the road. Guy went up to him and shook hands. 'I'm terribly sorry, old chap, but there's nothing we can do.'

We just had to drive away and leave him standing there. I kept looking back. I don't think I ever saw anyone look so lost and forlorn. Boris stared till he was out of sight. 'What's happening to Gigi? Why can't Gigi come?'

On we went to England. Guy took the gold and jewels and platinum and paid it into Cook's bank, each piece in the name of the person who had given it to him. Nothing written down; he carried it all in his head and he never made a mistake.

Boris's parents hadn't arrived and no message had come. I kept Boris with me. He came down to the beauty parlour while I had my hair shampooed, and stood there with his hand on my knee chattering away in German. I had the dryer on and I couldn't hear one word so I just said 'ja' or 'nein' at intervals and smiled at him. All the girls in the shop were very taken with him.

I said to Guy, 'If his parents don't get through, we'll adopt him. Do you agree?'

'Yes,' he said. 'I do.'

But the next day the phone rang. The parents were at a refugee camp on the south coast somewhere. Guy drove Boris down to them that afternoon. I hated parting with him but it was a very happy outcome. For everyone except Gigi.

But fate was on our side that trip. We woke at dawn with the telephone ringing in our room. It was the Harwich Immigration Authority. 'Sorry to disturb you Captain Morton. We have a person here who's given your name as his sponsor to enter the country.'

'Let me speak to him,' said Guy. 'Good to hear your voice, Gigi!'

Later in the day he arrived at the hotel and told us what had happened. He said when we drove off it was the loneliest, most terrible feeling he'd ever had in his life. He wandered back to the frontier town and sat drinking a cup of coffee in a café there. He watched a train, a shabby two-carriage local thing, puffing its way across the border to Belgium. So he began to ask questions. He found that the train came across from Belgium every morning bringing forty or so workers who were employed in a factory on the German side. And every night it returned them to Belgium. He guessed that the faces of the workers would be so familiar to the guard that the business of passport inspection wouldn't come up.

The next evening he got on to the train. When the guard came up to him and asked for his passport he assumed a strong English accent and made a lot of elementary blunders in his German. He hadn't got his passport, he said. They'd told him it wasn't necessary. He'd come across that morning with no trouble. He said he worked for an English engineering firm who'd sent him out to look at the German factory that they had ties with.

The guard looked puzzled. He hadn't come across anything like this before. 'How do I know you're English?' he said. 'You might be a criminal trying to leave the country.'

Gigi fumbled round in his pockets then hauled out a couple of English pound notes. 'Look, I've still got some of the money I brought across with me.'

'That's all right then,' said the guard. 'We have to be careful you know.' And he let him through.

'How lucky you were!' I said. 'However did you happen to have English money in your pocket?'

Guy and Gigi grinned at each other. 'The same way I happened to have the key of that Turkish prison in my pocket,' Guy said.

The penny dropped. 'You passed them to Gigi when you shook hands and said goodbye.'

'That's right. I'd folded them small.'

Oh, Guy was quick thinking in an emergency! I hadn't noticed a thing and neither had the frontier guard. That trip was an outstanding success. The routine business was less spectacular.

I remember one man who came to us. An ordinary little German-Czech he was, neither young nor old, a simple, respectable citizen. He'd worked for years in a bank and he'd risen to be branch manager. He had a neat little house in the suburbs and a neat little wife and one child. When the occupation occurred it made no difference to his routines. He was one for minding his own business and getting on with his job.

One day he arrived at the bank and found on his desk a notice that said NO JEWS WANTED HERE. He pushed it aside and settled down to work.

After a while the assistant manager came in. 'Didn't you see the notice?' he said.

'Yes, I saw it. But it's nothing to do with me. I don't hire the staff; they're sent from the main branch. In any case none of them in this branch are Jews.'

'One is!' said the assistant-manager looking at him. The Germans had gone and looked up his records – or maybe the assistant-manager had. His maternal grandmother was a Jewess. He had no idea. It had never been mentioned in the family. His other grandparents were Aryan and all were Lutheran protestants. It didn't matter. One grandparent was enough. He was a Jew.

He came to us in a desperate state. 'What can I do? I'm classed as a Jew. I don't know any Jews. I don't know anything about them. I've never had anything to do with them. Now I can't get a job anywhere and I can't leave the country. What can I do?'

For him there wasn't any answer. Or if there was, we didn't know it.

Girls had a better chance of getting away. Especially if they were pretty and rich. One day we were invited to a wedding by some wealthy Czechs that Guy had met. It was a lovely house and a beautiful wedding breakfast, all very formal and lavish. Champagne and rice and much gaiety. The only odd thing about it was that there was no bridegroom. There was a telephone with a long distance call linked and a young man standing in as proxy for the groom. The bride was a Jewess, the groom an English boy. We drank his health as an absent friend. The next day with a new passport, a new name and a new nationality, she flew to England.

Both the boys, Nowell and Roy, got at least one proposal a week. Nowell told me he was very tempted sometimes. Pretty girls, wealthy girls begging him to marry them. They'd promise him anything, anything, if only he'd consent. They'd divorce him as soon as they got to England. It was hard to refuse but he did. It must have been even harder for Roy. He was more amenable. There was one girl in particular . . . I think Roy may have married her in the end. I hope he did.

She was such a pretty girl – really an outstanding beauty and she came to us in terrible distress. Two years before her mother had been having a bridge party. They were sitting around the table and they started talking about Hitler. 'Oh, that man!' the mother said. 'He ought to be hanged! Let's forget him and get on with the game!'

When Hitler arrived and people were in real danger someone obviously thought that they'd get in well with the Nazis by reporting the casual remark to the Gestapo. The woman was arrested for plotting against the life of Hitler. It was grotesque.

The Gestapo took her away. When the father came home and found what had happened he went straight down to Gestapo headquarters demanding to know where his wife was.

'Oh, you want to know where your wife is? Come on in!' they said and they sent him to the concentration camp for a fortnight. I knew the man quite well but when they let him out of the camp and he came knocking at our door I didn't recognize him. In that one fortnight his skin had changed colour and his movements were all uncertain and trembling. And he had a dreadful look in his eyes.

When he started telling us just what they had done to him I fainted. I came to on the bed; Guy had carried me out. After that he never let me listen to anyone who had actually been in a concentration camp. We never saw the wife again and there was no way we could help the man away. While we were still trying to work out a way to help the girl a train of events started that rushed us along to a crisis.

It began with some Jewish boys whom Guy was taking across to England to school. I remember that after they left their mother came to see me. She didn't really know what was going to happen to them or whether she'd ever see them again. And of course she was in danger herself. When she was going – I can see her now – she stood with her hand on the door and turned back to me.

'You can't understand,' she said bitterly. 'I hope you never have to go through this.' It was true of course. We always had the comforting thought that whatever happened we could almost certainly escape with our lives and at that stage we hadn't yet been in real danger.

Guy got the boys across successfully. While he was in England he went to see Mrs Roger Smith about future adoptions.

'I do wish I could see your side of the work,' Mrs Smith said.

'You can. Put on your coat and come with me.'

'Oh!' she said. 'But I haven't got anything – only my passport.'

'That's all you need.'

'I haven't any money and the bank's closed.'

'Don't worry,' Guy said. 'I'll pay for everything and when you get back to England you can pay me back.'

So she packed a suitcase, put on a coat and got in the car with Guy.

She stayed with us for a week finding out all sorts of things about the work. She also treated all four of us to the opera, bought herself a suit and a fur hat, a dinner-service, all handmade, and a box of Czech glassware.

'Whatever does all that come to?' she said at the end of the week, sounding guilty about her extravagance. Guy worked it out in English money. 'With your fare, six pounds,' he said. By this time an English pound was worth nearly 1,000 Czech crowns. No wonder we were getting rich!

While Mrs Smith was with us a Jewish woman and her three small children arrived in terrible danger. They had to be got out immediately. Guy took the big air-cooled Tatra and in the early morning he slipped away with this pathetic family. He told Nowell to see Mrs Smith home when she was ready to go. She was thinking of leaving the next day.

But the next day, early in the morning before any of us were up, there was a ring at the doorbell. It was the mother of the children – the woman Guy had set off with the day before.

I got a terrible fright. Where was Guy? And what she said was what I'd been dreading hearing for months. 'It was the Gestapo. They took the Captain.'

I thought of the man who'd been in the concentration camp and what I'd heard before I fainted.

She told us there had been an accident. The children had been in the front seat with Guy. She thought that one of them had grabbed the wheel. The car hit a bank and rolled. The next thing she knew the car was on its side and there were rings and brooches and cigarette cases scattered around. And two men with swastikas on their armbands were trying to help all of them out through the window.

'It was just bad luck that a car with S.S. men in it should be behind us,' she said. 'They took us down to headquarters and they made me show my passport.' She didn't have to tell us what was on it. 'They sent us back,' she said. 'What am I going to do now?' She was frantic, trying to think of a way to save her children.

All I wanted to hear about was Guy. 'I don't know what's happened,' the woman said. 'I watched Gestapo headquarters till the train came that we had to catch. The captain never came out in that time.'

We couldn't do anything for that woman. It was just hopeless. The three of us – Nowell, Roy, and I – talked for a long time. There didn't seem to be anything we could do for Guy either. It wasn't even any use ringing the consul. We didn't know what story Guy had told and we couldn't risk upsetting any bluff he might be trying. There was just one thing. He'd told Nowell to take Mrs Roger Smith to England. If he got away we knew that's where he would wait for us, at the Cumberland Hotel. It seemed unlikely that with the Gestapo on his tail he'd risk ringing us at home wherever he was.

We decided that Roy should stay and look after things in Prague – though he couldn't do much without the rest of us. Nowell and I would take Mrs Roger Smith home. I just couldn't sit around and wait. I had to go and see if Guy had got to England.

Before we left there was one urgent piece of business that the boys wanted to finish. They wanted to try what they called 'one of the Boss's tricks.' There was a child, a little boy, Herbert someone. An adoption had been arranged for him in England through the official Refugee Committee. But for some reason, I forget what it was if I ever knew, little Herbert wasn't allowed to enter Prague. So it was stalemate as far as the Refugee Committee was concerned. They, the official lot, never did anything illegal. That was the difference between them and us. The Morton crowd didn't mind how many laws they broke. Nowell and Roy set off that morning. I don't know what they did; I was worrying too much about Guy to take much notice.

Late at night they arrived back with 'our 'Erb' as we called him – a plump little boy, very dirty, very tired, very scruffy. We called Anna and asked her to put him straight in the bath. She washed him and then all his clothes and had them clean and ironed by morning.

When he was dressed Roy took him round to the Refugee Committee's headquarters. They were back again within an hour. There wasn't a chance in the world of getting through to that office, Roy said. The queue was so long that even if he'd stood there all day he wouldn't have got more than half way along it.

We couldn't think what to do so I rang the Baron. He told me he'd be round in half an hour and in the meantime to dress myself up in my most expensive clothes. He arrived wearing his chauffeur's uniform and driving his huge luxurious car with a Union Jack on the front. He looked at me and nodded approval. I looked ultra fashionable and rich enough to match the car. I got in the back of the car with our 'Erb and the Baron drove us to the Refugee Committee Headquarters.

It was on the fourth floor of a big building. The queue stretched four deep right down the stairs, out the door, and down the street for the length of two big blocks. All women waiting for that tiny chance of having their children sent to England. It was a dreadful sight. They couldn't have taken one in a hundred of those that were waiting. There were smartly dressed women and poor women with shawls over their heads – every kind of woman. It was heartbreaking.

There were policemen patrolling the queue. We drove up and one of them, seeing this enormous car with a chauffeur and a British flag, came up and opened the door. The Baron, like a good chauffeur, stood to attention as our 'Erb and I got out. The policeman made a path for us through the queue and escorted us up the four flights into the office. There was a young Englishman behind the desk, very kind, very worried, very proper.

'Have you got Herbert—on your list?' I asked.

'Yes, we have. But we can't get hold of him,' he said.

'Here he is.'

'How did you get him?'

'Well, that's another story. Can he go across today?'

'Certainly. We've had his papers ready for a long time.'

Later that same day Nowell and I set out to take Mrs Roger Smith back to England. We took the Ford V8 and raced across Germany on the beautiful autobahn. As soon as we were clear of Nazi territory we stopped and I rang the Cumberland Hotel.

'Is Captain Morton there?'

'Yes, Madam. Just one moment please.'

I couldn't believe it till I heard his voice.

The story, when we heard it, was typical Morton. The Gestapo had held him all day for questioning but he'd bluffed his way out. He told them that the woman who was with him had just asked him for a lift. He barely knew her – what was wrong with that? The Gestapo were determined to get him. Guy's briefcase had sprung open in the accident and all that expensive stuff had been sprayed over the car. If he wasn't doing anything worse at least he was smuggling. The Gestapo called in the Customs officials. The Customs people were always very correct and formal and like a lot of ordinary officials they rather resented the Gestapo. It didn't matter to the Customs who Guy had had in the car, only that he was smuggling valuables across the frontier. The rule was that British citizens could take out their own property but nothing else.

'It *is* my property,' Guy said.

'How can one man own seven gold cigarette cases?' they asked.

Guy put on his most haughty expression. 'Surely you don't expect me to mix my Craven A's with my Ardaths?'

He got away with it. They asked him for his address in England. Cigarettes were very much on his mind at that moment. He had a packet of Three Castles in his pocket. 'I own three castles,' he said. 'Which address would you prefer?' They let him go.

We drove Mrs Roger Smith home, then Guy, Nowell, and I had a conference.

'Now look,' Guy said. 'There's nothing against either of you or Roy. I'm the one who's been breaking the law and I'm the one they're on to. You two go back by train. I'll keep the V8 because I haven't got a car here now. (The Tatra had been put out of action when it rolled.)

When you get back to Prague, take a look around and see what's happening. If things look calm and ordinary, let me know and I'll come out again. There's a lot of unfinished business – we'll carry on a bit longer if we can. But if the Gestapo come around asking questions about me, just pack the Persian carpets and come quietly away.'

It sounded safe, the sensible thing to do. The boys and I could manage it easily.

Nowell and I travelled back by train. We were light-hearted with relief and we had a hilarious time. I had great wads of German marks in my handbag. We broke our journey in Germany and stayed in a royal suite. It was incredibly luxurious. The walls were covered with figured silk brocade instead of paper.

We reached Prague and went up to the flat. I had a key with me in my handbag – look, I have it still. That's the one.

We opened the door and went in. It was terribly quiet.

'Roy!' we called. No answer.

'He must have gone out,' Nowell said. 'He'll be back soon.'

Then Anna must have heard our voices and she came running from the kitchen calling to us. 'Gracious Lady, Gracious Lady, you're safe! You're safe!' and she grabbed my hand and kissed it.

I knew what had happened right away. They'd taken Roy.

'It was the Gestapo!' Anna said. 'They will be back, I know. Oh Gracious Lady, what shall we do? I'm so frightened for us all!'

Right away Nowell went out and rang the consul – we didn't dare use our own phone. The consul knew all about it. He'd been able to see Roy. 'They say they'll keep him for a fortnight and then release him. Don't worry about him. There's nothing you can do for him now. Just get out yourselves as fast as you can. If you stay around Prague you'll end up in the same place. Today is Tuesday. Thursday is a public holiday. I imagine even the Gestapo will be on holiday – or at least they'll be spread a bit thin. Try and get out then. It's really your only chance. At all costs you must prevent Guy coming back. I'm sure he's the one they really want.'

It was all very well to say get out. It wasn't so easy. The catch was that to travel anywhere you had to have a Gestapo permit. We used to get them for a fortnight at a time. You could make one journey in and out on them. We'd used up the last journey on our current permit when we returned to Prague. We couldn't go to Gestapo Headquarters and ask for a new permit – we might just as well have knocked on the gate of the prison. And we couldn't cross the frontier without a permit. We'd got ourselves into a trap.

Anna cooked us a meal and brought it in herself.

'Where's Maria?' I asked.

'Maria! Don't speak to me of Maria! Maria has run away. Gracious Lady, it is she that has made all this trouble. There's been a boy calling for her lately. Three nights ago he knocked at the door. Jesus Maria! He was wearing a Gestapo uniform!'

She served our meal. 'What will become of us all?' she said. There was nothing to be done that night and we were too tired to think clearly. I went to bed. I was just drifting off to sleep when I started wide awake, thinking I heard footsteps on the landing. I lay there tense waiting for the thump thump thump of a fist on the door. Nothing happened. I lay staring into the dark. I heard the lift coming up. My heart was pounding. Nothing happened. I couldn't lie there all night.

I got up, put on a dressing-gown and wandered out to the sitting-room. Nowell was there in the same state. Both of us were terrified. We huddled together on the sofa all night – holding on to each other for comfort and trying to make plans. Whatever we thought of always there was this blank wall in front of us. How could we cross the frontier without permits?

About three o'clock in the morning I had the second great brain wave of my life.

'Tomorrow is Thursday, the holiday. The consul said there wouldn't be many Gestapo around then. Suppose you go down to the station this morning as soon as it's light and buy tickets for both of us for Friday's International train. Book seats all the way through to London and pay for them in English money. That way the station people will be sure to notice you and remember. It'll be reported to the Gestapo for sure. They'll be waiting to pick us up at the station on Friday morning.'

'Well, how's that going to help us?'

'We'll go by car. We'll go tomorrow. They won't have alerted the frontier guards because they'll be expecting us to turn up at the railway station on Friday. The consul said there wouldn't be many Gestapo around on Thursday and we may be able to bluff our way across the frontier.'

It wasn't much of a plan but it was better than nothing. Nowell elaborated it. 'We can't sit around here all day waiting for them to come.

We'll go and buy the tickets and we won't come back to the flat. Where can we go for a day and a night? I know – Freddie's!'

It sounded ludicrous. Freddie didn't fit into a world of concentration camps and jackboots and torture. The most suspicious Gestapo agent in the world couldn't suspect him of anything. It sounded wonderful.

As soon as it was light we dressed and got ready. I just took the suitcase packed as it was from my one night trip to England. If the Gestapo came to the flat there mustn't be anything missing to suggest we weren't coming back. What with fear and shock and lack of sleep, I was stupid. I took off the travelling dress I was wearing which was really lovely and one of my favourites and I left it there in the wardrobe. I put on a suit I wasn't nearly so fond of. I felt badly about leaving Anna but she was only in danger because of us. She was pure Czech, no Jewish blood. The kindest thing we could do for her was just get out. We told her we were going and I asked her if she would take care of Dizzie for me. She wept and kissed my hand. We handed her all the Czech money we had – to her it seemed an enormous amount and she wept even more.

We drove openly to the station in my conspicuous white Jaguar. Nowell bought the tickets, a great roll of them, and paid for them in English pound notes. Then we drove to the little town beyond the outskirts of Prague where Freddie and Mary lived. No one attempted to stop us.

It was another world, Freddie and Mary in their little two-roomed flat in the village. It felt like an ordinary cheerful neighbourly call. That night we sat around talking about the problem of the frontier.

'I wouldn't mind driving you across,' Freddie said, 'seeing it's a holiday tomorrow.' He might have been offering us a lift to the shop.

'Freddie,' I said, 'is your travelling pass in order? Have you got a Gestapo permit?' The permits were stamped inside one's passport. (See, my passport is full of them for 1938 and 39. That's the Gestapo stamp – the swastika with the eagle on the top.)

'I always keep my permit up to date,' Freddie said. He sounded mildly reproachful. *He* wasn't irresponsible.

The next morning the four of us drove into Prague. Freddie and Mary in their car (which was really ours) and Nowell and I in the white Jaguar. When we reached the flat Nowell parked the Jaguar out on the roadway instead of in the garage – an open advertisement that we were around. Then we hopped into Freddie's car and just drove away.

We didn't take a thing – not a single Persian carpet, none of my clothes, not even the money from the safe. Nothing. We just drove away. The only thing we stopped for was to pay the bill at my dressmaker's on the way out.

It was early May. A lovely spring day, the trees in young leaf. The sort of day when concentration camps seemed such an obscenity you couldn't believe they existed. Freddie drove along placidly enjoying the countryside, pointing out this and that to us and sedately pulling up every ten miles or so to relieve himself. I thought, 'How on earth can this innocent get us across the frontier? We would have been better off on our own.'

Time was passing. If we could get across we could board the International train at Dresden. Although Czechoslovakia had been occupied the frontier between it and Germany still existed, not as two separate boundaries with no-man's-land between them but as a single barrier where passports and travelling permits were checked and stamped. I had no idea what Freddie was planning to do or even if he realized that he'd have to do something.

Then suddenly it was upon us. The guard had carried a little table outside the guardhouse and was sitting there quietly enjoying the spring sunshine. Freddie pulled up. He gathered up our four passports and stacked them, his own on top, then Mary's, Nowell's under that, then mine.

He ambled across cheerfully to the guard. Beside the road there was a huge horse-chestnut tree. I can see it now, it's imprinted on my brain forever, those big treacly brown buds just about to burst. I was looking at the tree, but out of the corner of my eye I could see what Freddie was doing. He handed the man the top passport, his own. It was stamped and returned. Then Mary's. Then I heard him say in his awkward German, 'We are going into your lovely country. We thought we should see Dresden.' He handed the guard Nowell's passport.

'Ah, Dresden!' said the guard. 'It is the most beautiful city in the world. You will be enchanted by Dresden.' He stamped the passport and handed it back.

'I don't know much about the hotels there,' Freddie said. 'What's a good place to stay in?' And he handed over my passport.

'Well, now, I'd have to think about that,' the man said. My passport devoid of a permit was lying in front of him. He stared at it absently. 'The Bellevue Hotel is a very fine place but it is also a trifle expensive. Perhaps you would prefer . . .' and he named two or three other hotels. 'At any of them you will be very comfortable.' And he stamped my passport and handed it back.

Nowell grabbed my hand and held on tight. Freddie thanked the guard and strolled back to the car. 'I'll never laugh at Freddie again,' I thought. 'He has just saved me from the concentration camp.'

We trundled on our way. The excitement had done no good at all to Freddie's bladder. The International train had left two hours before we reached Dresden. Obviously Nowell and I were going to have to spend the night there. And if we went on the next day, Friday, we'd be on the very train that we'd so painstakingly advertised that we were going to travel on. We'd got safely through the first barrier. But there was still the frontier between Germany and Belgium to cross.

We had a meal together and we all went and sat in the Zwinger – my beautiful place that I loved so much. Freddie with his box camera, took a photo of Nowell and me sitting there in the spring sunshine. It felt wonderful just to be alive. I could feel Nowell's eyes resting on me wherever I went. He made excuses to take my arm or touch my hand. Shared danger does that to you. Even I felt it. I had to keep reminding myself how old I was, how young he was.

Freddie and Mary went back. Nowell and I had become fatalistic. We would take our chance on the train the next day. We took only the elementary precaution of avoiding the hotels the guard had named and choosing an inconspicuous one in the suburbs.

The next day we caught the International train. We took sleeping berths in different cars. Guy had taught me that trick: if there's anything wrong with your passport, travel in a sleeping berth. The other passengers have their passports individually checked at the frontier. But in a sleeping car you simply hand your passport to the steward. He passes them in altogether at the frontier. Anyone dealing with a whole batch together is less likely to notice irregularities.

For a long time that night I couldn't sleep. The journey seemed to go on and on. I couldn't believe we hadn't reached the frontier. Then I must have dropped off because the next thing I knew Nowell was shaking me and shouting.

'We're in Belgium! We passed the frontier twenty minutes ago! We've made it!' We hugged each other and danced round, almost hysterical. I didn't violate my marriage vows then, or ever, but I won't say I wasn't tempted that night.

Brussels. Oh, it was lovely to feel safe again! We had a few hours to fill in before the boat train left for Ostend. Nowell was collecting beer coasters so we wandered round to all sorts of funny little places and he drank one glass of beer in each of them. The only thing I was worried about now was that Guy might have gone back to Germany to rescue me. The consul in Prague had told Nowell that he'd sent a message to Guy telling him Roy was arrested. He had a private line to London. We couldn't get hold of Guy at the Cumberland so we decided we should let the consul know we were safe. But he was a very cautious man and we didn't want to involve him or embarrass him. After all we were being sought by the police of the country he was stationed in.

In the end we hit on a way. We bought a postcard of Brussels and addressed it to him. We wrote the message in English and left it unsigned. THE SPROUTS ARE BEAUTIFUL.

The Channel crossing, a four hour trip. We got in at midnight. The closer we got the more I worried about Guy. We looked and looked as we berthed. All of a sudden we saw him, waiting on the wharf. He'd been meeting boat after boat, in a panic because he'd sent us back into danger.

Guy had brought the Ford V8. We drove back to London, me in the front seat next to Guy. All the way he was gripping my knee beside him. From the back seat Nowell was gripping my shoulder on the other side.

Oh, it felt good! We talked about all the things we'd left in the flat – not really sad about it though. We were too pleased to be out ourselves unharmed.

'The only thing I regret is my dress suit,' Nowell said. It was his first and he was so proud of it.

'Get yourself another,' Guy said, 'Savile Row. I'll pay for it.' And he did.

Now that we were back my nerves gave way. I wasn't ill, just terribly tired and shaky. We went down to Cornwall for a holiday. It was the most beautiful June in living memory in England. We went sailing – which I loathed but Guy loved – and lay on the beach – which I loved – and soaked warmth and sun every day till Czechoslovakia became an unreal memory.

At the end of four weeks of complete rest we sat up and looked at each other and said, 'What are we going to do next?'

It sounds a stupid thing now with hindsight, but in that June of 1939 we didn't think there was going to be a war. It seemed to us that Hitler would take anything he wanted to and that nobody would lift a finger to stop him. But we didn't think that he would go any further – or not much further. He'd taken the places which had a large German population; he'd united the Germans in one country. He wasn't interested in non-Germans; why should he advance any further?

So we thought and talked and planned as though there would be peace for years to come. We asked each other where we'd most like to live. The answer was the south of France of course, but we didn't have enough money to be able to live that kind of life.

I said, 'I'd like to go to America. I just loved America.'

'I couldn't live amongst the Yanks!' Guy said.

'Shanghai,' I suggested. 'Let's go back to my dear Shanghai!' But that didn't appeal to Guy either. Just as well, considering what happened when the Japanese invaded.

'Well,' I said, 'how about going to the colonies?'

Guy looked thoughtful. Yes, he liked the idea of a colony. 'Canada?' he suggested.

'I couldn't live in Canada,' I said. 'It's far too cold!'

'Australia then? That's warm enough even for you.'

'Oh, I couldn't,' I said. 'I can't stand their dreadful accents! How do they speak in New Zealand, Guy?'

'As far as I know they talk quite decently there.'

That was the 19th of June. Three days later we were on the *Rangitata* headed for New Zealand.

We spent the intervening time at the Cumberland. Guy had just come back from booking our passages, first-class of course, and we were still in a flurry of trying to decide all in a rush what we ought to buy for the journey, when there was a call from the desk that two visitors were asking for us. It was Freddie and Mary.

What they had to tell us was the end of our own story in Czechoslovakia. A few days after Nowell and I left they had gone to our flat to see if they could save some of our things. The flat was in a shambles, utterly stripped. Dizzie was running round barking and Anna rushed out to them in terror. She grabbed Freddie's hand. 'Everything is gone! The Gestapo has taken everything!'

All the furniture had gone, the Persian carpets, our clothes and china and ornaments and pictures. The safe was broken open and empty, the door swinging on its hinge. What hadn't been taken had been wrecked. Anna rushed through to the kitchen and came back with the electric jug in her hands. She thrust it into Freddie's hands, saying, 'Take it to the Gracious Lady. Tell her it was all I could save.'

It was then that Freddie and Mary began to be frightened. Roy in prison, the flat rifled and smashed. Freddie rang the consul. And the consul agreed it might be better if they didn't stay. They packed up slowly and deliberately and came away with all their possessions.

'What are you going to do?' they asked us.

'We're going to New Zealand.'

They both looked wistful. We owed them a lot. Freddie had got me across the frontier. If they hadn't been involved with us there wouldn't have been any reason for them to leave Czechoslovakia.

Guy and I looked at each other. 'Why don't you come with us?' Guy said.

Freddie and Mary still looked wistful. They hadn't enough money.

'Don't worry about that! Pay what you can and we'll fix the rest.'

Guy went out and changed the booking from two first-class passages to four second-class ones.

I felt humiliated travelling second-class and so did Guy, but it was the only way we could manage to pay the fares. Later it seemed like a shadow moving in front of all that was to come.

(3)

NEW ZEALAND

It was raining when the *Rangitata* passed through Pencarrow
Heads into Wellington Harbour; the bitter squally rain of early
spring. The Mortons' passage was booked to Dunedin.

'I suppose it'll be warmer there,' said Grace, momentarily slipping
into a familiar association – south equals heat, go south to the sun.

A New Zealander standing near laughed cynically. 'That'll be the
day!' Of course, she remembered, everything here works in reverse,
everything is upside-down.

'Why don't we get off here, Guy?' she said, huddling in her one
surviving Czechoslovakian fur coat. 'Don't let's go where it's any
colder.'

The New Zealand passengers crowded the rails, the sweet tears of
returning exiles in their eyes and voices.

'Oh, look! Look!' a woman cried, pointing, trembling, 'There's
the Dee-eye-see!' Grace, catching the passion in the voice, cried
'Where? Where?' expecting – what? A monument, a Statue of
Liberty, an ancient venerable rock?

'There! See the sign!'

'But that's a shop, isn't it? A department store?' How pathetic,
she thought.

The town, glimpsed between squalls of rain looked ridiculously
small; wooden houses on the hills, dolls' houses, not real, not for
real people.

Guy said, 'Am I right in thinking Wellington is one of your larger
towns?'

'It's the capital,' he was told. 'That's parliament over there, that
grey building, with the pillars.'

Guy and Grace avoided each other's eyes. A parliament for two
and a half million people?

In spite of the rain the harbour, end-stopped in all its explorations
by abrupt hills, was spacious and beautiful.

'It reminds me rather of Hong Kong,' said Grace. 'Let's get off here, Guy!'

On the wharf the returning New Zealanders disappeared into the arms of their healthy relatives and were borne away. The oblique rain bruised faces and legs, the winds found chinks in overcoats and sent comfortless draughts scurrying through underclothes. Before they were through the customs they were chilled to the bone.

'Come to New Zealand, the land of sunshine,' quoted Grace, remembering the Underground posters.

Guy said, 'Let's go to the hotel, darling. I'll collect the car later.' The stewardess who looked after them on the voyage had recommended the St George.

Through streaming taxi windows they glimpsed a street or two of shops with odd makeshift looking verandas sheltering the pavement. Grace was too tired and too cold to react to anything. The lobby of the St George was mercifully warm and soft underfoot. The end of a twelve thousand mile journey, a new country, a new hemisphere.

Guy signed the register. It was four o'clock in the afternoon. 'Would you have tea sent up to our room immediately please?'

'Tea's off,' said the receptionist.

Tea was on the next morning whether you wanted it or not. A knock on the door woke them in the early dawn.

'Whatever's the matter?'

'Seven o'clock, dear! Here's your cuppa!' A woman, stringy and capable, slapped a cup down for each of them. Grace swam up through sleep to find her, incredibly, still standing there hand on hip, telling her life story to Guy.

'My husband, he was cut in half by a circular saw, you know . . .'

Grace didn't know, and didn't want to, especially at dawn on a wet cold morning at the wrong end of the world.

It would have been easier, she thought, if the people hadn't spoken English. Then you could have accepted it for what it was, a foreign country, utterly different but with its own grammar and sense. But because you heard English around you, a kind of English, you expected familiarity and the unfamiliar seemed as weird and distorted as the sinister distortions of dreams.

If they're going to speak English why can't they learn to speak it correctly, Grace thought. They put their mouths in position to say "air" and then just keep them like that whatever they're saying. It was weeks before she recognized their familiar greeting with its gulped first vowel and long dipthonged second as the local version of 'Good day'.

They larded their conversation with strange, uncouth expressions. 'What a dag!' they said. (She was horrified when she found what a dag was.) When they meant 'think' they said 'reckon'. When the weather depressed them they grunted, 'Cow of a day!'

It was a cow of a day every day for the first nine weeks. Trees shivered to flower and leaf but the rain and cold persisted. On the very first morning Grace found her way to the tear-provoking D.I.C. and equipped herself with warm underwear which helped a little.

In the streets the women wore a rough, bowdlerized version of the clothes she had worn in Shanghai seven years ago. Less well-cut and on lumpier figures. It seemed strange to her that they were not embarrassed by their own appearance. She passed a cinema. The film advertised was one she'd seen a year ago in Czechoslovakia; the next cinema reached further back to Shanghai days. Where am I? What am I doing here? The world slipped out of focus; she kept expecting to wake up.

When she met New Zealanders, had conversations in shops or the lounge of the St George, there was something in their reactions to her that she could not quite identify. Oh, they were kind enough, perfectly amiable in their slightly rough-textured way, but they never, she felt, reacted to her personally. It was a routine kindness, a sort of all-purpose bland amiability. Once or twice when she or Guy spoke she had seen a kind of opaqueness come into their eyes. She had heard the word 'Pom' but didn't then know what it meant. Not that she minded how they reacted. After the danger, the pace, the camaraderie of Czechoslovakia it all seemed terribly tame – a people and a country singularly lacking in flavour and style. And she had never cared for provincialism.

But for better or worse they were in New Zealand. The question was, what were they to do for a living? Guy had come with an introduction in his pocket to a certain local magnate, Sir Charles Norwood, chairman of nearly everything it seemed from the

Chamber of Commerce to a local yacht club, and of half the company boards of directors as well. An ex-mayor of the capital city and rumoured to be a millionaire.

Guy presented himself and his credentials to Sir Charles one Saturday morning. And came back laughing. 'You'll never believe it. He was digging the garden. In dirty old flannel trousers and a jersey out at the elbows. His wife made us a cup of tea.'

In a mood of amused disbelief they decided to explore further before deciding on a place to settle. Auckland after all was the biggest town – presumably somewhat nearer to a real city.

'It's a long drive,' they were told, 'and the roads aren't all that good. Better go by train.'

The express left Wellington in mid-afternoon but showed no inclination to hurry itself unduly. About six o'clock it drew in to the small station of Marton Junction. Unaccountably and apparently with a single impulse all the passengers in the carriage, apart from the Mortons and one other couple, emptied themselves on to the platform and joined in what seemed to be a charging stampede of blind panic. From her first-class window Grace could see the finishing line, the four-deep press round the refreshment counter, the long communal table where the lucky ones gobbled up their prizes with silent single-mindedness.

The only other remaining woman in the carriage gave tongue. 'For cryin' out loud,' she cried out loud, 'will ya look how these people live!'

The passengers dribbled back on to the train, many balancing on top of great thick white cups and saucers, a further saucer weighted with a pie or a wad of sandwiches or a tombstone of fruit cake. They took the pies up in their hands and ate them cheerfully and unashamed. Sometime later when the train was under way a porter wandered through the carriages collecting the empties in a kerosene tin bucket.

'What time would you like to have dinner, darling?' asked solicitous Guy.

'Oh, about half past seven, I suppose.'

They made their way up the jolting train, till they found a mild old guard.

'Which end is the dining car?'

'Dining car? Oh well now, they don't have them now. We used

188

to, you know. That'd be quite a time back. Let's see. I reckon it'd be – oh say, back in 1928. That'd be when they took them off. Somewhere about then.'

The hungry Mortons were hurtled through the night. Guy slept. Grace stared out of the black window. No lights in this landscape. She dozed a little, half-waking each time the train jerked to a stop. It was raining heavily. For the first time she became aware, with an inward shudder, of the emptiness of this country. The end nowhere. Nothing between me and the frozen Antarctic.

Once she woke more fully and peered out. She could hear the rain beating on the corrugated iron of the station roof. Through the distortion of water on the pane two or three lights blurred. A long unpronounceable name full of vowels was nailed up like a goal-post close to the window. Her own face peered back at her, a second self palely drowning in the New Zealand night. Who gets off at a station like this? Who gets on in the middle of the night? From what lonely farms, by what rough and winding roads have they travelled in the rain? The train gathered its energy again and a minute later there was only rain and blackness.

Later she woke again. Sleep had fitted words for her to the rhythm of the train. 'Lors alack a daisy, lors alack a daisy.' At first they were nonsensical; then, from the old Ning-hai Mission Compound in a less alien land that held mother and Mother Goose, the old rhyme shyly emerged.

> There was an old woman as I've heard tell,
> She went to the market her eggs for to sell,
> She went to the market all on a market day,
> And she fell asleep on the King's highway.
>
> There came by a pedlar whose name was Stout,
> He cut her petticoats all round about,
> He cut her petticoats up to the knees,
> Which made the old woman to shiver and sneeze.
>
> When this little woman first did wake,
> She began to shiver and she began to shake,
> She began to wonder and she began to cry,
> 'Lors alack a daisy, this be none of I!'

Auckland. 'What does one do here in the evening?' Guy asked the waiter at the Station Hotel. 'Where would be the best place to go and dance?'

The waiter looked puzzled and said 'Just a minute, sir.' Later he returned and gave them one name and address. 'I think this place'll be open.'

The taxi drew up at a building that was uncompromisingly unlit and unopen. 'Oh yes, of course!' the driver said. 'It's Wednesday. They never open on Wednesday nights.'

In that bitter Spring of 1939 Auckland was as cold as Wellington. Which meant that as a place to live Wellington won easily on points – more beautiful, more cosy, more full of character. The Mortons, having returned, went house-hunting.

An agent showed them through a house in Oriental Parade. 'The lounge . . . the bedrooms . . . the kitchen. The laundry . . . it's small of course but I'm sure Mrs. Morton will find it quite convenient for washing for just the two of you.'

Guy and Grace looked at each other and began to laugh.

'You!' Guy spluttered. 'You! Do the washing!'

'Captain Morton, I've just got on to a very handy little proposition. Just up your street, I'd say. Several people are after it but I told them, "I'll be frank with you. I'm going to let Captain Morton have first refusal and I've got a hunch that there won't be any refusing going on."' He is a businessman always on the point of closing a deal, always on the edge of making a fortune. Buying and selling everything from wholesale groceries to land. And doing very nicely, thank you.

The handy little proposition is a fishing lodge coupled with a garage and a store at Turangi beside lovely Lake Taupo. Guy goes up to inspect it and comes back cheerful, completely sold. He is sure that it will provide a living for them and for Freddie and Mary as well. Guy and Grace will supervise the operation while it gets going. Freddie and Mary will understudy them. Once it is established as a going and profitable concern the Mortons will be able to leave Freddie and Mary to take charge of the business and staff in the off season while they winter in the more congenial climate of Fiji. The future suddenly looks inviting.

190

No one talks to them about experience.

No one explains that in New Zealand (unlike China and Czechoslovakia) there is no cheap labour to exploit; that if you want to make a living out of a fishing lodge then you work it with your own two hands, cooking and cleaning, book-keeping and gardening, and even then it is a living you will make, not a fortune.

If anyone had explained, it is doubtful whether the Mortons would have listened. The English, as traditional colonizers, have a propensity for knowing more about local affairs than the locals. Which may have been why nobody did explain.

The day the Mortons drove up to take possession it was bitterly cold. They had arranged to spend the night at the Chateau, the ski-resort hotel on Mt Ruapehu. At six in the evening they were still an hour's run from the Chateau and weather was worsening as night fell. They stopped at a garage and rang through to the hotel. Yes, they were told, the road was still open.

As they drove up the mountain the snow was thicker and when they arrived at the bottom of the slope that leads up to the Chateau there were four empty cars ahead of them, obviously stuck.

There was nothing for it except to get out and walk. Carrying their suitcases they staggered up the slope. Grace's thin-soled shoes were soaked, her feet frozen. They were both very angry.

It was after seven when they stepped into the Chateau. Dinner, they were told, was off.

Guy sent for the manager and his rage boiled over. 'Of all the stupid things! To let this happen at a ski-resort! You call yourself a manager!'

'Hold on!' said the manager. 'I can't control the snow. It doesn't ask my permission to block the drive. What can I do?'

'Do what any decent ski-resort in any decent part of the world does! Get yourself horses and a cart of some sort. In winter take the wheels off and put skids on the carts. Then have your sleigh waiting at the end of the road so that people don't have to lump their own baggage.'

'So that's what you'd do? It's an idea,' said the manager. 'We'd better talk it over while you get some dinner inside you.' The discussion was long, amiable, and not confined to luggage and sleighs.

As the Mortons left in the morning the manager said, 'When you get this fishing lodge of yours off the ground you'd better come over and stay for a week-end. On the house.'

Turangi. On the first day while Guy and Freddie and Mary were making up beds and preparing rooms and Grace was ineptly sweeping the veranda, a prolonged and jolting crash shook the house. They rushed outside. There was (at that time) a bridge with a bend in it spanning the river not far from the lodge. A heavy army-type lorry had failed to take the bend and hurtled into the river.

Local inhabitants sprang up from an apparently deserted landscape. It was probably a sound they had cause to recognize. Everyone rushed into the water and two men were extracted from the cab of the drowning lorry. Shocked and shivering, and wrapped in blankets from the newly-made beds, they were the Mortons' first guests. The second lot, two policemen, arrived minutes later and took possession of the first. They were escapees from a nearby prison, the police explained. They had knocked out the guards of an outdoor working party and commandeered the prison lorry.

As an omen it didn't seem too favourable.

Entry from *Wise's New Zealand Index*, 1939: '*Turangi* 150 miles sth of Hamilton by motor. East Taupo County. Telephone and p.n. office. Fishing and shooting. Roads good. Named after a Maori chief called Turangi Tukua. Nearest post office Tokaanu. Doctor at Taupo.'

Dollimore's *New Zealand Guide*, 1954, adds 'Pop. 378 (c), predominantly Maori. Fishing lodges. Stores.'

This particular fishing lodge had ten bedrooms and a dining-room. Guy and Grace used the very last of their capital to build a large pleasant detached lounge. Everything they owned was now sunk in this venture.

From their predecessors they had inherited a French cook who was very capable when he was sober, which he was quite often. Grace went up to Auckland to engage proper staff. The man in the employment agency lectured her. 'Now Mrs Morton, you're English and in New Zealand people don't expect to be slaves when they work for somebody.'

She thought of dear Juji and of Humpty and she was furious. What did this presumptuous little man know of the quality of those strong, enduring loyalties?

'I've had servants all my life and I've never treated them as slaves. We've been the greatest of friends!'

'Well, Jack's as good as his master in this country.'

When the lecture was over she was able to engage some staff, one of them a very capable English woman. Who only lasted a few weeks.

'I'm sorry, Madam. I'll be leaving next Friday.'

'Oh no! Why? Is it the conditions?'

'No, Madam. The conditions are very satisfactory. It's the others, the other servants. They make fun of me.'

'Oh, surely not! Why should they do that? Perhaps you're imagining it.'

'No, Madam. I'm not imagining it. They laugh at me all the time. Because . . .'

'Because what?'

'Because I call you "Madam". And the Captain "Sir".'

'Whatever is there to laugh at in that?'

'I don't know, Madam. But they think it's funny.'

The drunken French cook was replaced by a married couple. The wife did the cooking and relieved Grace of the necessity of dealing with the rest of the staff, whom Grace still thought of as 'the servants' (though she had learned that that was a dirty word in New Zealand and was best not spoken aloud). It was the old Chinese system, transplanted as nearly as possible into this alien soil. Nurserymen had been engaged to plan the garden and to ship down all the shrubs and trees that would be needed.

Sufficient waitresses and housemaids had been found. A capable local Maori boy who was an experienced mechanic would run the garage with the help of two or three underlings and with Guy around to supervise. Freddie was to take charge of the store. Mary was supposed to understudy the cook and help in the kitchen but she found any duties onerous; Grace's sex instruction had paid off – she was very pregnant.

Grace ordered the food and other provisions and kept the accounts. Finding herself busy, and unaware that she was doing anything unusual, she employed a local girl as her personal maid to wash and iron her clothes. She discovered her mistake when several of the treasured handful of garments she had brought from Czechoslovakia went missing. When she told New Zealanders about the loss she thought that something harsh and gleeful grinned through their token sympathy. You could almost hear them saying, 'Serve you right.'

Guy was general manager, supervisor, co-ordinating officer in chief. The staff at full muster numbered thirteen, not counting the Mortons themselves.

The fishing lodge had barely opened for business when the Second World War broke out. The Mortons had no money, no way to return. They listened to the relayed B.B.C. news, and on short wave to the German version of events. Voices, distorted in transmission, spilled their urgencies in the quiet New Zealand night. Cultured English voices tolling disasters, guttural Germans crackling with triumph. Outside the moreporks hooted. Far from home.

New Zealand drained herself of men for this distant war. Troop-ships, crammed with territorials, hastily trained, and airmen barely out of the A.T.C., slid out of Wellington and Auckland harbours on their dangerous journey through mined and torpedo-ridden seas. They rarely got away unnoticed. Wives and girlfriends watched them as though their eyes could keep the ships safe in port. Rumours leapt to life, were contradicted, re-established. 'It'll be half-past seven tomorrow morning, I'm telling you. I had it straight from...'. 'This girl I know's married to the chief engineer. She says....' Usually someone had it right, or guessed right.

With posters, with radio warnings, with press advertisements the authorities tried to curb the proliferation of rumour. CARELESS TALK COSTS LIVES! WALLS HAVE EARS – DON'T TALK! Information on troop movements was certainly being relayed from New Zealand to enemy sources.

Way up in Turangi, Guy and Grace Morton listened at night to Nazi broadcasts from Germany. Guy and Grace Morton admitted to speaking and understanding German. Guy and Grace Morton were foreigners from goodness knows where.

'They say they're English – that's what they say!'

'They lived in all those Nazi countries. They told me themselves. Said it right out.'

194

'The police say there's someone up this way sending out messages.'

'Mrs Morton, is your husband a spy?' asked one of the simpler minded locals.

Flippant, Grace said, 'Certainly. He keeps a submarine in Lake Taupo. Haven't you seen it?'

A group of local women met in the newly-built lounge of the Lodge to knit socks for soldiers and roll bandages. Grace looked out of the window.

'Here comes my husband. He's a spy. Haven't you heard?'

Some weeks later an embarrassed detective called.

'Mrs Morton, we have to investigate any report that's made to us. Is it true that you told several women in this room that your husband was a spy?'

This is ludicrous! I'm dreaming.

She explained.

'I'm afraid I'll have to ask you some questions. You took over the running of this lodge in August? How many times have you left Turangi since that date?'

'Let me see. I've been three times to Auckland, and once, no twice, down to Wellington.'

'Is that all? Isn't it true that you went to Wanganui as well?'

My God, they are watching my every move with their hostile little eyes and their narrow, jealous little minds.

'Yes, yes, I did. I drove down but I didn't like the look of it so I came straight home again.'

'And what was the purpose of these journeys?'

'To keep me sane. Good Heavens, if you lived in a place like this wouldn't you want to get out.'

The detective laughed. 'Yes, come to think of it, I would. I'm sorry about all this and I'm glad you're taking it so well. We have to question quite a lot of people and some of them get really upset.'

'But they'd be Germans, wouldn't they? We're English. We were chased out of Czechoslovakia by the Gestapo. We put ourselves in danger to help people. We lost all our possessions. Do you think we'd be here, in this hole, if it hadn't been for the Nazis?'

'I'm sorry, Mrs Morton. Stories go around you know. We have to investigate even when they're ridiculous.'

She never forgave them. Forty years later New Zealanders were

195

still the people who spied and watched and gossiped and accused her of being a traitor.

The story died hard. A young friend, an airman in training who often spent his leave at the lodge, came to Grace one day and took her hand, embarrassed, moved.

'Mrs Morton, I'm so sorry. Is there anything I can do to help you?'

'What is it? Why do you want to help me?'

'I know what's happened,' he said.

'What has happened?'

'Guy was seen when he was at the station being taken down to Somes Island.'

'Is that so?' said Grace. 'Guy! could you come here a minute?'

Guy wrote to the government offering his services. He explained that he spoke German like a native and would be willing to be interned on Somes Island with the enemy aliens in order to act as a government agent. There had already been escapes from the island and other outbreaks of trouble. Guy's offer, perhaps not surprisingly, was refused.

It was the war that finally ruined the fishing lodge. Petrol was rationed. Who could spend their precious coupons on trips to Turangi? Business fell away, suddenly and almost completely.

In the final trickle of guests one woman became friendly with burdened Mary.

'What are you going to do when the baby comes?'

'I don't know.'

'Have you been to the Plunket?'

'What's the Plunket?'

'My dear, this is no place for a pregnant woman. You need to be where you can get regular medical attention. Why don't you come back to Auckland with us? Your husband will have no trouble finding a job there and we'll help you look for a nice little flat.'

Freddie and Mary left and dropped out of the Mortons' lives.

The staff was dismissed. Guy travelled down to Wellington to save what he could. He located the confident, confidential gentleman who passed them the handy little proposition in the first place.

'We have to sell. The business just isn't coming in. Do you think you could find a buyer? Someone who'd like it for a private home?'

'What do you mean sell? You don't own that place.'

'Good Heavens, man! We bought it from you yourself barely a year ago. You can't have forgotten.'

'Oh no! What you bought was the lease. That's Maori land. It can't be bought or sold. You knew that. Don't come at that with me!'

'Listen – we put up a building on that land – it's increased the value of the property enormously. We must be able to get something back on that!'

'Sure. You can move it away. Set it up somewhere else. Sell it. I suppose you built it on skids?'

'What the hell are you talking about? It's built decently on solid foundations.'

'That's too bad. Build it on skids and you can move it. Put down foundations and it's part of the estate. That's the law, old man.'

At the same time the international licence on their car expired. They had to register it anew. But cars with left-hand drive were not legally allowed on New Zealand roads in those years. To convert it would have cost more than the Mortons could afford. They sold it to a mechanic for a fraction of its value.

What do you do without money in a strange country where no one wants the skills you have? Where the very thing that used to be your greatest asset, your voice with privilege and position in its vowel sounds, proves an enemy provoking defensive hostility or contempt or amusement. ('A pom with a plum in his mouth. Hell, they're arrogant! Up themselves.')

Guy found himself a job as a mechanic at General Motors in Lower Hutt. Grace once again stayed behind to tidy away the tag ends of an enterprise. As at Uzhorod, the unpaid bills poured in. But this time there was no way she could settle them – they remained unpaid.

Guy Morton passed into bankruptcy.

He was nearly sixty. Grace looked thirty but her birth-date said that she was in her forty-fifth year.

✻   ✻   ✻   ✻

Laings Road, Lower Hutt. An upstairs flat. Grace with a basket on her arm pirouetting and parading in front of Guy.

'Look at the suburban housewife off to do the shopping!' They both laughed.

But Grace actually putting parcels in her necessary basket thinks, 'Suppose one of my Shanghai friends saw me now!'

'Whatever happened to Grace Botham? That well-dressed, witty woman. The one that was always in demand. Grace Botham the professeur?'

'Oh, Grace! She lives in a dull house in a dull street in a dull suburb in a dull country. She cooks and sweeps and irons her husband's shirts.'

'Not Grace, no, you're thinking of someone else!'

For the first time in her life she lives without a maid. Sweeping and ironing are fairly easily learned though they are never second nature to her as they are to women brought up to them. But cooking is a daily nightmare, a horrible exam that she must sit, unprepared, every night of her life. She buys herself a text but no cookery book is elementary enough. She goes to her neighbours for help – isn't that what you do when you're in trouble?

'It says here to steam it. What does that mean? Do I put it in hot or cold water?'

They laugh at her in shocked disbelief. 'Go on! You do what it says. Steam it.' She never asked them anything again.

With her basket on her arm she visits the butcher's shop, lingering till she is the only customer.

'I don't know anything about buying meat. I want something I can cook tonight for two people.'

He suggests fillet steaks. 'How do I cook them?'

Step by step he tells her. Grace Botham of Shanghai is grateful to a butcher for his sensitive courtesy.

The preparing of the meal takes hours each day. Guy eats what she serves with every sign of enjoyment and asks for more.

'Do you like it, Guy?'

'It would have been all right if you'd . . . if you hadn't . . .'

And when the periodic storms of violence shake him, he yells at her. 'You serve me muck! How can any woman be so stupid?'

Her good mind tells her that she is learning, that the meals she serves are savoury and satisfying, but deep within her a frightened voice agrees with every criticism. Always, all her life, the smell of cooking is to her the smell of failure.

It is all part of her sense of alienation. The sky is strange here, strangely marked and coloured; gross bare hills threaten. The forest (which the natives perversely call the bush) is the wrong shade of green, flowers bloom in winter, and there is a plentiful absence of snow. The very man in the moon is unrecognizable upside-down.

Textures worry her. The memory of the thick woollen socks of the farmers who came to fish at Turangi fills her with a sense of physical repugnance, their scarred and calloused hands horrify. She remembers dancing at the Chateau and noticing that the New Zealand women in the room could be identified by their red, weathered hands.

'They may have to clean and cook and scrub but you'd think they'd have pride enough to conceal it,' thinks Grace, understanding only one brand of pride. She buys rubber gloves and hand-lotion to preserve the pallor of her own.

She listens to the accents around her, vainly trying to classify them as a clue to a social scale more definite and extreme than exists here. She imagines she is complimenting a fourth-generation New Zealander when she says, 'No one would know you were born here.'

But not for nothing is she Nellie Botham's daughter. Her upper lip is outwardly stiff. Already she knows that New Zealanders, in the face of criticism, may reply cruelly, 'If you don't like it, why don't you go home?'

Where is home?

Her nostalgic misery, rammed down into her own bowels – she must keep cheerful for Guy – turns sour there and corrupts. Heart sickness turns into physical lethargy and an unidentifiable, but apparently permanent, sense of bodily distress. She thinks of her old enemy, anaemia. Has it turned pernicious? Or could it be cancer? Reluctantly she tells Guy.

Guy, alarmed and solicitous, takes her to a doctor.

'Not a thing wrong with you,' he says heartily and suggests she take cascara. They score it up, another entry on their slate of sins this country has committed, and look for a specialist.

Guy discovers the admirable and amiable Dr Pacey who examines Grace very carefully.

'Do you really not know what's wrong with you?' She waits for the worst. 'You're pregnant.'

'That's impossible. I can't be!'

'Well, it's either a three-months foetus or a tumour.'

'At my age,' cries Grace, 'let's hope it's a tumour!'

Pregnancy tests are a new and cumbersome technique involving live rabbits and a considerable time lapse. But the results are reliable.

'Firmly positive. And everything seems to be in order. Shall we say December?'

After the first shock the baby rejuvenates them. They are again the adventurous, dashing Mortons. Who else would conceive a child when they total between them more than a century of experience? It also rescues Grace from the horror of cooking in the Laings Road flat. They move to a Wellington boarding-house. Guy has found himself a more congenial and lucrative job in the office of the Wellington branch of Lloyds.

1942. Twice, in June and again in August, the earth stirs and heaves. Precariously perched Wellington shakes alarmingly. In pyjamas and curlers, citizens spill out into the streets. In Customhouse Quay a huge concrete parapet crashes from a building on to and through the pavement below. But it is night time and Customhouse Quay is deserted. No one is hurt. Grace is sitting in the circle of the Majestic Theatre when the second quake comes. Her pregnant woman's instinct for survival gets her down the stairs to the lobby before she is consciously aware of having moved.

All the news from overseas is bad. Singapore falls to the Japanese. They are pressing south towards Australia. Wellington becomes a base for American troops, the streets take on an olive-green tint as marines in their thousands move in. American accents everywhere, Camel cigarettes and Lucky Strikes, condoms in the shop doorways. Coffee shops selling real coffee flower in Willis Street and Lambton Quay.

But Grace, with her private miracle within, is insulated from the stirrings of war. Now that she and Guy have adjusted to the idea of a child they are delighted. 1942 is their late and secret spring.

Standing in a picture theatre for the national anthem, Grace suddenly laughs. It is the eighth month. Dr Pacey has told her that day that the baby has turned with its head well down ready for birth.

'What's the matter with you,' whispers Guy.

'I've just thought – how funny, my son stands on his head for God Save the Queen!'

December, summer, six shopping days to Christmas. On the 17th of the month Grace goes into labour. She has known it will not be easy. To bear a first child at the end of your fruitful years is a dangerous business.

In a private hospital in Willis Street Dr Pacey administers Twilight Sleep to her but her drowsiness is punctuated by huge red throbs of pain so that her body is a drum beaten for three days to a barbaric and mounting rhythm. Over and over again she is moved into the theatre and then out again to make way for yet another swifter queue-jumping birth. Dr Pacey swims into her nightmare and out again. Guy hovers helplessly at the gates of hell. On the 20th her rhythm crashes to a climax. A son is born, vigorous, healthy.

Dr Pacey, triumphant, drives up to Brooklyn himself to tell Guy who after lingering so long has slept throughout the final act.

In the calm aftermath Grace watches from her window a huge magnolia tree. Every morning the great cream flowers open to the sun and, following its passage, droop and die as it sets. Christmas Day. Guy, brimming with goodwill, shares the hospital's festive dinner in Grace's private room. It smells of roses and joy as well as lamb and mint sauce. They are never to be so happy again.

While Grace has been dawdling in the life cycle of the magnolia flowers, Guy has found his family a flat in lovely Oriental Bay and has moved in. The windows overlook the harbour, only the road between them and the beach. As the baby grows, whenever Wellington weather is kind, Grace spends whole days with him on the sand running back to the flat only to fetch his bottle or orange juice or sieved vegetables.

He grows satisfactorily, this miraculous baby, but not in unruffled calm. He is delicate. With the autumn cold he develops asthma. Night after night Grace sits by his bed till daylight, gently pushing to expel the air from his choking lungs. She feels for the first time the full weight of her years. So, apparently, does Guy.

The old problems – housework, money, Guy's moodiness, reassert themselves and dominate lives worn thin by fatigue.

To both Grace and Guy it is unthinkable that a house should not be clean and neat in every particular. It is the nature of houses to be so and, if they are not, then clearly there is somewhere a dereliction of duty.

Tired, Grace cannot meet her own standards or Guy's. There are no maids or chars in New Zealand but there is an occupation that to an outsider looks the same, called 'Help in the House'. It may be a local euphemism so that New Zealanders can have what they in theory deplore, or it may be that by changing the name they hope to expel the sad social connotations of domestic work.

Grace acquires a woman to help in the house. She has already discovered that in the topsy-turvey antipodean social structure doctors occupy the top position. It is mildly surprising to find that her help is a doctor's sister. When one of Grace's friends drops in, the help serves a beautiful afternoon tea then pours herself a cup and sits down with the ladies to drink it and chat. Grace thinks wistfully of unobtrusive Humpty and Juji, but is more amused than annoyed.

It is Guy who upsets the delicate balance by complaining that the bathroom floor has not been adequately polished, nor the shelf where he keeps his razor wiped down.

'I'm not a charwoman, Mr Morton,' says the help and, taking her coat from the peg by the front door, leaves never to return. The difference is apparently not just one of nomenclature.

Money and rage are more basic problems.

To Guy, money is not the measure of man's worth but it is the outward manifestation of that worth. To look poor and act poor is more humiliation than he can stand especially in a country that has, he thinks, nothing else to judge by. He carries his image proudly – a free-spending gentleman – and there is little of his salary left over for such mundane stuff as meat and groceries and the power bill. He is happy to live in debt, it's a gentlemanly failing. Grace, with the missionary ethic behind her, loathes it.

Their money troubles are rocks that surface regularly. The sudden squalls from nowhere are a worse threat.

They are no less violent now than they have always been. Grace, who can look before and after, knows she will weather them. But how can you explain away a shouting violent adult to a terrified toddler?

Friday evening Guy is breaking glasses against the kitchen door. David is screaming, beside himself with fear. Grace picks him up and carries him, hysterical, through to the bedroom. And while she walks the floor with him, calming and comforting, acknowledges at last that this is unendurable and must stop.

As residents, they avoid the beach in summer weekends when Wellingtonians crowd there to swim and sunbathe. But the next fine Sunday Grace lures Guy out for a walk and knowing she is safe from physical attack with a couple of hundred witnesses around, she issues her ultimatum. 'Either you control yourself or I take David and go. I still love you and you can say what you like and I'll forget it, but I can't take any more violence.'

Guy, as much a victim of his own destructive cycle as any of them, is sad and contrite. 'I don't know why I'm like that. I do love you both so much. I swear I'll never let it happen again.'

And for five weeks it doesn't. He is loving, kindly Guy. Grace begins to relax. Then inevitably the eruption comes, the worse for having been bottled up so long.

Grace has already seen a lawyer who has told her she has grounds for divorce. Guy's lawyer advised legal separation. Very quietly at the end, with much sadness, they part.

✳   ✳   ✳   ✳

Grace had a woman friend living at Island Bay. She and David moved in to share the house. She had a little money scraped together from a radio talk or two, and one good run of private coaching. It was soon exhausted. Guy, predictably, paid the maintenance he was legally obliged to, reluctantly, and at irregular intervals. Soon it stopped arriving altogether. David was too delicate and too young to be left to a child-minder while Grace went to work. For the first time in her life she saw poverty from the underside. It was an ugly sight and she looked at it alone.

> When this little woman first did wake,
> She began to shiver and she began to shake,
> She began to wonder and she began to cry,
> 'Lors alack a daisy, this be none of I!'

The Social Security system was then in its infancy, a clumsy giant not come to its full powers. It would be two years before a Labour government introduced the Child Benefit; thirty years before the Domestic Purposes Benefit arrived to make life possible for just such people as Grace and David. Nevertheless Grace's solicitor advised her to apply to the Social Security Department. 'It exists to help people who for one reason or another can't work,' he told her. 'You're merely claiming a right. So don't feel badly about it.'

But she did. Already she had sold all her saleable possessions, including the old and beautiful jewellery that had come to her from Aunt Mollie. Now she joined the procession of the desperate and the hopeful passing through the lobby of the Social Security Department. She was raw with humiliation. 'I, Grace Botham of Shanghai, asking for public charity, for a hand-out.'

No decent privacy screened the transaction. At the first interview she gave details of her position to a clerk, and went home; was later sent for, passed through a long room full of desks to the very last desk where a large fat man was in possession.

'Now, Mrs Morton,' he told her, 'we've investigated your case and we find that your husband is quite able financially to pay you maintenance: therefore the Department cannot assume the responsibility of supporting you. The man for you to see is the maintenance officer. If you put in a request to him he'll undertake the negotiations with your husband. In the meantime, all we can do is allow you a small weekly sum to assist you.'

He passed her across a voucher. She read the amount printed on it. Three shillings. It would in those days have paid for bread and milk for the week – but only just and not a crumb left over. She had travelled in from Island Bay for this.

'Do you realize,' she cried, 'that it's a shilling each way by tram? Would you accept a shilling a week?'

The fat man looked embarrassed. 'No,' he said. 'I wouldn't.'

'Well, neither will I!' She dropped the voucher on the desk and walked out.

Never again.

All the same the clumsy ham-fisted young giant of a department did occupy itself in her service and one day the maintenance officer sent for her, beaming.

'You'll be all right now. We've got a whole year's maintenance paid in advance.'

He handed her four cheques, three of them post-dated. Each one was for three months maintenance and each was properly signed by Guy.

With money in her purse to be husbanded she looked for a cheaper, pleasanter way of living, and found it near the tiny Manawatu town of Feilding where a farmer's wife offered board and lodgings to paying guests.

Gentle orchards, a few cows. Grace and David live in a bach in the garden.

The days are peaceful and she is glad to draw breath in this unexpected haven. Loneliness and fears return at night.

She wakes to a panting and puffing and crying that should be David in the grip of asthma, but is definitely not. Outside the four walls of this bach alone among the trees someone is choking and dying, gasping for breath. Common humanity demands that she go to his aid; that she run through the black garden and hammer on the sleeping farmhouse door. Lights, doctor, lights!

She cannot do it. Coward! It's no good, she can't face the dead alone in the sightless night. Dear God, let someone else hear him and come, let him get better and go away. Please God, just this once, and I'm sorry I don't believe in you.

God obliges. The spasms pass away. The victim is either recovered or dead. The morning will be soon enough to find out.

The girl who brings breakfast across to the bach has noticed no stray corpses in the garden. 'Tell me again what that noise was like.'

Grace gives a fair imitation. The girl giggles. 'An opossum! That's what it would be. They often make noises like that!'

The breathing space that Grace has won for herself and David amongst the Feilding fruit trees is short. When she tries to cash the second of Guy's post-dated cheques she is not altogether surprised to find it bounces. The account is closed. After a certain length of time you give up fighting. Grace accepts the fact that she must provide for David herself.

Live in position required by certificated teacher. One dependent child. Salary less important than comfortable home.

She imagines a spacious sheep station, David running free and rosy in the country air. What she gets is a private boarding-school in

Taranaki. A single bedroom, 8 foot by 9 foot, with an extra bed jammed into it for David. He is not allowed to sit beside her at the staff dining-table. Only the little boarders, homesick for a pet, welcome him, spooning his food in at the communal table and mopping his face for him. To Grace it is made clear that he is a black mark against her and she'd better mind her p's and q's.

As soon as his legs have muscles enough to push pedals, she escapes from these constrictive walls. They move into lodgings in town and trundle along to school together each morning, David on three wheels, Grace – wobbling somewhat, thirty years out of practice – on two.

It's a stop-gap solution; the 'Situations Vacant' columns of *The Dominion* remain her favourite reading. This pays off in the end. She is appointed headmistress of a small church school in Marton. Seventy children, mostly girls, with a few boys in the mixture in the infants. The one other teacher, humorous and warm, becomes Grace's friend for life. David begins school happily, one of her flock of babies.

There is a creek near the school that rises in winter. The second year of Grace's tenure it is dangerously high. 'Out of bounds,' she tells the children and their parents. 'Any child who goes to the creek will be expelled. I can not take the responsibility.' A few days later a bevy of little girls, thrilled at such wickedness, rush in to gasp that two boys are playing by the creek and they'll be expelled, won't they Mrs Morton? One is David. Solemnly Grace expels him.

He could be sent off each morning, with a schoolbag jogging on his back, to the state school down the road where the children of butchers and clerks, dustmen, doctors, and railway workers tumble along together. But to Grace, long conditioned to selective schools, this is unthinkable. David is seven; it is time for the shaping process to begin that will mould him into a gentleman.

She asks questions everywhere and finds at last what she wants – a 'pre-prep.' school where, amid forty acres of bush and gardens, a privileged handful of boys are educated. Every term, neatly labelled with his name and destination, he is flown 200 miles to school.

To pay for this luxury she reduces her own life to an unalleviated routine, heroically dull. She wakes at night with sudden starts, columns of pounds, shillings, and pence in her head, refusing to come to the right answer. She takes up again the struggle to extract money from Guy, and schools herself to the acceptance of poverty.

'Thank God for my tiny two-roomed flat,' she writes in her diary. 'It is quite unnecessary to compare it with the Cathay Mansions, for that and all similar luxury are gone from my plane.'

At ten, David graduates to a private prep. school, nearer at hand. The sums in Grace's head dance more frantically. To her, New Zealand-born David is no more a New Zealander than she, China-born, is Chinese. It is her duty, as it was her mother's before her, to return her son to the unpolluted fountainhead.

'David simply must have a good English public school education. Then it's all up to him.' What she has in mind is Bedford School where Mark spent seven years. But where on earth is the money to come from?

You have to spend money to make it. She scrapes together the fees for a correspondence course on writing and lays out a precious ten shillings a week – hire-purchase of a typewriter. She sells a couple of short articles then:

'On Sunday night I went to bed with an inspiration and after nearly seven hours of thrill I conceived the whole idea of a plan of a book . . . It is based on the story of Nancy Chan.'

Every day for a year when the energetic practical day was finished she plunged back to Chefoo and Shanghai with the joy of a homecoming. When the manuscript was finished she sent it off to her former literary agent in England. A few months later he wrote to say that he thought it quite possible he could place it with a publisher.

Suddenly there were possibilities round the corner again. She asked David's headmaster to prepare him for the Bedford entrance examination, she inquired about teaching jobs in England, she began a second novel.

The bright bubble burst one Friday afternoon.

There was one child in school who was dyslexic and could not learn to read. There was a boy who had been expelled for attacking the girls with any weapon that came to hand. There was an older girl who had not been awarded a bursary she thought was her due. These three dissatisfied parents – three out of seventy – went to the committee without my knowing. The vicar sent for me and told me that he had been getting complaints and that it was a very unhappy school.

'I wonder if you'd mind getting hold of the last inspector's report', I said, because I knew what had been written there. 'This is a very happy school.'

But the vicar couldn't find it.

So I said, 'If it's unhappy, I'm not staying.' I'm the wrong person to have that sort of thing said to me. I handed in my resignation and walked out that afternoon, just the way I did from that private school when I was a girl.

I went down to Wellington and stayed with a friend. I was terribly shaken and upset at what had happened and worried stiff about the future. How was I to pay David's school fees, let alone save for him to go to England and Bedford. Everything seemed black and horrible.

I arranged for David to go to a private prep. school in Wellington as a day boy, but he was heartbroken at the thought of leaving his boarding-school.

Then out of the blue Guy paid me £22 maintenance and the next day I got a letter signed by all the children of the school and a cheque from the parents for £95. That was a really large sum in those days, equivalent to more than $1000 now. My confidence was restored; it was clear I had been liked and appreciated and, best of all, it meant David could stay on at boarding-school.

Still I had to set about finding a job and making a new home for myself and David. I was fifty-seven then but I looked younger and I still had plenty of energy.

She went to the Education Board and became a long-term relieving teacher in the Wellington area. Island Bay, Brooklyn, Wadestown, Karori, Newtown, Mt Cook, Te Aro – Wellington trams rattling up hills, deposited her at some time or other in every corner of the city. She lived in shared houses, rented rooms, boardinghouses. This was in the 1950s, the years of the great housing shortage. A flat was a prize for a hundred applicants to scrabble for.

Ultimately she was one of the lucky ones. The ground floor of a big old home in Karori. Everything was on a grand scale: David's bedroom was 23 foot long, his favourite occupation rowing a boat around the lake in the grounds.

To pay for this spaciousness Grace took in boarders, cooking for them and cleaning the house when she got home from school. Her two novels had never found a publisher and the dream of an English public school dissolved. She accepted what was possible, Scots' College, Wellington.

'David was growing up without a father. The least I could do was send him to a private school where the classes were small enough for the masters to take a personal interest in all the boys.'

To make ends meet, Grace took private pupils, coaching them in French and English two evenings a week.

At sixty she wrote in her diary, 'After a day at school I am too tired to do anything but go to bed when all the chores are done . . . I feel a longing for the next life whatever it may be like. If it were not for books I don't think I could stand it without losing my sanity.'

A hand stretches out from the past. Dapper Uncle Harry in New York has finally dismissed life after a hundred years and one day. Courteously he salutes her from the grave, slipping her a legacy of £200 – enough for a car.

'Joy, I feel less like a stranded whale and I don't get so crying tired.'

Somewhere amongst these hills and bays, Guy was living out his life too. For a long time Grace saw neither flesh nor shadow of him. Then, when she was living at Karori . . .

somehow I got word of Guy – I can't remember how. I knew he'd married again and his third wife had divorced him just as Meggie and I had done. Now I heard that he was very ill, in hospital. I thought, 'If he's bedridden and impotent I'd be delighted to have him and look after him. Here I am in this big flat – he could have the veranda bedroom and David would have a father and I'd have someone to look after and someone to talk to whose company I really enjoyed and if he got into a temper – why, I could just walk out of the room.'

I went to the hospital all prepared to say, 'All is forgiven. Come home!' I found the right ward and the sister was telling me which room he was in when Guy himself came stalking down the corridor, big as ever with his hair going white and the dressing-gown on that I knew so well. I moved towards him and spoke but he just gave one look at me and stalked right past.

I didn't know then that he had married again for the fourth time. Thinking back on it, I think he may have assumed that I'd come to beg for maintenance – he owed me an awful lot. But that was the last glimpse I ever had of Guy.

❊   ❊   ❊   ❊

The years passed. David graduated to university. Grace was teaching at Marsden School and living in a delightful little flat in Khandallah. There was a complex of three houses; a lawyer and his wife lived in one, a bank manager and his wife in another, and the widow of an army officer in the third where I had my flat. They were just my kind of people. I was happy there. I hadn't been happy in so long I'd forgotten what it was like.

I'd been having a bit of trouble with my ankle and I had to see the doctor. One day I said to him, 'I don't know if I'm being hypochondriac, but could you look at this little spot on my head. It's sort of throbbing.' He looked at it and shone a light into my eyes.

Then he said, 'It's something no doctor wants to tell anyone. You've got shingles and the infection is in your eyes.' He told me to go home to bed.

'All right,' I said. 'I'll go and collect the books I've got to mark . . .'

'You're not to go back to the school at all,' he said. 'You're to drive straight home and get into bed and stay there.'

So I drove home stopping only to buy a nice bedjacket. If I'm going to be an invalid, I thought, I might as well look civilized.

I needn't have bothered. I felt so ill for three weeks I didn't care how I looked. I had spots all over my face and the pain was terrible.

The three ladies in this little nest of houses were wonderful. They wouldn't let me go to hospital. They looked after me, taking turns at bringing my meals to me and doing my washing. I don't know when I've had such marvellous true friends. The doctor came often for the first ten days, then he said, 'You're on the mend now. I don't need to call again. You'll be able to come to my rooms in a week or so,' and he made an appointment for ten days ahead.

But I didn't get better. I just got blinder and blinder. When the day came for the appointment I had to be driven to the surgery and I felt my way in, unable to see a thing.

The doctor had a fit when he saw me and he bundled me straight off to a specialist. The specialist told me I would be blind for months.

'Am I going to be blind altogether?' I said.

He barked at me, 'Don't be so dramatic!'

I was blind for five months. I thought fate had finished with me. You get knocked down a few times in life and you think, 'Well, that's it, I've had my share!' And you begin to get on your feet again so fate gives you one more knock.

But I had good friends to help me. John, a teacher who had boarded with me once, was married and living in Christchurch. He called and said, 'You made your home mine, now we're going to make our home yours.'

My flat had to be packed and the car sold. I couldn't do anything. Every time I put something down on the bench or table it fell to the floor and smashed. 'All the less to pack,' David said cheerfully.

I worried about money because I'd suddenly stopped earning but that was fixed up for me too. Because David was at university I'd been getting

210

the child benefit for him still. Someone saw the Social Security Department and they got to work on my case immediately with the result that in one week I switched from receiving the Child Benefit to receiving Universal Superannuation.

I had a friend in Taranaki from the days when I taught there. As soon as she heard the news she told me to come straight up to her. John and David put me on a plane and the air hostess looked after me marvellously. At New Plymouth she led me by hand across the tarmac till my friend's hand was on my arm.

I lived with John and Christine in Christchurch for some months. I wasn't in pain any more and though being blind was unpleasant and frightening, the doctor had assured me I wouldn't lose my sight permanently so I just kept thinking, 'If you live through it, you'll see again.'

And the doctor was right. Gradually, gradually, my vision returned. After a while I could see to walk in a general way and I wandered round Christchurch exploring, with my hand up shading my eyes from the sun like a criminal. I began to be able to read again, at first with a strong magnifying glass and then in the usual way.

After a few months we saw an advertisement for a flat in Barbadoes Street. So I got my home and my independence again and I lived there for four years.

As soon as I could see properly I looked around for a job. At first I took French classes on Saturday mornings at the technical college. They were nice people at that school but the money wasn't good so I went to the Education Board and applied for a job as a relieving teacher of French.

They sent me to a Catholic school for girls. At first I couldn't tell the nuns apart. While I'd been partially blind I'd got used to recognizing people by their shape and colour, but with nuns all you have to go on is the face.

The nuns are lovely people to work with, so kind and nice, but they've no idea what life is like for people out in the world. They don't understand that if you want to eat you've got to pay for it. Clothes, food, the roof over their heads are all supplied free. I was supposed to be paid every fortnight but they kept forgetting to draw my pay for weeks on end. I told them if it happened again I'd leave. And it did.

I wrote to my friend in Palmerston North, the one who'd been my infant mistress at the Marton school. Almost immediately I got a telegram back. HAVE FLAT FOR YOU HAVE PAID MONTH ADVANCE RENT. So I packed up and moved to Palmerston North.

I had another reason for the move. I always used to think that though I'd had most experiences a woman could have, I'd never be a grandmother because I'd done my own child-bearing so late. But while I was in Christchurch, David married and within a few years I had a granddaughter and a grandson. It was a tremendous thrill. I flew north and helped when the babies were born and most of my teaching money went on air fares. At least in the North Island I'd be closer to them.

The first flat was tiny but soon I got a bigger one in a beautiful old home. Universal Superannuation wasn't enough to cover the rent there and my food as well.

There was a coaching college in town so I taught there two nights a week and did knitting and crocheting as well for a little fashion shop. I managed to supplement the pension and live quite comfortably.

Then my eyes began to give trouble again. 'Cataracts', the specialist said, 'in both eyes.' I was shocked and despairing. Despite the shingles I'd always had perfect sight, and I knew now what it felt like to be blind. I cried myself to sleep every night for a while.

But Dr Henderson told me that he would operate and remove the thickened lens first of one eye, then of the other and that, with glasses to supply an artificial lens, I would be able to see again. I trusted him completely – he's a wonderful doctor.

The whole process took six years to complete, two before the first eye was ready for the operation and another four before the second was. And all the time getting blinder and blinder.

I taught as long as I could. But when I got to the stage of using a magnifying glass to see the books with I gave up – it was too stupid altogether. I could still crochet by feel without looking at the work.

Finally I went to the public hospital and had the first operation. I had a terrible reaction to the anaesthetic. I can't describe it – sheer terror filling every part of me. I imagine that's what a bad L.S.D. trip must be like.

For two or three days after the operation I was alone in a room flat on my back with bandaged eyes. I even had to drink my tea flat on my back. Then I was moved into a ward with six people, all more or less blind feeling their way around.

When the time came for me to be going home, the doctor and the sister inquired very carefully about how I would manage living alone. But I had arranged everything. Below my flat there was a girl living, a solo mother who had trained as a nurse. She was to come up every day to help me through my bath and prepare my meals. I had saved a little money and Olive had sent me a cheque so I was able to pay for three weeks' help.

The first thing that happened when I got home was that a blood vessel burst in my eye so that I had to lie down flat again for a fortnight. The second thing that happened was that the girl who was to help me told me she was broke – with Christmas just a week or so away – and she asked me if I could pay her in advance. I gave her $40, just about all I had. She took it and off she went on a holiday with her boyfriend.

There I was, blind and penniless, with no one to look after me. It was dreadful. One of the worst moments I've ever had in my life.

There was a gardener who took care of the grounds for all the flats and he was a dear. He arrived at the door with my mail at the same time as my good friend Margaret called to see me. They were both horrified at what the girl had done.

'I've got a daughter who's getting married in a few weeks' time,' the gardener said. 'I'll ring her up.'

He did, there and then, and she came to stay with me until she got married. Margaret provided the food and every day that lovely girl gave me my evening meal and slept in my sittingroom. Before she left for work in the morning she prepared a lunch tray for me and left it on the top shelf of the fridge. Once a day I would feel my way to the kitchen and without having to bend (you mustn't bend at all) I'd locate the tray and eat my meal blind. Some of it went in my mouth.

Finally I was able to get up and potter round. I still felt desperate – not for physical help any longer or for money, but for mental stimulation.

I couldn't read and I wanted to know what was going on in the world. I used to get out my magnifying glass and try to read the paper. One day the first thing I saw was, NEED A FRIEND? RING SAMARITANS.

So I jolly well did.

'Can we help you?' they said. I told them my problem.

They sent along Richard, a young chap in his third or fourth year at Massey University. He was a good friend to me. I never knew when he was coming but he'd pop in two or three times a week usually on his way back from Massey and he'd always bring me something interesting. And we talked and talked. We discussed everything under the sun except the crops – he was an agricultural student.

About the same time I got in touch with the Mothers' Help organization. They send people to help with housework where there is a need for it. You pay something for the service, but it's very cheap – a lot of the labour is given voluntarily. The same woman came to me once or twice a week for four years, and she became a really good friend. She helped with housework and the gardening and the washing and she used to read aloud to me. Richard had introduced me to *The Lord of the Rings* and week by week she read it to me.

By this time another old friend of mine was living in Palmerston on the other side of town. 'There are some nice senior citizens' flats near our place, Grace,' she said. 'Why don't you apply for one? Then I'd be able to pop in and see you all the time.' So finally I did.

Just before my name came to the top of the list and I was allocated a flat, this friend rang me up and said, 'I won't be along to see you today. I'm feeling a bit off-colour.' A fortnight later she died of cancer.

They're dear little flats – they really are! And I'm lucky to have one at the end of a row. They're just as comfortable as any luxury flat with the bathroom leading out of the bedroom and a sunporch off the livingroom.

The only difference between these and a luxury flat is that here you're the person in the kitchen.

When the government began to charge tax on Universal Superannuation I humiliated myself by changing to the Old Age Pension which is a few dollars more a month. I don't feel humiliated about it now though because, when I think of all the New Zealanders I've taught, it seems to me that I deserve it. So now I'm a full-blown, full-blooded pensioner.

Bland Papaioea Place accommodates her, another tenant with a unique load of human experience. She rests with her feet up – doctor's orders – but her mind goes on adventuring.

There was the song contest she entered, composing words and music with one eye and a magnifying glass, on a piano bought with a surrendered insurance policy. At seventy-six she enrolled as a student at Massey University for an extra-mural course in philosophy. That venture was interrupted by her second eye operation.

The operation was successful. With strong glasses she can read again, and does so voraciously. The house-bound library service links her to the world. Every fortnight comes an armful of the newest publications on the subjects that fascinate her – the nature of matter and of man, mysteries of the human mind, past civilizations, the possibilities of the planets, animal behaviour and intelligence. There have been losses:

Guy is dead now. About four years ago I had a vivid dream. I thought Guy was standing by my bed leaning over me in a loving way. I said, 'O Guy, I'm so glad you still love me!' and I woke up hearing my own voice saying this aloud. I was quite sure that he must have just died. Much later an old friend came to see me. We were catching up on news of this and that person we'd known.

'And your old man's gone too,' she said.

I said, 'Yes, about two and a half years ago.' I'd heard nothing of his death but I was so sure from the dream.

'Yes,' she said, 'that's when I saw it in the paper.'

Last year I was struck down myself by pancreatitis. It's a terribly sudden and painful disease and I was rushed to hospital more dead than alive. For several weeks I was too ill to be much aware of anything beyond my bodily discomfort. I remember once when I was lying on a hospital bed all trussed up with wires and tubes, I looked up and saw a swarm of solemn worried faces all staring down at me. I thought, 'Now I know what it feels like to be the corpse at an Irish wake.' Gradually, as I recovered, I realized that my room was full of flowers and that there were always friends popping in to

214

see me. Even when I went home the procession continued. I had no idea I had so many friends. I woke in the night and thought, 'I'm not a stranger here any more.'

Her illness left a residue of dizziness and pain, reminders of death's proximity. Nevertheless, her flat abounds with life – friends, music, books, exotic flowering pot-plants. Students still seek her out for help with French or English but she will no longer accept money from them.

I teach because I love it. I don't need the money and I don't want to feel obligated to give lessons if I don't feel up to it. Most of my pupils have remained my friends. Some come to see me regularly and others write to me from all over the world.

Letters come from David, too, wandering in Turkey and Greece, his father's old haunts. Her grandchildren come to visit, teenagers with Botham features and eyes.

I'm eighty-two now, she says, and I seem to have lived a number of different lives. I'm not a bit afraid of dying (though I hope it won't be from something as painful as pancreatitis). There are just two things though. I would like to see my grandchildren grow up and I do want to know if there's intelligent life in some other part of the universe. I refuse to die until I know that.

❖   ❖   ❖   ❖